W9-BZL-137

The Family Tree Guidebook to EUROPE

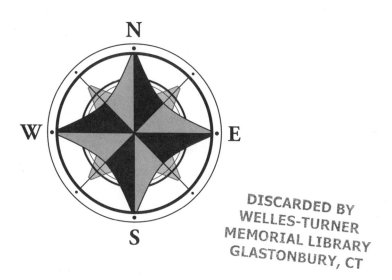

In memory of
WILLIAM "SAM" KOWALSKY
and
DOROTHY S. KOWALSKY

The Family Tree Guidebook to EUROPE

YOUR ESSENTIAL GUIDE TO TRACE YOUR GENEALOGY IN EUROPE

ALLISON DOLAN
and the Editors of Family Tree Magazine

FAMILY
TREE
BOOKS

Cincinnati, Ohio

shopfamilytree.com

CONTENTS

1 INTRODUCTION

By Lisa A. Alzo

A GUIDE TO EUROPEAN RESEARCH

Crossing the pond: Most genealogists end up doing it at one time or another. Whether your ancestors sailed over on the Mayflower, sought to escape Ireland's Great Famine or were part of the mass migration starting in the late 1880s, your research trail will likely lead you to Europe—perhaps not literally, but definitely mentally.

Of course, the journey back to the old country isn't always a smooth one. Name changes, confusing geography and records in unfamiliar languages and formats can easily intimidate even experienced researchers. But don't let these challenges hold you back. With our 11 tips for tracing your ancestors "over there," you'll sail right through these potentially rough research waters.

STEP 1 ✦ Exhaust US Sources First

Gather as much information as possible on this side of the ocean before you try to cross it. You'll want to learn your immigrant ancestor's hometown in Europe, his original name and other details to help you identify him in foreign records. Believe it or not, the best place to begin researching is at home. Talk to your relatives and ask them for copies of family documents such as birth certificates, passports, naturalization records, correspondence and other papers likely to contain clues to ancestral origins.

Next, search genealogy records. The old standby, the federal census, usually provides only a country of origin. Even immigrant passenger lists can be hit or miss—sometimes they give a village or town; other times, just a province or region. Birth, marriage or death certificates and military papers may offer clues. Obituaries may list where an immigrant was born, but because a relative or associate provided the information, it may not be accurate. In 1917 and 1918, male US citizens and aliens born from 1872 to 1900 had to fill out WWI draft registration cards, searchable online at **<ancestry.com>** and on microfilm at the Family History Library and National Archives. If the person had a Social Security Number, request his SS-5 (Social Security number application) through the Social Security Administration. It costs $27 if you know the number or $29 if you don't. (See **<www.ssa.gov/foia>** for more information.)

Keep in mind that immigrants often traveled together and put down roots among relatives and friends, forming "cluster communities." They ran their own churches and schools, established newspapers and formed social organizations. Don't overlook repositories specializing in these immigrant communities, such as the Balch Institute for Ethnic Studies at the Historical Society of Western Pennsylvania **<hsp.org/genealogists-community-historians>**, the Immigration History Research Center at the University of Minnesota **<ihrc.umn.edu>** and the Slovak Institute in Cleveland **<slovakinstitute.com>**. An ethnic-based genealogical society **<cyndislist.com/societies/ethnic>** might yield even more results.

STEP 2 ✦ Get the Immigrant's Name Right

It'll be hard to find your ancestor "William Smith" in Germany if he went by Wilhelm Schmidt there. The names you find in North American records may be Americanized versions of their European equivalents, or altogether different. But don't buy into the family lore about your ancestor's name being changed by immigration officials at Ellis Island (or other ports). This simply didn't happen; read more at **<www.ilw.com/articles/2005,0808-smith.shtm>**.

Many immigrants changed their own names once they arrived in America to make the name appear "more American." Often, they'd change or drop a few letters. For example, the Polish name Jabłoński might become Yablonski, or the first name Jan would become John. Or they'd switch to a phonetically similar name (Stanislaw becomes Stanley). Some bosses or teachers called immigrants by names that were easier for Americans to spell or say.

Connecting with others researching the name might help you determine its original form. A Google **<google.com>** search is a good start, but you might have better luck on a genealogy-oriented site such as Cyndi's List **<cyndislist.com/surnames>** or RootsWeb's Surname Resources Page **<resources.rootsweb.ancestry.com/surnames>**. Whatever the name, search for all conceivable variations and phonetic spellings in indexes and online databases.

STEP 3 ✦ Learn Naming Practices

Studying European cultures' naming customs can often help clue you in to previous generations and extend your family tree. They can also be useful in determining siblings' birth order or determining whether there were other children. For example, children's names can give you important clues to likely names of the grandparents. In the Italian tradition, the firstborn son is named for the paternal grandfather, the first daughter for the paternal grandmother, the second son for the maternal grandfather and the second daughter for the maternal grandmother.

Carpatho-Rusyns often named the eldest son after the father and the second son after the paternal grandfather. The third son was named after the maternal grandfather. The eldest daughter would be named Mary; the second, Anna; and the third, Helen. Subsequent children would be named after other relatives. This explains why the same given names seemed to be repeated through the generations in many of my own family lines.

Learn how different cultures use patronymics for hints to a father's first name. In Scandinavian languages, the patronymic surname is formed by adding suffixes to the father's first name: -son or -sen to indicate "son of," and -dotter, -dóttir or -datter for "daughter of." The Spanish use double surnames; when a woman marries, she keeps her last name, and adds her husband's surname (Maria Pérez Álvarez).

STEP 4 ✦ Brush Up on History

Finding out the why behind your ancestors' lives is just as important as the who, what, when and where. Sociologists and historians studying the migratory patterns of humans often refer to "push" and "pull" factors causing such movements. "Push" factors are conditions that drive people to leave their homelands, such as crop failures, epidemics, scarcity of land, poverty, high taxes, political or religious persecution, obligatory military service and wars. My paternal grandfather left Slovakia before his 17th birthday to escape a mandatory three-year service in the Austro-Hungarian army.

"Pull" factors attract people to a new area, typically by providing the potential for social and material betterment. These include the promise of political or religious freedom, or the availability of land or jobs.

Creating a time line with family and historical events can help you see what influenced their decisions. Start with our free biographical outline <**www.familytreemagazine.com/basicforms**>. You also can generate a time line from your genealogy software or with Genelines <**progenygenealogy.com/products/timeline-charts.aspx**>.

STEP 5 ✦ Study Geography

In order to successfully trace an immigrant ancestor, you'll need the name of his town or village of origin. Knowing that an ancestor came from Ireland or Germany usually won't help you research an ancestor in the old country. And even knowing that an ancestor came from London, Paris, Kiev or some other large city might not be enough. That's because in most foreign countries, the majority of records were kept on a local level, in a town hall or parish office. For US sources, immigrants often would give a large city as their place of birth simply because it was a more familiar point of reference.

To know where to look for records, you'll need to know how boundary changes might've affected your family's town (wars and political moves may have changed its name or the country it was in) and have a working knowledge of historical and current geography. Start with the map

resources listed in each country's chapter in this book, and then look to your library.

Most cities, and even smaller towns or villages, have websites. Try a Google <google.com> search for town or village name (such as Donegal Ireland); add a province or county name if needed. To get more specific, consult gazetteers—these geographical dictionaries list the towns in an area and tell you about political jurisdictions (provinces, counties, districts) and where a town's inhabitants went to church. The Family History Library (FHL) <familysearch.org> has gazetteers in print and on microfilm (see step 8). For more help putting the place name into context, see *Place Names of the World: Europe Historical Context, Meanings and Changes* by John Everett-Heath (Palgrave Macmillan).

SEARCHING FOR THE RIGHT RECORDS

Even when researching in a foreign land, you'll often seek the same types of records as on this side of the pond. Although availability and coverage vary by country, here are the top sources for tracing Europeans.

- **Civil registrations:** official documentation of births, marriages and deaths, similar to US vital records
- **Parish records:** registrations, baptisms, marriages, burials and sacraments such as confirmations
- **Cemetery markers:** provide birth and death dates
- **Military records:** give age, place of birth and other personal details; may contain parents' names
- **Census:** regular counts of an area's residents; provide family members' names, place of residence, religious affiliation, occupation, livestock owned and more
- **Emigration:** lists of those leaving a country kept by departure ports or police
- **Land/manor records:** provide names of successive property owners and may list hereditary tenants or laborers
- **Tax records:** show landowner, tenant, type of land, tax valuation and amounts
- **Family histories:** published genealogies covering noble families
- **Town or village histories:** may contain information on common surnames, notable residents, significant events and more

STEP 6 ✦ Bypass Foreign-Language Barriers

Don't expect key records to be written in English. The same applies to websites and correspondence. Therefore, you'll want to learn some basic genealogical terms such as *baptism*, *marriage* and *death*; *husband*, *wife*, *mother*, *father*, *occupations* and so forth. Check out our list of genealogical words in Dutch, French, German and Spanish in the Appendix on page 262.

For short, rough-but-serviceable translations, try the free online translators available from Google **<translate.google.com>** or BabelFish **<babelfish.com>**. Just type in a word or block of text, choose from a list of languages and click Translate. Consult a professional for tougher jobs (see step 10).

STEP 7 ✦ Find Online Records

"Crossing the pond" doesn't mean you have to hop on a plane or ship. Thanks to the internet, you can make great progress even on your laptop. Explore the free FamilySearch Record Search **<familysearch.org>**, a growing project of the Church of Jesus Christ of Latter-day Saints (LDS) to digitize records and post them online for free.

Subscription site Ancestry.com's World Deluxe subscription includes records from the United Kingdom, Germany, Italy, France, Sweden and other countries. UK-based FindMyPast **<findmypast.com>** has more than 500 million records, including censuses, military documents, and civil registrations. This book lists many country-specific databases, including Sweden's Genline **<genline.com>**, ScotlandsPeople **<scotlandspeople.gov.uk>** and, for the UK and Ireland, GENUKI **<genuki.org.uk>**.

STEP 8 ✦ Use FHL Microfilm

Although FamilySearch's digital records are making headlines now, the Family History Library has been a great resource for years. It has the largest collection of genealogical records in the world: 2.4 million rolls of microfilmed records, including vital, census, land, probate, immigration, church and more from 100-plus countries, with extensive coverage of Europe. The FamilySearch Research Wiki **<wiki.familysearch.org/en/Browse_by_Country>** can tell you what records to look for from your ancestral homeland. Search the online catalog at **<familysearch.org/catalog-search>** for microfilm you can order for a small fee via one of the FHL's 4,600-plus branch FamilySearch Centers (FSCs). Search the catalog by a place or a keyword, rather an ancestor's name. To search by place, click on Place Search and type in a place, such as *Naples*. You can also fill in the optional "Part of" search field—entering *Italy* will make sure you see records from the Naples in Italy, not the one in Florida. A keyword search helps get you to a specific record group or topic (for example, *1869 Hungarian Census*).

When you find records of interest, print the listings and take them to your local FSC. Bring payment in cash—film rental fees are due when you order and most centers can't accept checks or credit cards. You'll get a phone call in four to six weeks when your film comes in; you'll have 30 days to view the film on the FHC microfilm readers. For more help, see **<familysearch.org/learn/wiki/en/Introduction_to_LDS_Family_History_Centers>**.

The FHL has a vast collection of books, gazetteers and other reference materials that don't circulate to FSCs, so you may want to save up for a trip to Salt Lake City to do some heavy-duty researching.

STEP 9 ✦ Write to Archives

Of course, the FHL doesn't have all the records for all the countries in the world. Your next move may be to contact archives or churches of the area you're researching. Knowing where records are located gives you a huge advantage. The chapters of this book list organizations and archives for each country. Check the *International Vital Records Handbook*, 5th edition, by Thomas Jay Kemp (Genealogical Publishing Co.) and *In Search of Your European Roots* by Angus Baxter (Genealogical Publishing Co.). Or see Repositories of Primary Sources **<uidaho.edu/special-collections/other.repositories.html>**, which links to more than 5,000 websites of repositories worldwide.

Once you've identified the appropriate archive, search for its website on Google. Many archives give instructions and fees for research requests online. Responses will vary depending on an archive's location, facilities, equipment, staff and communications protocol, but these tips will set you up for success.

1. Follow all policies and procedures, and make your request as specific as possible.
2. Be brief and simple, use short sentences, and request information about only one ancestral line at a time.
3. Heed the European style for writing dates—day, month, year (as in 10 February 1897).

SAMPLE REQUEST LETTER FOR FOREIGN ARCHIVES

{Date}

{Your Street Address}
{Your City, State and ZIP Code}
{phone and/or e-mail address}

{Name of Institution}
{Street Address of Institution}
{City, State and Zip Code}

Dear Sir or Madam:

I am currently researching my family history and am requesting a copy of a {record type} for {full name of person}. The {name of event, such as birth, death, marriage} took place on {date or approximate date} in {town, village, county of event}. This individual's parents' names were {parents' names, if you know them}.

Please inform me of the cost for obtaining a photocopy of the record and how this payment may be sent to you. I have enclosed a self-addressed envelope for your convenience.

Thank you for your attention to my request.

Sincerely,
{Your Name}

CHAPTER ONE

IRELAND

By Sharon DeBartolo Carmack

REGIONAL GUIDE

The late English author Pete McCarthy, who was Irish on his mother's side, decided to travel the length of Ireland in search of his roots. His method of research? Stop in every pub called McCarthy's and talk with the people there. Certainly if you're of Irish descent, a trip to Ireland should be in your future—if for no other reason than to say you've been to every pub that shares your surname. But you don't have to venture across the Atlantic before shouting, "*Erin go bragh!*" Our seven-step guide will get your Irish roots search going right here at home.

STEP 1 ✦ Learn a Wee Bit of History

You probably realize that exploring the history of your ancestral homeland helps you understand why your ancestors left it and where they settled. Between 1851 and 1921, 4.5 million people departed Ireland, with 3.8 million coming to the United States. According to the 2000 census, 30.5 million US residents claim Irish ancestry—more than seven times the 4.2 million living in the Republic of Ireland today. The island of Ireland's population peaked around 8 million before the Potato Famine, perhaps the most famous emigration impetus, which lasted from 1845 to about 1849.

All of Ireland merged with the United Kingdom in 1801; a 1921 treaty partitioned the island into the independent Irish Free State (now the Republic of Ireland) and the six counties (Antrim, Armagh, Londonderry, Down,

Fermanagh and Tyrone) of UK-governed Northern Ireland. Disputes over the treaty led to civil war until 1923. A 1998 agreement officially ended "the Troubles," a period of civil unrest between nationalists (primarily Catholic) and unionists (primarily Protestant) in Northern Ireland. For more history, see *The Course of Irish History*, 5th edition (Roberts Rinehart Publishers).

STEP 2 ✦ Know What You're Up Against

Researching any ancestral line can bring about obstacles. Apart from identifying your ancestors' place of origin in the Emerald Isle, two main stumbling blocks are common to Irish researchers:

FINDING THE ARRIVAL DATE: You'll probably encounter your biggest Irish research challenge if you have a famine immigrant in the 1840s or 1850s who had a common name. As in many cultures, Irish names tend to repeat over generations. You may find yourself trying to keep straight the arrivals of a half-dozen Patrick Kellys and 17 Molly Malones. Passenger lists for the heavy Potato Famine immigration era are helpful only if you can identify your common-named ancestor by linking her to another family member or to a fellow traveler with an unusual name. (Search NARA's online database of immigrants who arrived in New York during the famine at **<www.archives.gov/research/arc/topics/immigration>**.)

As much as you'd like to find relatives' passenger lists, however, those prior to about 1891 probably won't specify where your ancestor came from, other than "Ireland." Remember, too, many Irish first went to Canada and then traveled to the United States. The best you may be able to get is a narrow span of years when your forebear came to this country. But that's OK. I've never found the passenger-arrival list for my Great-grandma Delia Gordon, but I've stood in front of the house in County Leitrim where she was born. I'll take that over a passenger list any day!

KNOWING IT'S YOUR ANCESTOR: Gathering enough identifying information is important to researching your ancestor in US and Irish records. I might as well have been searching for John Smith in New York when I tried to figure out who John Donovan's Irish-born parents were. By 1885, he'd received a land patent in North Dakota and settled his family there. His wife's name was Maria. Census records said his place of birth was either Illinois or Iowa. Wanna guess how many John Donovans appear in the 1880 census index for Iowa and Illinois? I pieced together information from a variety of records in the United States to ensure I'd found the right couple and learned the true identity of John's parents.

Fortunately, John used a middle initial, *W.*, which helped narrow my search. There was a John W. Donovan in 1880 in Waukon, Allamakee County, Iowa, with a wife Maria, both the right ages to be the couple I sought. Living with them was John's brother "Neily," a nickname for Cornelius. I found a civil marriage record that gave Maria's maiden name but no other helpful clues except the minister's name, Father David Slattery. I researched him to learn what parish John and Maria were married in. Then, from the church records, I added another relative: Margaret Donovan, a baptism sponsor for John and Maria's first child. I'd also researched

John and Maria's North Dakota children, and by obtaining the children's death certificates and obituaries, I was able to confirm I had the right Iowa couple.

I braved Iowa's 1870 census indexes, looking for a John, a Cornelius or Neil, and a Margaret or Maggie of the right ages in one household. In a printed 1870 census index, I found several households with children of these names. But only one fit the age configuration: the household of Martin Holverson and his wife, Catherine, included the three children, plus six more. Going on the assumption the Donovan father had died by 1870 and his wife remarried, I checked for a probate in Allamakee County. There I found one for Daniel Donovan, naming his wife Catherine and nine minor children including John, Cornelius and Margaret. The estate wasn't settled until all Daniel's children had come of age in 1887, 22 years after he died. John was recorded in the probate as John W. Donovan, with wife Maria, then residing in North Dakota. I'd found the immigrant ancestors, so I could next focus on searching for where in Ireland they came from.

STEP 3 ✦ Understand Ireland's Geographic Divisions

To find records in Ireland, you'll need to learn not only your ancestors' Irish county, but also the townland—which isn't a town. Townlands are the smallest administrative division in Ireland, similar to our neighborhoods. Be aware of several other geographic divisions, too: Your ancestor's "address" may be something like the townland of Knockavinnane, Poor Law Union of Tralee, Parish of

TIME LINE

500 B.C.	Celtic tribes arrive in Ireland.
460 A.D.	St. Patrick, the patron saint of Ireland, dies on March 17.
841	Vikings build their first settlements in Ireland.
1169	Normans, Welshmen and Flemings invade Ireland.
1200	Modern Irish grammar standardized.
1446	The Blarney Castle, home of the famous Blarney Stone, is built.
1607	English government confiscates part of Northern Ireland.
1613	English and Scottish Protestants colonize Ulster.
1649	English Protestant Gen. Oliver Cromwell arrives in Ireland to crush rebellion.
1690	English King William defeats the exiled English King James II at the Battle of the Boyne.
1695	Law forbids Irish Catholics from voting or joining the armed forces.
1759	Arthur Guinness starts brewing his famous dark beer at St. James' Gate.
1780	Irish nationalist leader Henry Grattan calls for home rule.
1791	Society of United Irishmen is formed to fight for political, economic and social rights for all Irish.
1793	Catholics can vote.
1800	Dublin Parliament dissolves itself; England and Ireland unite as one country.

1845 ◆	Potato famine drives 1.6 million Irish to migrate to the United States between 1847 and 1854.
1900 ◆	Nationalists demand freedom from British rule.
1914 ◆	Home rule bill becomes a law but is delayed until the end of World War I.
1916 ◆	Hundreds of Irish rebels die in unsuccessful Easter Rising.
1921 ◆	Southern Ireland becomes a free state; six northern counties remain part of the United Kingdom.
1923 ◆	Poet and playwright William Butler Yeats wins Nobel Prize.
1972 ◆	British troops fire on crowd of civil rights protesters on Bloody Sunday; protesters destroy British embassy three days later.
1993 ◆	Prime ministers of GreatBritain and Ireland sign declaration promising peace to Northern Ireland.
1997 ◆	Frank McCourt wins the Pulitzer Prize for *Angela's Ashes*.
1998 ◆	Voters approve the Good Friday Agreement, outlining Northern Ireland's relationship to Ireland and the United Kingdom.
1999 ◆	Ireland adopts the euro as its official currency, dropping the Irish pound. Northern Ireland continues to use the British pound.
2009 ◆	Ireland's economy falls into a depression, leading to the emigration of tens of thousands of people.

Ballymacelligott, Barony of Trughanacmy, County Kerry, Province of Munster.

Don't worry if this sounds like a bad tongue twister. To sort out these geographical divisions, start with the Administrative Divisions of Ireland explanation **<rootsweb. ancestry.com/~fianna/guide/land-div.html>** and the *General Alphabetical Index to the Townlands and Towns, Parishes and Baronies of Ireland* (Genealogical Publishing Co.). At **<www.seanruad.com>**, you can search on a townland and get the name of its province, Poor Law Union, county, parish and barony.

STEP 4 ◆ Pinpoint the Place

Your next challenge is to identify that specific place of origin on the Emerald Isle. Although the island of Ireland is about the size of Indiana, it can seem as big as Jupiter if that's all you have to go on.

Of course, learn all you can about your Irish ancestor in American records, and with a bit of Irish luck, you might discover her origins. Leave no Blarney Stone unturned in your search, including tombstones. The Irish are known for including the county and sometimes the townland of origin on their headstones—for example, Bridget McNamara's Richmond, Va., headstone says she was a native of Kildysart, County Clare, Ireland. Be sure to look for obituaries, death certificates and church records in America, as Catholic priests with largely Irish congregations might have included this information in records of marriages, baptisms or burials (see the February 2004 *Family Tree Magazine* for church records how-tos). But a place of origin can turn up in any record, so gather every document your ancestor might've created in America.

Expanding your search to all family members' records is key, too, as I learned when researching my great-grandmother Delia Gordon. She and her twin sister, Mary, emigrated from Ireland. Some relatives thought they were from County Cork. Records for Delia, Mary and their immediate families said only "Ireland." When Mary attempted suicide in 1906, a newspaper article mentioned another sister, Annie, whom I hadn't known about. I started tracking Annie's family, and her husband's naturalization gave Annie's origins as County Leitrim. Because of my lengthy search far the three sisters, I could give the County Leitrim Heritage Centre (part of the Irish Family History Foundation's network of genealogy centers) enough information to find the Gordons in church records. Turns out they lived in the townland of Ardvarney.

To find Irish Heritage Centres and learn what records they have, go to **<www.rootsireland. ie>**. A growing online database, RootsIreland.ie is run by the nonprofit Irish Family History Foundation (IFHF) with a goal to create a mega-database of Irish records from local historical societies, clergy, civil authorities, county libraries and government agencies.

The site currently has extracts from more than 18 million records: baptismal and birth records, marriage records, burial and death records, census records, gravestone inscriptions, passenger lists and Griffith's Valuation of Rateable Property. When you visit the home page, click the map of Ireland on the right. Color coding tells you which counties have records online: Only a few areas—a pocket in Dublin and counties Clare, Carlow, Kerry and south Cork—haven't yet put their records on the site.

If you're still coming up empty on the place of origin, broaden your search to people associated with your ancestor, such as witnesses to baptisms, deeds and other records, as well as Irish-born neighbors listed in the census. Immigrants tended to migrate with and settle near people they knew from their homeland.

STEP 5 ✦ Search for Descendants

Still not finding the place in Ireland? After you've exhausted all the records that the Irish immigrant, her family and associates might have created, start researching the lines forward. Use censuses, vital records, city directories, online phone directories and message boards to research the children and grandchildren of the immigrant generation. Information on family origins might have been passed down in another branch as oral history or a document that's now in the hands of a second cousin.

A word of caution, though: Family stories may claim your ancestor came from County Cork (as they did for my great-grandmother), Dublin or Londonderry. While it's certainly possible, these were also sites of major ports of departure. It's possible your immigrant left from one of these places but was born and raised elsewhere. If these areas come up, activate your genealogy radar and dig deeper.

STEP 6 ✦ Explore Irish Record Resources

Once you find an Irish place of origin, you might be surprised how many records from Ireland are available to you here in America. The Church of Jesus Christ of Latter-day Saints' Family History Library (FHL) **<familysearch.org>** in Salt Lake City has more than 11,500 rolls of microfilmed Irish records and 3,000 microfiche, You can visit a branch Family History Center (FHC) to order films for viewing there. (See **<familysearch.org>** to find a center near you.)

The bounty includes census, lands probate, military, vital (both civil and church) and other records—more Irish research material in one place than just about anywhere else. The FHL also has maps and more than 3,500 reference book, directories and periodicals covering Irish history, genealogy and geography.

To learn more about the FHL's microfilmed records and get additional tips for tracing Irish roots, see **<www.familysearch.org/learn/wiki/en/Ireland>**.

The sheer numbers of Americans claiming Irish ancestry translates into plentiful online resources. Start sorting them out at Cyndi's List **<cyndislist.com/ireland.htm>**. GENUKI **<www.genuki.org.uk/big/irl>**, a free site for UK and Ireland research, is a must-visit destination. Select your ancestral counties or "all of Ireland" for how-tos, historical information, surname list, recommended references and links to sites with genealogical records.

Visit the Ireland GenWeb Project **<www.irelandgenweb.com>** and the Northern Ireland GenWeb Project **<rootsweb.ancestry.com/~nirwgw>** for mailing lists and record abstracts. (Volunteers oversee each county site, so content varies.) As for subscription-based websites, Irish Origins' **<www.irishorigins.com>** records include Griffith's Valuation, a will index and the 1851 Dublin city census.

STEP 7 ✦ Get Your Hands on the Records

Following is an overview of the records with which you'll start your Irish ancestral research, plus a few more. Keep in mind that while some websites link search results to record images, much of what you'll find online is abstracted information from the actual record. Look for source details and seek the original record whenever possible.

CENSUSES: Irish censuses were taken every 10 years starting in 1821 through 1911. But because the Irish Civil War disrupted the next enumeration, it didn't happen until 1926. (This and later censuses aren't open for research.)

Unfortunately, few of those census records are left. The 1922 Four Courts fire in Dublin, sparked by Irish patriots, ruined all but fragments of returns from 1821 through 1851. The government destroyed those from 1861 to 1891 after compiling population statistics. So the only ones you can use are the 1901 and 1911 censuses.

The schedules give each person's name, relationship to the head of the household, religion, literacy, occupation, age, marital status, county of birth and ability to speak English or Irish.

The National Archives of Ireland has made 1901 and 1911 census records free online **<www. census.nationalarchives.ie>**.

Until then, since there's no microfilm index, you'll need to find the FHL film with your ancestors' county and district electoral division (DED). Find the DED in Townlands in 1901–1911 Censuses of Ireland, Listed by District Electoral Divisions, on FHL microfilm rolls 1544947 through 1544954. Then run a place search of the FHL catalog on the county and civil parish, and look for a 1901 or 1911 census heading.

You may be able to locate online indexes or abstracts for some areas. Check the county listings at the Ireland and Northern Ireland GenWeb sites, and see Census Online **<www.census. nationalarchives.ie>** and Census Finder **<www.censusfinder.com/ireland.htm>**.

We mentioned before that most of the 1841 and 1851 Irish censuses were destroyed (only the 1841 enumeration of the parish of Killeshandra in County Cavan survived). But here's some good news: During the 1910s, Irish clerks used the 1841 and 1851 censuses to prove age on Old Age Pension applications. They searched census returns and recorded what they found on pension forms. Even if your ancestor left Ireland before the 1910s, one of his family members who stayed behind might have applied for an Old Age Pension. The forms provide the applicant's address at the time he applied, names of the applicant's parents (including the mother's maiden name), and the applicant's address in 1841 or 1851 (county, barony, parish, townland and street, if in a town). Some pension clerks even recorded the names and ages of everyone in the census household, so it's worth a look even if your ancestor was one of those pre-1910 immigrants.

The original pension forms are at the National Archives of Ireland **<www.nationalarchives. ie>** (for counties now in the Republic of Ireland) and the Public Record Office of Northern Ireland **<www.proni.gov.uk>** (for counties now in Northern Ireland). Pension records for Northern Ireland and County Donegal also are online at Ireland Genealogy **<www.ireland- genealogy.com>**, where it costs about $3 per record view.

For both the Republic of Ireland and Northern Ireland, the pension forms also are on FHL microfilm, "Census search forms for the 1841-1851 censuses of Ireland" **<www.familysearch. org/search/catalog/1039474>**. The indexes and forms are arranged by county, then barony, parish and townland. First look for your ancestor in the index, which will tell you from which census the form was compiled. Copy the reference number from the index, as this is what you'll need to find the form on microfilm. You can rent the film by visiting your local Family History Center.

CHURCH RECORDS: Look for baptisms or christenings, marriages, burials and meeting minutes. Though today's Irish citizens practice many religions, pre-20th century Irish were predominantly Catholic, Protestant (Church of Ireland, the state church), Presbyterian, Methodist and Quaker (Society of Friends). Each denomination had its own systems for keeping and retaining records. The FHL has microfilmed a third of all Catholic parish registers, some transcriptions of Church of Ireland and Presbyterian parish registers, and a good number of Quaker parish registers. Run a place search of the online catalog on your ancestors' county, then look for a church records heading. Visit the GenWeb sites for your counties of interest, too—they may have abstracted church records.

An 1876 law required Church of Ireland parishes to send their registers to the Public Record Office in Dublin. This law was amended in 1878 to let parishes with sufficient storage keep their records, so not all parish records went to Dublin. Further, some ministers copied records before sending on the originals. That means you still can find many Church of Ireland records despite the 1922 fire.

If the FHL doesn't have your ancestors' church records, you can find out where to request them by consulting the 11-volume *Manuscript Sources for the History of Irish Civilization* by Richard J. Hayes. Look in the subject indexes under Parish Registers and Vestry Books for Church of Ireland records; look by denomination for other churches' records. In the place indexes, look for church records by county and then town, city or parish.

The National Library of Ireland also has many parish registers; see its guide at **<www.nli.ie/en/parish-register.aspx>**.

CIVIL REGISTRATION: Ireland's civil birth, marriage and death records begin in 1864. (For earlier dates, you'll need to look for vital statistics in church records.) Civil registration records are organized into districts. The originals stayed with district registrars, with copies forwarded to the General Register Office in Dublin **<www.groireland.ie>** (staff there can respond to record requests but can't do research for you). Records for Northern Ireland were moved to the General Register Office or its district offices **<www.nidirect.gov.uk/gro>**.

The FHL has many of the birth, marriage and death indexes and registers for Ireland and Northern Ireland on microfilm. Births from 1864 to 1958, marriages from 1845 to 1958, and deaths from 1864 to 1958 are also searchable at **<familysearch.org/search/collection/1408347>**. Before 1878, the indexes are arranged by year and alphabetically by surname; after that, they're alphabetical by quarter year.

The place name you'll find recorded in the index to civil registrations is the district where the event was registered. So, for example, the index might show, "Gordon, Mary. Manorhamilton. vol. 10 page 501." Manorhamilton is the registration district, but not necessarily the place where Mary was born. You would need to look at the record to learn the townland where this Mary Gordon was born. And to determine what county that registration district is in, go to **<www.connorsgenealogy.com/districts.htm>**. You can see a map of the districts at **<www.connorsgenealogy.com/RegistrarDistrictsMap.jpg>**.

GRIFFITH'S PRIMARY VALUATION AND ORDNANCE SURVEY MAPS: Between 1848 and 1864, every civil parish in Ireland made a valuation of taxable property. These Griffith's Primary Valuation records name the head of household and the landowner, and tell the property acreage, value of the property and the tax assessed—making them a good substitute for the lost 19th-century population censuses. The lists are organized by county, barony, civil parish and townland.

Additionally, each townland has a map number so you can locate the property on Ordnance Survey maps—detailed maps first created in the 1830s. Using these resources, you may be able to identify the exact location of your ancestors' land and even their still-standing cottage.

You'll find Griffith's valuations and survey maps online (except for counties now in Northern Ireland) at Irish Origins. There, you can search records from 1847 to 1864 on a person's name or a place and narrow results by townland or other administrative division. Irish Origins is the only place online to get all the valuations, including images of the original records. Griffith's Valuation is also searchable (without images) at **<www.askaboutireland.ie/griffith-valuation>**.

Ordnance Survey maps (1837 to 1913) also are available through fee-based sites such as PastHomes **<www.pasthomes.com>**. The FHL has maps from 1834 to 1845 on microfiche.

TITHE APPLOTMENTS: Predating Griffith's Valuation are Tithe Applotment Books, kept from 1823 to 1838. Everyone, regardless of religion, was supposed to pay a tithe to support Church of Ireland clergy. Tithes record the head of the household's name and the property value. In 1831, ancestors who defaulted on their tithes were recorded on another list—see FHL microfiche 6394360 through 6394367 to find out which counties have these records on film.

Like Griffith's valuations, you'll find tithe applotments online at commercial and volunteer websites, as well as in books and FHL microfilm.

If you're lucky enough to research in Ireland, consider adding these repositories to your itinerary: In the Republic of Ireland, go to Dublin and visit the National Archives and National Library, Genealogical Office **<www.nli.ie/en/heraldry-collections.aspx>**, General Register Office, Land Valuation Office **<www.valoff.ie/research.htm>** and Registry of Deeds **<www.landregistry.ie>**.

In Northern Ireland, stop by the Public Record Office of Northern Ireland, Presbyterian Historical Society **<www.presbyterianhistoryireland.com>** and General Register Office.

PRISON RECORDS: Harsh times called for harsh measures, and many of our Famine-era ancestors were arrested for crimes such as stealing from a neighbor's garden. From 1790 to 1924, drunkenness accounted for more than 30 percent of crimes reported and more than 25 percent of incarcerations, according to prison registers on subscription site FindMyPast.ie **<www.findmypast.ie>**. Considering that more than 3.5 million names (prisoners, as well as relatives and victims) are listed in the records when the Irish population averaged 4 million, the odds are good you might find a relative.

By 1822, Ireland was home to 178 prisons. FindMyPast.ie's Irish Prison Registers 1790-1924 collection covers a variety of institutions, from county prisons to sanatoriums for alcoholics. Many of the transgressions were minor, such as being "idle" or "a suspicious character." The registers give details such as the prisoner's name, address, place of birth, occupation, religion, education, age, physical description, next of kin, crime committed, sentence and dates of committal and release (or death date).

You can access the collection on FindMyPast.ie with a subscription or with Pay As You Go credits. Keep in mind that a county search on this site checks the county where the prison is located, not necessarily the county of birth or where your ancestor lived. The original prison registers are at the National Archives of Ireland in Dublin **<www.nationalarchives.ie>**.

NATIONAL SCHOOL RECORDS: Irish National School records cover from 1831, when National Schools were established, through 1921. School registers typically give the name and age of the pupil, religion, father's address and occupation, and general observations about the student. Some may record the student's birth date, attendance, grades and when the pupil left the school.

Although most school registers are still in the custody of the local school or church, the National Archives of Ireland has them for about 145 schools in counties now in the Republic of Ireland. They date primarily from the 1870s and 1880s. For a list by county, see **<www. nationalarchives.ie/topics/Nat_Schools/ns.html>**. The FHL has some of these registers on microfilm. To see if any might cover your ancestor's school, run a Place search on the county (or city), then look for the subject heading of Schools. Read more about the registers at **<www. nationalarchives.ie/topics/Nat_Schools/natschs.html>**.

The Public Record Office of Northern Ireland's school records collection is much more substantial for the six Northern Ireland counties. That repository has more than 1,500 registers, most dating from the 1860s onward, though some date from the 1850s. Better yet, the FHL has these on 80 rolls of microfilm. Run a Place search of the online catalog on Ireland, then look for the subject category Schools. From there, look for "National school registers of North Ireland, 1850-1950: Down, Londonderry, Antrim, Armagh, Fermanagh, and Tyrone counties."

Then it gets messier: The records are cataloged by the name or location of the school. It might take searching through several registers for an area to find the school your ancestor attended. Additionally, there might be two registers for each school, one for female pupils and one for male pupils. Consult the finding aid "Descriptive Catalogue of Pre-1900 School Registers," which includes an alphabetical index of schools, on eight rolls of microfilm.

LAND RECORDS: Starting in 1708, land transactions were recorded with the Registry of Deeds in Dublin. This wasn't mandatory, so not all transactions were registered, but in these records you'll find deeds of sale, lease agreements, marriage settlements and wills.

Most likely, your ancestors didn't own land in Ireland, but that doesn't mean land records won't be valuable to your search. Many of our poor rural ancestors leased their small plots of land and cottages, and some leases were recorded among the land records. A common type of lease was a "lease for lives." This meant the persons named in the lease held the land for as long as someone named in the lease was still alive. Once no one on the lease was still living, the lease ended. The lease usually named three people—often a father, one of his sons and the youngest son, who presumably would be the longest-surviving tenant.

Leases could also be granted for a certain number of years, or land could be rented on an annual basis without a lease. I found the lease with my great-grandfather, David Norris, as the leaseholder, along with the amount of rent, after his father and older brother died.

After 1782, when some Penal Laws were relaxed against Catholics and dissenting Protestants, tenants could purchase land outright or "in fee." It might have taken several generations, though, for a family to save enough to purchase the land on which their homes stood. In the late 19th century, the government set up schemes to assist tenants in purchasing the property they leased.

The FHL has microfilmed indexes and deeds (1708–1928) from the Registry of Deeds for all of Ireland. In the library catalog, run a Place search on Ireland and look for the subject heading Land and Property. Then scroll down until you find "Transcripts of memorials of deeds, conveyances and wills, 1708-1929." The alphabetically arranged Surname Index includes only grantors (sellers). The grantor's name is followed by the grantee's (buyer's) name, county, year, volume number and deed number. There's no index to grantees.

It's easier to search the Land Index, which is arranged by county and barony. Look for all entries for your ancestor's townland (they won't necessarily be together or in any particular order). This index gives the parish, grantor, grantee, year, volume and deed number. After finding entries for the townland, search the column for grantees' names in that townland. You'll probably need to search many rolls of indexes; each index might cover only a five-year time span. If you find your ancestor in the index, look for the deed in the corresponding microfilm with that year and deed volume.

WILLS AND ADMINISTRATIONS: Most people in Ireland were too poor to leave wills, but don't make assumptions about your ancestors. Just as with land records, it's better to check a source and find nothing, than to assume your family isn't in the records. I didn't think any of my ancestors had anything of value to warrant a will, yet I found one for my great-great-grandfather John

Norris of Tamlaghtmore, County Tyrone, who died in 1898. Even though he didn't own land, he did own farming equipment.

Wills can be divided into pre-1858 and post-1858. The jurisdiction for keeping wills and administrations changed in 1858. Before, the Church of Ireland recorded these documents and transferred records older than 20 years to the Public Record Office in Dublin. Unfortunately, the records were destroyed in the Four Courts Fire. A good number of the church's indexes survived, however, as well as some abstracts. And don't forget to check the aforementioned Registry of Deeds, as some wills were recorded there.

After 1858, all probates and administrations were recorded at the Principal Registry in Dublin and at 11 District Registries throughout the country: Armagh, Ballina, Belfast, Cavan, Cork, Kilkenny, Limerick, Londonderry, Mullingar, Tuam and Waterford. Each registry includes several counties. County Tyrone, for example, is part of the Armagh Registry. For a list of counties within the districts, scroll down to the Districts subhead at **<www.from-ireland.net/ genealogy/Wills-%26-Deeds-Explanation>**. Original wills between 1858 and 1900 also were destroyed in the fire, but you can find transcribed copies from the 11 District Registries. Wills since 1904 are intact for all 12 registries.

If your ancestors were from Northern Ireland, you can search an index to the will calendar entries for the three District Probate Registries of Armagh, Belfast and Londonderry on the Public Record Office website. Calendars were published annually starting in 1858 and contain abstracts of wills and administrations. The calendars are arranged alphabetically by surname and can contain the name of the deceased, address, occupation, date of death, date of probate, whether a will or an administration (meaning no will, but sufficient enough estate to enter into probate) was filed, names and relationships of next of kin, value of the estate and the registry in which the will was proven. PRONI's database covers 1858 to 1919 and 1922 to 1943. Part of 1921 has been added, with remaining entries for 1920 to 1921 still to follow. The index links to digitized images from the copy will books for 1858 to 1900, some 93,000-plus images. And it's all free.

The Ulster Historical Foundation has an Index to Printed Irish Will Calendars, 1878–1900 (covering every Northern and Republic county) at **<www.ancestryireland.com/family-records/irish-will-calendars-1858-1878/>**; you must be a subscriber to search it.

The National Archives of Ireland is trying to reconstruct lost wills of the Republic of Ireland by using abstracts and requesting copies from families and attorneys. Consequently, it now has thousands of testamentary records you can search in the Irish Wills Index at subscription site IrishOrigins.com **<irishorigins.com>**. It covers only up to 1858, however.

You can find copies of surviving wills and administrations for the eleven District Registries on FHL microfilm. These can be difficult to find and use. In the online catalog, check under Ireland—Probate records, and also under Ireland—Probate records—Inventories, registers,

Census

Government censuses of the population are particularly valuable because they list nearly all the population at a given time. The Irish government took a census in 1813 (which no longer exists), then every ten years from 1821 through 1911. Due to the Irish Civil War of 1921–1922, another census was not taken until 1926. The next census was taken in 1936. Starting in 1946, censuses were taken every five years through 1971. Since 1971, censuses have been taken every ten years.

Only parts of the early censuses survive. The censuses from 1821 through 1851 were mostly destroyed in the 1922 fire at the Public Record Office in Dublin. The censuses from 1861 through 1891 were destroyed by the government after statistics had been compiled from them.

The 1901 census is the first complete census available for Ireland. The 1901 and 1911 censuses are available to the public, but all censuses taken since 1911 are not.

The 1821 to 1851 censuses are divided by county, barony, civil parish and townland. The 1901 and 1911 censuses are divided by county, electoral division and townland.

You will find the following information in the 1901 and 1911 censuses:

1901: The 1901 census lists each member of the household's name, age, sex, relationship to the head of the household, religion, occupation, marital status, county of birth (except for foreign births, which give country only), whether the individual spoke Irish and whether the individual could read or write.

1911: The 1911 census lists the same information as the 1901 census and adds for each married woman the number of years she had been married to her current husband, the number of children that had been born to them and the number of their children who were still alive.

catalogs. If you're at the library in Salt Lake City, look for the Irish Probates Register. It's easier to find the correct film using this guide than by using the catalog.

Another FHL microfilm source to check is "Calendar of the grants of probate and letters of administration made in the principal registry and in the several district registries, 1858–1920." Find these microfilms in the FHL catalog by searching under Ireland—Probate Records—Indexes.

Whether it's your mother, grandmother or some other relative who came from Ireland, 'tis a grand time to be an Irish genealogist. These often-overlooked sources and databases will help you find that "something in you Irish."

RESOURCES

ORGANIZATIONS AND ARCHIVES

BRITISH LIBRARY
Great Russell Street, London WCIB 3DG
England
E-mail: customer-services@bl.uk
<www.bl.uk>

GENERAL REGISTER OFFICE (IRELAND)
Government Offices, Convent Road,
Roscommon, Ireland
Phone: +353 (0) 90 6632900
Fax: +353 (0) 90 6632999
E-mail: gro@groireland.ie
<www.groireland.ie>

GENERAL REGISTER OFFICE (NORTHERN IRELAND)
Oxford House, 49-55 Chichester St., Belfast BT1
4HL, Northern Ireland
Phone: +44 (028) 9151 3101
E-mail: gro.nisra@dfpni.gov.uk
<www.groni.gov.uk>

IRISH GENEALOGICAL SOCIETY INTERNATIONAL
1185 Concord St. N, Suite 218, South St. Paul,
MN 55075
<www.irishgenealogical.org>

LINEN HALL LIBRARY
17 Donegall Square North, Belfast BT1 5GD,
Northern Ireland
Phone: +44 (0)28 9032 1707
E-mail: info@linenhall.com
<www.linenhall.com>

NATIONAL ARCHIVES OF IRELAND
Bishop Street, Dublin 8, Ireland
Phone: +353 (0)1 407 2300
Fax: +353 (0)1 407 2333
E-mail: mail@nationalarchives.ie
<www.nationalarchives.ie>

NATIONAL LIBRARY OF IRELAND
Kildare Street, Dublin 2, Ireland
Phone: +353 (0)1 603 0213
E-mail: info@nli.ie
<www.nli.ie>

PUBLIC RECORD OFFICE
The National Archives, Kew, Richmond, Surrey,
TW9 4DU
Phone: +44 (020 88) 763444
<www.nationalarchives.gov.uk>

PUBLIC RECORD OFFICE OF NORTHERN IRELAND
2 Titanic Blvd., Belfast BT3 9HQ, Northern
Ireland
<www.proni.gov.uk>

REGISTRY OF DEEDS (IRELAND)
Property Registration Authority, Chancery Street,
Dublin 7, DX 228, Ireland
Phone: +353 (0761) 001610
Fax: +353 (01) 804 8037
<www.landregistry.ie>

REGISTRY OF DEEDS (NORTHERN IRELAND)
Land & Property Services, Lincoln Building,
27-45 Great Victoria St., Malone Lower, Belfast
BT2 7SL, Northern Ireland
Phone: +44 (28) 9051 4635
Fax: +44 (28) 9025 1659
<www.dfpni.gov.uk/lps/index/
land_registration-2>

REPRESENTATIVE CHURCH BODY LIBRARY
Braemor Park, Churchtown, Dublin 14, Ireland
Phone: +353 (0) 1 492 3979
Fax: +353 (0) 1 492 4770
E-mail: library@ireland.anglican.org
<www.ireland.anglican.org/library>

VALUATION OFFICE
Irish Life Centre, Abbey Street Lower, Dublin 1,
Ireland
Phone: +353 1 817 1000
Fax: +353 1 817 1180
E-mail: info@valoff.ie

BOOKS

British Archives: A Guide to Archive Resources in the United Kingdom, 4th edition, by Janet Foster and Julia Sheppard (Palgrave Macmillan)

Directory of Irish Archives, 5th edition, edited by Seamus Helferty and Raymond Refausse (Four Courts Press)

A Genealogist's Guide to Discovering Your Irish Ancestors by Dwight A. Radford and Kyle J. Betit (Betterway Books)

Irish Records: Sources for Family and Local History, revised edition, by James G. Ryan (Ancestry)

The Irish Roots Guide by Tony McCarthy (Lilliput)

Quillen's Essentials of Genealogy: Tracing Your Irish & British Roots by W. Daniel Quillen (Cold Spring Press)

Tracing Your Irish Ancestors: The Complete Guide, 4th edition, by John Grenham (Genealogical Publishing Co.)

Tracing Your Irish Family History by Anthony Adolph and Ryan Tubridy (Firefly)

WEBSITES

AncestryIreland
<www.ancestryireland.com>

Association of Professional Genealogists in Ireland
<www.apgi.ie>

Center for Irish Studies
<www.stthomas.edu/irishstudies>

Emerald Ancestors
<www.emeraldancestors.com>

Eneclann
<www.eneclann.ie>

FindMyPast.ie
<www.findmypast.ie>

FromIreland
<www.from-ireland.net/genealogy>

GENUKI Ireland
<www.genuki.org.uk/big/irl>

Index to Printed Irish Will Calendars, 1878-1900
<www.ancestryireland.com/database.php?filename=db_wills>

Ireland Genealogy
<www.ireland-genealogy.com>

Irish Ancestors
<freepages.genealogy.rootsweb.ancestry.com/~irishancestors>

Irish Family History Foundation
<www.irish-roots.ie>

Irish Origins
<irishorigins.com>

Irish Times (1859-present)
<www.irishtimes.com/search>

Northern Ireland GenWeb Project
<rootsweb.ancestry.com/~nirwgw>

Origins Network
<www.origins.net>

RootsIreland
<www.rootsireland.ie>

CHAPTER TWO

ENGLAND AND WALES

By David A. Fryxell and Lise Hull

I f you're among the estimated 25 million Americans with English ancestry, there's never been a better time to explore your roots. Along with such sites as Ancestry.com **<ancestry.com>** and FamilySearch **<familysearch.org>**, your British cousins have gone on an online genealogy records spree. In fact, you can do so much genealogy research from your home in the States that you don't have to go on that dream trip to England to discover your roots there (but we won't mention that to your other half). These resources and research tips will acquaint you with your English and Welsh ancestors.

ENGLAND

We think of English arrivals in America as dating to the Mayflower and Jamestown, and it's true that England supplied a majority of the Colonial population. But even into the first half of the 19th century, English immigrants to the United States trailed only Germans and Irish. They actually outnumbered the Irish in the 1870 and 1880 censuses.

Look for English emigrants in the British subscription site FindMyPast. co.uk's **<www.findmypast.co.uk>** 1890 to 1960 lists of passengers leaving the United Kingdom. Although departure records for folks from England are rare before 1890, other resources can reveal your early immigrant's overseas origins. P. William Filby's *Passenger and Immigration Lists Index* (Gale Research), found in many libraries and on subscription site Ancestry.com (but not in the version of Ancestry.com you use at the library), is a good place to start finding early

US arrivals. The Family History Library (FHL) has "assisted emigrants registers" that give details on Englishmen who got a helping hand crossing the Atlantic (often as indentured servants). Clues also might lurk in nonimmigration records, such as probate files; many Americans were mentioned in wills back in their home country. The English birth data at FamilySearch.org can suggest places of origin for people matching your ancestors' names.

For English immigrants who arrived on US shores after 1820, use the passenger databases on Ancestry.com. You can search Ellis Island arrivals free at **<ellisisland.org>** and on FamilySearch. org **<familysearch.org>**. An index to passengers at Ellis Island's precursor, Castle Garden, is free at **<castlegarden.org>**.

Locating Places

Especially for earlier emigrants, make it your goal to narrow their locale in England to a particular parish, so you can consult the right church records. Landranger and other maps, available via **<www.ordnancesurvey.co.uk>** and **<www.streetmap.co.uk>**, can help you pinpoint English places; you can even search for house and farm names on these sites. The Institute of Heraldic and Genealogical Studies **<www.ihgs.ac.uk>** sells parish maps for every county in England as well as maps showing civil-registration districts. You can also consult the *Phillimore Atlas & Index of Parish Registers* by Cecil R. Humphery-Smith (History Press). The ever-helpful GENUKI site (for GENealogy researchers in the UK and Ireland) offers a searchable database of church locations at **<www.genuki.org.uk/big/churchdb>**.

When mapping your English ancestors, keep in mind that England changed its county boundaries in 1974. Pre-1974 counties are often referred to using a system of three-letter abbreviations called Chapman Codes ("NFK" for Norfolk, for example). You can find maps of pre- and post-1974 county configurations in FamilySearch's English research guide **<wiki.familysearch. org/en/England_Maps>**, and a guide to translating today's counties into the historic ones used at GENUKI at **<www.genuki.org.uk/big/eng/Modern.html>**.

The Family History Library catalogs its English records according to the place names used in John M. Wilson's work *The Imperial Gazetteer of England and Wales*, published about 1871. When you search for records in the FHL catalog on FamilySearch, select Place-names and type the parish or town name into the search box. You'll get suggestions for the county that town or parish is located in.

A wrinkle to remember in your research is that England switched from the Julian calendar to today's Gregorian calendar in 1752, omitting 11 days after Sept. 2 to align with the solar year. So the day after Sept. 2, 1752, was Sept. 14. At the same time, the year changed from starting on March 25 to starting on the familiar Jan. 1. (Previously, the day after March 24, 1565, would have been March 25, 1566.) To convert Gregorian dates to Julian ones (and vice versa), you can use the calculator at **<www.rosettacalendar.com>**.

Censuses

If your ancestors left Mother England relatively recently, you may be able to trace the family using the English census, which began collecting genealogically useful data in 1841 and every ten years thereafter. That first enumeration listed everyone in the household by name, sex, street, occupation and whether he or she was born in England. Ages are also given, but those for anyone over 15 were typically rounded down to the nearest multiple of five. This census was organized by county, "hundred" (an administrative division of land) and parish.

Censuses from 1851 on list name, age (no more quirky rounding), occupation, relationship to the head of household, and parish and county of birth. Foreign births may list only the country. These censuses are organized by enumeration district. If you can't find an ancestor in a given census, keep in mind that the English enumerations were a snapshot of the population on a given night—June 7, 1841, for example. So your ancestor may be listed at a workplace, boarding school or if traveling, a hotel.

You can search the 1841 through 1911 censuses for free at FamilySearch.org and link to record images at FindMyPast.co.uk (fees apply). Another free resource is the index on the volunteer site <**www.freecen.org.uk**>, where coverage varies by census year and county. FindMyPast.co.uk is the only site offering all the 1841 through 1911 census records. You can search by name or address, and all results are linked to digitized images. Ancestry.com has searchable censuses with

Time Line

AD 48	Romans invade Wales.
1039	Gruffydd ap Llywelyn unites Wales under one rule.
1284	Statute of Rhuddlan subjugates Wales to England.
1400	Owain Glyndwr begins uprising against English rule.
1536	King Henry VIII unites England and Wales.
ca. 1600	Shakespeare's Hamlet premieres
1642	Civil war begins as Oliver Cromwell seeks to overthrow the monarchy; record keeping from here until the end of the Commonwealth period (1660) is irregular.
1649	King Charles I is beheaded.
1660	Monarchy is restored under Charles II, who discourages emigration.
1662	Act of Uniformity forces conformity to the Established Church; Welsh migration to America begins.
1707	Act of Union forms Great Britain from the Kingdom of England and Wales and the Kingdom of Scotland.
1733	Parish registers switch from Latin to English.
1752	Gregorian calendar adopted.
1754	Lord Hardwicke's Act outlaws marriages outside the Church of England except for Quakers and Jews.
1768	First edition of the Encyclopedia Britannica published.
1778	End of Penal Laws; many Catholic registers date from this time.

1801 ◆	Ireland unites politically with Great Britain to form the United Kingdom of Great Britain and Ireland.
1814 ◆	Treaty of Ghent ends final war between England and its former American colonies.
1825 ◆	An overpopulated Great Britain repeals anti-emigration laws.
1837 ◆	Queen Victoria begins her reign (to 1901) and civil registration begins.
1843 ◆	Charles Dickens writes *A Christmas Carol*.
1847 ◆	"Treachery of Blue Books" blames Welsh language for poor state of education.
1859 ◆	Charles Darwin publishes *On the Origin of Species*.
1863 ◆	World's first subway opens in London.
1901 ◆	First wireless message across the Atlantic.
1916 ◆	David Lloyd George becomes first Welsh Prime Minister.
1921 ◆	Republic of Ireland separates from the United Kingdom.
1928 ◆	Oxford English Dictionary completed.
1940 ◆	Winston Churchill becomes prime minister and Hitler launches the Battle of Britain.
1952 ◆	Elizabeth II becomes queen.
1964 ◆	"British Invasion" begins with the Beatles' appearance on "The Ed Sullivan Show"
1967 ◆	Welsh Language Act passed.
2011 ◆	Prince William marries Catherine Middleton.

record images from 1841 to 1901; the 1911 data are now being added.

Other online options include the Origins Network **<www.origins.net>**, with an index and images of the 1841, 1861 and 1871 enumerations. World Vital Records **<www.worldvitalrecords.com>** lets you search and view the 1841 to 1891 enumerations. You can search the 1901 census at **<www.1901censusonline.com>** and the 1911 census at **<www.1911census.co.uk>** (a National Archives website, powered by Find-MyPast.co.uk). If you want to go the microfilm route, the FHL has microfilmed English censuses from 1841 through 1891, along with many different census indexes.

Supplement your census searches with directories of counties, towns and parishes (these are much like city directories in the United States). The FHL has a large collection; search on the county or city and look under the directories heading. The University of Leicester has created a searchable digital library of Historical Directories **<www. historicaldirectories.org>**, 1750 to 1919, with high-quality reproductions of many of these rare books.

Birth, Marriage and Death

English birth, marriage and death (BMD) records began not long before the census, on July 1, 1837, making that 1837 to 1841 period a key demarcation in English genealogical research. Full compliance with the new civil registration requirements, which were voluntary until 1874, sometimes lagged, but 90 to 95 percent of all pre-1875 births and nearly all deaths and marriages got recorded.

Birth registrations generally include the child's name, sex, birth date and birthplace, the parents' names (including mother's maiden name) and father's occupation. Death certificates usually give only the name, age, occupation, date, place and cause of death; a spouse's name is sometimes listed or, if the deceased was a child, a parent's name may be filled in the blank for occupation.

Marriage certificates typically contain the date and place; the church denomination if any, names and ages of bride and groom; whether each was single or widowed; their occupations and residences at the time of marriage; plus the names and occupations of each father. It's often noted whether either father was deceased. When looking for marriage certificates, remember that weddings most often took place in the bride's parish.

Researching in civil registrations is a two-step process. First, look for an ancestor's event in the quarterly indexes produced by the UK Office for National Statistics. The earliest indexes list only name, registration district, and the volume and page number of the certificate. After 1865, death indexes include age at death. After June 1911, birth indexes also list the mother's maiden name. And post-1911 marriage indexes give the spouse's surname, handy for cross-referencing.

The FHL has microfilm copies of all these indexes through 1980 but doesn't have any copies of actual certificates. The volunteer-transcription FreeBMD project **<www.freebmd.org.uk>** has transcribed and made searchable more than 200 million individual index records to date. If you can't find your kin for free, FindMyPast.co.uk has fully indexed and searchable birth, marriage and death records. Another pay site, BMDIndex **<www.bmdindex.co.uk>** also lets you search birth, marriage and death indexes from 1837 on—covering a total of 255 million events.

Once you've found an ancestor in a BMD index, step two is to obtain a copy of the full birth, marriage or death certificate from the General Register Office. You can take advantage of an online ordering service at **<www.gro.gov.uk/gro/content/certificates/default.asp>** and charge fees and overseas postage to your credit card. For standard service with the index reference supplied, orders are sent on the fourth working day after receipt, not including weekends or bank holidays **<en.wikipedia.org/wiki/Bank_holiday#List_of_current_holidays>**.

Church Records

For early arrivals to the United States—and to push your research back beyond 1837—you'll need to turn to church records. (These continued after 1837 and can be used to double-check BMD records or as a way to fill in a gap.) The Church of England began keeping records in the 1530s, and beginning in 1598, parishes were required to make copies ("bishop's transcripts") for their local bishop. The originals and copies may differ slightly in details, so it's worth checking both. Even if your ancestors were "nonconformists" (they didn't belong to the Church of England) their marriages may have been recorded there. For other nonconformist records, see the pay site BMDRegisters **<www.bmdregisters.co.uk>**.

English Census

The English government has taken a census every 10 years since 1801 (with the exception of 1941, due to World War II). Prior to 1841, the censuses are merely a head count of the people in a certain area, with no real genealogical use; however, some parishes collected the names of their parishioners and a few of these lists still survive.

The 1841 census was conducted on June 7. All censuses between 1851 and 1931 were taken between March 31 and April 8. Only the people who spent the night in each household were enumerated; those traveling, away at school or working nights were listed where they spent the night.

The following information is included in these censuses:

1841: This document lists the members of every household, including name, sex, address, occupation and whether they were born in England. Note that census takers rounded the ages of those over age 15 down to a multiple of five, so 48 became 45.

1851 AND LATER: Here you will find the names, ages, occupations, relationship to the head of the household, and parish and county of birth (except foreign births, which may only give a country).

The censuses are organized by civil registration districts and then subdivided into enumeration districts. The 1841 census is an exception, arranged by "hundreds" (administrative subdivisions of land). On census films, you will find a title page with the district number and a description of the area covered by each enumeration district.

The original census records for 1841 to 1901 are held in the National Archives' Public Records Office (PRO) <**www.nationalarchives.gov.uk**>. Keep in mind that records less than a century old are confidential. You must provide the name and address (at the time of the census) of the individual you are seeking, as well as the written consent of the person on the record or a direct descendant.

Church records include christenings, marriages and burials. Marriages became separate registers beginning in 1754, and separate preprinted forms were introduced for all records in 1813. Most English church records are actually now kept in county record offices, which were considered safer, and they have been extensively microfilmed by the FHL.

Christenings, usually within a few weeks of birth, were recorded with at least the date and infant's name; you may also learn the father's name and occupation, mother's first name, the infant's birth date and legitimacy, and the family's place of residence. Beginning in 1813, the form asked for the date, child's given name, both parents' first names, family surname, residence, father's occupation and minister's signature. The birth date was sometimes included.

Marriage records can be more sparse, listing only the date and names of the bride and groom. Especially after 1754, you may also find each person's status (single or widowed) and place of residence, plus the groom's occupation. In addition to the marriage register, you may locate ancestors in a register of banns (announcements of intent to marry); check the FHL catalog by parish for these. Marriage licenses might have been issued in lieu of the three-week banns process; these are mostly kept in county offices and may be found in the FHL catalog under the name of the county (look under Church Records).

You can also consult several marriage indexes, the largest of which is *Boyd's Marriage Index*, covering 4,375 parishes. It's available from the FHL.

Prior to 1813, burial registers list the deceased's name and burial date and may also give age, place of residence, cause of death and occupation. A wife's entry may give her husband's name, and a child's record might list the father's name. The forms introduced in 1813 call for name, age, place of residence, burial date and the minister's signature.

You might also investigate cemetery records, as "monumental inscriptions"

Telephone booth, London

(MIs) on tombstones often give not only birth, marriage and death data but also cause of death, military service or occupation. Prior to the Burial Acts of 1852 and 1853, which led to the establishment of town cemeteries, most people were buried in church graveyards. Many MIs have been transcribed by volunteers; click on your ancestor's county at **<genuki.org.uk/big/ eng>** to explore these lists.

Online, the best way to dive into English church records is via FamilySearch.org's International Genealogical Index of transcribed records, which in the updated version of the site are in databases such as England Births and Christenings, 1538-1975. FamilySearch.org also includes some digitized parish records. The ever-growing FreeREG project is transcribing parish records and posting at **<www.freereg.org.uk>**. You can also click to online church records and other marriage records at Ancestry.com, British Origins, World Vital Records and FindMyPast.co.uk.

Wills and Probate

Probate records are another valuable resource for delving further back into the past, especially if your English ancestors were relatively well-off. Only about 10 percent of English estates prior to 1858 went through probate in court, but it's estimated that a quarter of the population either left a will or was mentioned in one. It's worth looking for probate records for your English ancestors.

The Church of England, which was in charge of probating estates until Jan. 11, 1858, had more than 300 special probate courts. To find the right court, consult the FHL's 40-volume series of color-coded maps and probate keys. First you'll need to use the book or paper maps (available at many Family History Centers) to find the court. Then use the key (available along with the maps, as well as on microfilm and microfiche) to find the FHL call numbers for available records.

If an ancestor died between 1796 and 1858, you may be able to take a shortcut through indexes of estate-duty registers, which don't require exact knowledge of the deceased's residence. The actual registers, which recorded payment of a tax on all estates valued over 10 pounds, may also contain details not found in the original will. They are especially useful for estates in Cornwall, Devon and Somerset, where local probate records have been destroyed.

For later probate records, you can consult FHL microfilm of nationwide indexes to all wills and administrations of the Principal Probate Registry, which was created in 1858. Look in the catalog under England—Probate Records.

You can also search will records online in several collections at British Origins, which recently added the British Record Society Probate Collection of records from more than 20 counties dating as far back as 1320. FindMyPast.co.uk has a database of probate and wills from 1462 to 1858, and an index to death duty registers from 1796 to 1903. And the British National Archives' Discovery **<discovery.nationalarchives.gov.uk>** includes wills dating from 1384 to 1858 from the Prerogative Court of Canterbury and country court death registers between 1796 and 1811. Searching is free, with a small fee to download an image.

Military Records

Your English ancestor's military service opens another avenue of possible inquiry. Army records begin in 1660; prior to 1847, most English soldiers made a lifelong career of military service. Records before 1872 are organized by regiment, so it's useful to consult the regimental histories at the FHL (run a place search of the online catalog for Great Britain and look under the military history heading).

London Skyline, with the Thames, House of Commons, House of Lords, Parliament, Big Ben

English naval casualties are also included in the graves database. Other naval records date as far back as 1617; many are available only through the National Archives. You may find your English sailor ancestor in both the navy and the merchant marines: Seamen often moved back and forth and until 1853, enlistment was informal, typically lasting just three years.

Online, FindMyPast.co.uk offers an extensive collection of military databases. If your ancestor was an English "army brat," don't miss the databases of armed forces births between 1761 and 2005, and marriages between 1796 and 2005.

If an ancestor died while serving in one of the world wars, look in the Debt of Honour Register of the Commonwealth War Graves Commission **<www.cwgc.org>**. It lists 1.7 million members of British Commonwealth forces. (Note that it also includes 67,000 civilians who died as a result of enemy action in World War II.)

For more assistance in your search for English ancestors, see the suggestions and research guides in the free GENUKI site. You also can search the British National Archives' Access to Archives **<www.nationalarchives.gov.uk/a2a>**, which, won't serve up old ancestral paperwork but can tell you where to look for it among the 400-plus repositories across the UK. If all else fails, well, there's always that trip to jolly old England you've dreamed about.

WALES

On the Wales side of the Severn Bridge, a red dragon signals "Croeso i Cymru: Welcome to Wales." You have entered a tiny nation with its own Celtic language, rich heritage and distinctive landscape.

Boasting the cities of Cardiff, Swansea and Newport, South Wales is the most heavily populated part of Wales. It is dominated by English speakers and industrialization, thanks to King Coal, which has been mined and exported from the Valleys since the onset of the Industrial Revolution. Highlighted by rich, undulating farmland, West Wales features Pembrokeshire, long known as "Little England Beyond Wales," and Carmarthenshire, with its vocal pocket of Welsh-speaking residents whose voting strength helped create the National Assembly. Scenic Mid Wales, with its small villages, seaside vistas and Welsh-speaking communities, is often unwittingly bypassed by travelers anxious to reach Snowdonia National Park, where hulking grey crags are scattered not just with sheep but also with hikers. In the late 13th century, the mountainous terrain offered refuge to Welsh rebels fighting Edward I's army. Though the English king's mighty fortresses still dominate North Wales and slate mining has reshaped the land, the region is renowned for its beauty.

Emigration to America

You probably don't know that the Welsh actually discovered America well before Columbus sailed the Atlantic. In about 1169, Prince Madog ab Owain, a son of Owain Gwynedd, King of North Wales, voyaged from Wales to seek his fortune. Upon his return, he bragged of visiting a new land where the people lived peacefully. Many believe the land was America, and plaques commemorating the discovery have been laid at Rhos-on-Sea in North Wales, Madog's departure point and also at Mobile Bay, Ala., the prince's landing site across the ocean.

Despite Madog's momentous discovery, it took another 500 years before the Welsh began emigrating to America. According to David Peate, who details the pathway of Welsh emigration in Welsh Family History, "Despite the Toleration Act of 1688, religious dissenters were still excluded from many aspects of the political and social life of the nation. The American colonies offered the golden opportunity of relief; there was land available and the real prospect of religious and political liberty. It was against this background that the first sizeable emigrations from Wales occur." By the end of the 17th century, some 3,000 Welsh people had sailed to America, clustering together to continue practicing their individual religions.

In the 1790s, Wales suffered a severe economic and agricultural depression, which led to another wave of emigration. Sailing from Liverpool, Bristol, Milford Haven, Caernarfon and other ports, thousands of Welsh farmers, weavers, artisans and gentry sought relief in America, where land was abundant and inexpensive and the economy was stable. Others emigrated to Australia, Canada, New Zealand and South Africa.

Between 1815 and 1850, Welsh emigration to America soared, with new residents settling in New York, Pennsylvania, Vermont, Ohio, Wisconsin and Illinois. Some journeyed west to California to take advantage of the 1849 gold rush, while later in the century, opportunities in the higher paying industrial areas of Pennsylvania attracted Welsh miners and ironworkers. By 1900, Welsh settlers had also moved into Iowa, Kansas and Missouri, and a large number headed to Utah to join the Church of Jesus Christ of Latter-day Saints. Ultimately, Peate says, "On a rough and ready basis, it is considered that, during the years from 1820 to 1950, a conservative estimate of emigrants from Wales to the United States exceeds 250,000."

Consider joining your local St. David's Society or attending a *gymanfa ganu* to learn more about Wales and network with others digging up their Welsh roots. Gather as much information as possible, not only about your particular Welsh ancestor but also about the nation and its history.

Naming Conventions

Before delving too deeply into your roots, you will need to educate yourself about Welsh surnames. Even though their Anglo-Norman conquerors had fixed surnames, the Welsh continued to use the patronymic system of naming, at least in some parts of the country, until well into the 19th century. While most people use fixed surnames, some modern-day Welsh are reasserting their national identity by returning to patronymics, whereby children are identified in relation to their father.

Derived from "mab," which is similar to the Scottish "mac," the use of "ap" (before a name beginning with a consonant) or "ab" (prior to a name beginning with a vowel) indicates "son of." So, Madog ab Owain indicates that Prince Madog was Owain Gwynedd's son. Likewise, Llywelyn ap Gruffydd, the first and last native Prince of Wales, was the son of Gruffydd ap Llywelyn. Indeed, like most medieval Welshmen, Llywelyn claimed a lengthy pedigree: Llywelyn ap Gruffydd ap Llywelyn ab Iorwerth ab Owain ap Gruffydd ap Cynan ... and so on

Common Welsh names such as Bowen and Powell reflect patronymic origins. Bowen derives from ab Owain or ab Owen and Powell from ap Hywel. Price comes from ap Rhys, while Pritchard originated as ap Richard.

Besides using "ap" or "ab," the Welsh also added an **s** at the end of a father's forename to reflect kinship ties. So, John's son adopted the surname Johns, Jones or Jenkins. The same rule applies to Roberts, Williams and Richards. You need to be aware of these variations and cross-verify records to be certain you have identified the correct ancestor.

Sheila Rowlands adds, "Daughters were known by their father's name: Gwenllian *verch* (*ferch* in modern orthography) (daughter of) Rhys; the relationship was shortened to *vch* or *vz* in documents and appears also as *ach*. Traditionally, this led to women retaining their maiden names (that is, their father's name rather than their husband's)."

The idiosyncrasies of the Welsh language also affect the research process. For example, over time, Llywelyn ap Gruffydd's name may have been mutated to Gruffudd, Griffith or Griffiths, or even Guto. Madog may also be spelled Madoc; Maredudd has become Meredith; and Evan, Bevan, Jeavons and Ieuan are all variants of John.

Study one of the following books to bone up on the nuances of Welsh surnames: T.J. and Prys Morgan's *Welsh Surnames* (University of Wales Press), John and Sheila Rowlands' *The Surnames of Wales: For Family Historians and Others* (Genealogical Publishing Co.) or Sheila Rowlands' "The Surnames of Wales," in *Welsh Family History: A Guide to Research* (Federation of Family History Societies).

Parishes and Counties

Once you have determined your ancestor's name and any spelling variations that you might want to double-check, you need to locate the parish where the person lived. Again, it's not as easy as it sounds. As Bedwyr Lewis Jones states, "The main concern of family historians is to be able to identify and locate parishes. In doing this, there is one thing which has to be remembered—namely, that until fairly recently the spelling of place-names, even in official documents, could vary considerably. It is especially true in Wales where Welsh place-names have often been recorded by persons unfamiliar with the Welsh language. Cricieth in Caernarfonshire can appear as Crickaeth, Crikeith, Krickieth, Criccieth, etc."

To add to the confusion, Lewis Jones says, "In Wales, as in other countries, the same name may be borne by more than one parish." Trefdraeth is the Welsh name for Newport in Pembrokeshire and the name of a parish near Aberffraw on the Isle of Anglesey, yet the newest city in Wales is Newport, Monmouthshire. So, when you note which parish your ancestor was associated with, be sure to write down what county or diocese they belonged to as well. Then you can use that information as a good starting point for searching parish records or bishop's transcripts.

And just when you thought you had the parish and county figured out ... be aware that in 1974 and 1996 Wales underwent major structural reorganization. Counties came and went. Local authorities were carved out of historic counties; historic counties were reborn. Whereas Newport is now in Monmouthshire, it has also been part of Gwent. The Pembrokeshire Newport has also been in Dyfed. Most records refer to the pre-1974 counties, so it's vital that you identify the correct historic county for your search. Take a look at the Data Wales website **<www.data-wales.co.uk/walesmap.htm>** for help verifying a place or parish name. Family-Search has begun digitizing microfilmed Welsh parish records—see what's currently available at **<familysearch.org/learn/wiki/en/Welsh_parish_registers_on_microfilm>**.

Resources in Wales

Wales has made great strides in putting genealogical resources online. The National Library of Wales (NLW) has digitized a number of records and resources for family historians—you can

see the full collection at Digital Mirror <**www.llgc.org.uk/index.php?id=122**>, which includes photograph archives, historical manuscripts and Welsh biographies. The library's page of links to electronic resources at <**www.llgc.org.uk/index.php?id=electronicresources**> includes:

- **Crime and Punishment** <**www.llgc.org.uk/sesiwn_fawr/index_s.htm**>: the gaol files of the Court of Great Sessions in Wales from 1730 to 1830
- **Manorial Documents Register** <**www.nationalarchives.gov.uk/mdr**>: records include court rolls, surveys, maps, land terriers and all other documents relating to the boundaries, franchises, wastes, customs or courts of a manor.
- **Newsplan Cymru** <**www.newsplanwales.info/s001.htm**>: a newspaper microfilming initiative where you can search for Welsh newspaper holdings.

Once you've located a Welsh ancestor in the index at <**www.freebmd.org.uk**>, you can easily order copies of vital records from as early as July 1837 from the General Records Office <**www.gro.gov.uk/gro/content**>. You can search for wills proved in the Welsh Ecclesiastical courts before 1858 at <**cat.llgc.org.uk/cgi-bin/gw/chameleon?skin=profeb&lng=en**>; you can view scanned images online and order digital or printed copies for a fee.

Once you have exhausted all research avenues at home, it's time to visit the land of your fathers. When you arrive, head to the NLW in Aberystwyth or to the county archives office where your ancestor's records may be stored. According to assistant archivist Eirionedd Baskerville, the best place to start at the NLW is the Department of Manuscripts and Records.

Generally speaking, each county archives office holds copies of parish registers and/or bishop's transcripts (in some cases dating to the 16th century); civil registrations of births, marriages and deaths after 1837; other ecclesiastical records; school, hospital and council records; census records; wills and other probate records; maritime records; trade directories; tax records; and quarter-sessions records. They also hold copies of regional publications and newspapers, maps, poor-law union records, police records and even medieval manuscripts and town charters.

Contact the NLW or archives office prior to your arrival to set up an appointment, to be certain they have the information you seek and to prepare the staff for your visit. Staff are more than willing to work with you and to advise you on what documents they may have related to the names you are interested in. In many cases, they will even photocopy information if you cannot go there in person. However, some county archives will charge you to undertake postal research, and others don't have enough staff to do private searches.

Last, but certainly not least, remember to explore the "old mountainous Cambria, the Eden of bards." When you return home, don't be surprised if you, like so many before you, suffer from the malady called *hiraeth*, a gut-level yearning to return to the land of your forebears. You may just find yourself returning time and again.

ORGANIZATIONS AND ARCHIVES

BRITISH ISLES FAMILY HISTORY
2531 Sawtelle Blvd., PMB #309, Los Angeles, CA 90064
<rootsweb.ancestry.com/~bifhsusa>

BRITISH LIBRARY
96 Euston Road, London, NW1 2DB, England
Phone: +44 843 208 1144
<www.bl.uk>

BRITISH LIBRARY NEWSPAPER READING ROOM
Colindale Avenue, London NW9 5HE, England
<www.bl.uk/reshelp/findhelprestype/news/blnewscoll>

FEDERATION OF FAMILY HISTORY SOCIETIES
Box 8857, Lutterworth, LE17 9BJ, England,
Phone: +44 1455 203133
E-mail: info@ffhs.org.uk
<www.ffhs.org.uk>

GENERAL REGISTER OFFICE
Certificate Services Section,
Box 2, Southport, PR8 2JD, England
Phone: +44 300 123 1837
E-mail: certificate.services@ips.gsi.gov.uk
<www.gro.gov.uk/gro/content/certificates/default.asp>

GUILDHALL LIBRARY
Aldermanbury, London EC2V 7HH, England
Phone: +44 20 7332 1868
<www.cityoflondon.gov.uk/things-to-do/visiting-the-city/archives-and-city-history/guildhall-library>

HISTORICAL MANUSCRIPTS COMMISSION
Quality House, Quality Court, Chancery Lane, London WC2A 1HF, England
Phone: +44 20 8876 3444
<www.nationalarchives.gov.uk/archives-sector/hmc.htm>

INSTITUTE OF HERALDIC AND GENEALOGICAL STUDIES
79-82 Northgate, Canterbury, Kent, CT1 1BA, England
Phone: +44 1227 768664
<www.ihgs.ac.uk>

THE NATIONAL ARCHIVES
Kew, Richmond, Surrey, TW9 4DU, England
Phone: +44 20 8876 3444
<www.nationalarchives.gov.uk>

THE OFFICE FOR NATIONAL STATISTICS
Customer Contact Centre, Room 1.101, Government Buildings, Cardiff Road, Newport, South Wales, NP10 8XG
Phone: +44 1329 444972
Fax: +44 1633 652981
E-mail: census.customerservices@ons.gsi.gov.uk
<www.ons.gov.uk/ons/guide-method/census/1991-and-earlier-censuses/guide-to-earlier-census-data/index.html>

BOOKS

Ancestral Trails: the Complete Guide to British Genealogy and Family History, 2nd edition, by Mark D. Herber (Genealogical Publishing Co.)

British Archives: A Guide to Archive Resources in the United Kingdom, 4th edition, by Janet Foster and Julia Sheppard (Palgrave Macmillan)

Directory of British Associations & Associations in Ireland, 20th edition, edited by Tony Chalcraft (Emerald Group Publishing)

The Family Tree Detective: Tracing Your Ancestors in England and Wales by Colin D. Rogers (Manchester University Press)

A Genealogical Gazetteer of England by Frank Smith (Genealogical Publishing Co.)

Genealogical Research in England and Wales, 3 volumes, by David E. Gardner and Frank Smith (Bookcraft Publishers)

A Genealogist's Guide to Discovering Your English Ancestors by Paul Milner and Linda Jonas (Betterway Books)

Genealogical Resources in English Repositories by Joy Wade Moulton (Hampton House)

Guides to Sources for British History Based on the National Register of Archives: Guide to the Location of Collections Described in the Reports and Calendars Series 1870–1980 (Her Majesty's Stationery Office)

In and Around Record Repositories in Great Britain and Ireland, 3rd edition, by Rosemary Church and Jean Cole (Federation of Family History Societies)

In Search of Your British and Irish Roots by Angus Baxter (Genealogical Publishing Co.)

An Introduction to the Census Returns of England and Wales by Susan Lumas (Federation of Family History Societies)

Making Sense of the Census by Edward Higgs (Her Majesty's Stationery Office)

Making Use of the Census, 2nd edition, by Susan Lumas, (PRO Publications)

Marriage and Census Indexes for Family Historians, 7th edition, edited by Jeremy Gibson and Elizabeth Hampson, (Federation of Family History Societies Publications)

The Phillimore Atlas and Index of Parish Registers by Cecil Humphrey-Smith (Genealogical Publishing Co.)

Pre-1841 Censuses & Population Listings in the British Isles by Colin R. Chapman (Clearfield) *Tracing Your English Ancestors* by Colin D. Rogers (St. Martin's Press)

WEBSITES
1901 Census Online
<www.1901censusonline.com>

1911 Census Online
<www.1911census.co.uk>

Absent Voters of Grimsby & Cleethorpes 1919 (England)
<www.angelfire.com/de/delighted/voters.html>

Access to Archives
<www.nationalarchives.gov.uk/a2a>

Alan Godfrey Maps
<www.alangodfreymaps.co.uk>

Ancestry Search, Staffordshire, United Kingdom
<www.ancestrysearch.co.uk>

ARCHON Directory
<www.nationalarchives.gov.uk/archon>

Ashover Parish, Derbyshire
<www.ashover.org>

Birmingham and Midland Society for Genealogy and Heraldry (Staffordshire, Warwickshire and Worcestershire)
<www.bmsgh.org>

BMDIndex
<www.bmdindex.co.uk>

BMDRegisters
<www.bmdregisters.co.uk>

British Heritage
<www.thehistorynet.com/BritishHeritage>

Commonwealth Graves Commission

Cornwall GenWeb
<rootsweb.ancestry.com/~engcornw>

County Free Look-ups
<www.genealogy-links.co.uk/html/lookups.index.html>

County Record Offices
<www.oz.net/~markhow/englishros.htm>

Cyndi's List: England
<www.cyndislist.com/uk/eng>

Derbyshire Family History & Genealogy
<www.ashbourne-derbyshire.co.uk>

DocumentsOnline
<www.nationalarchives.gov.uk/documentsonline>

England GenWeb Project
<rootsweb.ancestry.com/~engwgw>

English Origins
<www.englishorigins.com>

Family History Unit—Kingston up Hull City Libraries
<www.hullcc.gov.uk/genealogy>

Family Tree Magazine
<www.family-tree.co.uk>

Federation of Family History Societies
<www.ffhs.org.uk>

FindMyPast.co.uk
<www.findmypast.co.uk>

FreeBMD
<www.freebmd.org.uk>

FreeCEN UK Census Project
<www.freecen.org.uk>

FreeREG Parish Registers
<www.freereg.org.uk>

Gazetteer of British Place Names
<www.gazetteer.co.uk>

Genealogy 4U, North East Lincolnshire
<genealogy4u.co.uk>

GENUKI
<www.genuki.org.uk>

Hampshire Genealogical Society
<www.hgs-online.com>

Herefordshire-Gen UK
<www.herefordshire-gen.co.uk>

Local History and Genealogy Reading Room: Sources for Research in English Genealogy
<www.loc.gov/rr/genealogy/bib_guid/england.html>

National Archives 1911 Census
<www.1911census.co.uk>

Notes on medieval English genealogy
<www.medievalgenealogy.org.uk>

Old Yorkshire; Yorkshire's local and family history magazine
<www.oldyorkshire.co.uk>

Ordnance Survey
<www.ordnancesurvey.co.uk>

Origins Network
<www.origins.net>

Streetmap
<www.streetmap.co.uk>

The National Archives: Discovery
<discovery.nationalarchives.gov.uk>

UK Mailing Lists
<rootsweb.ancestry.com/~jfuller/gen_mail_country-unk.html>

UK Street Maps
<www.streetmap.co.uk>

Your Archives Wiki
<yourarchives.nationalarchives.gov.uk>

WALES RESOURCES

ORGANIZATIONS AND ARCHIVES

ANGLESEY COUNTY RECORD OFFICE
Shire Hall, Llangefni, Anglesey, Wales LL77 7TW
Phone: +44 1248 752080
<www.anglesey.gov.uk/community/
birth-marriage-and-death/
tracing-your-family-tree>

ASSOCIATION OF FAMILY HISTORY SOCIETIES OF WALES
Geoff Riggs, Peacehaven, Badgers Meadow, Pwllmeyric, Chepstow, Wales NP16 6UE
E-mail: secretary@fhswales.info
<www.fhswales.org.uk>

CARMARTHENSHIRE ARCHIVE SERVICE
Parc Myrddin, Richmond Terrace, Carmarthen, Wales SA31 1HQ
Phone: +44 1267 228232
Fax: +44 1267 228237
E-mail: archives@carmarthenshire.gov.uk
<www.carmarthenshire.gov.uk/English/
leisure/archives/Pages/archivesrecords.aspx>

CEREDIGION ARCHIVES
Old Town Hall, Queen's Square, Aberystwyth, Ceredigion, Wales SY23 2EB
Phone: +44 1970 633697
E-mail: archives@ceredigion.gov.uk
<archifdy-ceredigion.org.uk>

CONWY ARCHIVE SERVICE
The Old Board School, Lloyd St., Llandudno, Wales LL30 2YG
Phone: +44 1492 577550
E-mail: archifau.archives@conwy.gov.uk
<www.conwy.gov.uk/section.
asp?cat=772&Language=1>

DENBIGHSHIRE RECORD OFFICE
Archive Service
46 Clwyd St., Ruthin, Denbighshire, Wales LL15 1HP
Phone: +44 1824 708250
Fax: +44 1824 708222
E-mail: archives@denbighshire.gov.uk
<www.denbighshire.gov.uk>

FLINTSHIRE RECORD OFFICE
The Old Rectory, Rectory Lane, Hawarden, Flintshire, Wales CH5 3NR
Phone: +44 1244 532364
Fax: +44 1244 538344
<www.flintshire.gov.uk/wps/portal/english/
services>

GLAMORGAN ARCHIVES
Clos Parc Morgannwg, Leckwith, Cardiff, Wales CF11 8AW
Phone: +44 2920 872200
E-mail: glamro@cardiff.gov.uk
<www.glamro.gov.uk>

GWENT ARCHIVES
Steelworks Road, Ebbw Vale, Blaenau Gwent, Wales NP23 6DN
Phone: +44 1495 353363
E-mail: enquiries@gwentarchives.gov.uk
<www.gwentarchives.gov.uk>

GWYNEDD COUNCIL ARCHIVES
Caernarfon Record Office, County Offices, Shirehall Street, Caernarfon, Gwynedd, Wales LL55 1SH
Phone: +44 1286 679095
Fax: +44 1286 679637
E-mail: archives.caernarfon@gwynedd.gov.uk
<www.gwynedd.gov.uk>

HAVERFORDWEST LIBRARY
Former Youth Club, Off Dew Street, Haverfordwest, Pembrokeshire, Wales SA61 1ST
Phone: +44 1437 775244
Fax: +44 1437 767092
E-mail: haverfordwestlendinglibrary@
pembrokeshire.gov.uk
<www.pembrokeshire.gov.uk>

LLYFRGELL GENEDLAETHOL CYMRU/THE NATIONAL LIBRARY OF WALES

Aberystwyth, Ceredigion, Wales SY23 3BU
Phone: +44 1970 632800
Fax: +44 1970 615709
<www.llgc.org.uk/cac>

MADOG CENTER FOR WELSH STUDIES

University of Rio Grande, Box 500, Rio Grande, OH 45674
Phone: (800) 282-7201
E-mail: cnapora@rio.edu
<www.rio.edu/madog>

NORTH AMERICAN ASSOCIATION FOR THE STUDY OF WELSH CULTURE AND HISTORY

E-mail: ellisjs@umflint.edu
<www.naaswch.org>

NINNAU—THE NORTH AMERICAN WELSH NEWSPAPER

11 Post Terrace, Basking Ridge, NJ 07920
Phone: (908) 766-4151
Fax: (908) 221-0744
E-mail: ninnaupubl@cs.com
<www.ninnau.com>

PEMBROKESHIRE RECORD OFFICE

Prendergast, Haverfordwest, Pembrokeshire, Wales SA61 2EF
Phone: +44 1437 775456
E-mail: record.office@pembrokeshire.gov.uk
<www.pembrokeshire.gov.uk/content.asp?id=15732&d1=0>

POWYS COUNTY ARCHIVES OFFICE

County Hall, Llandrindod Wells, Powys, Wales LD1 5LG
Phone: +44 1597 826088
<archives.powys.gov.uk>

WELSH-AMERICAN GENEALOGICAL SOCIETY

60 Norton Ave., Poultney, VT 05764
<rootsweb.ancestry.com/~vtwags>

WELSH NATIONAL GYMANFA GANU ASSOCIATION

Megan Williams, Box 1054, Trumansburg, NY, 14886
Phone: (607) 279-7402
Fax: (877) 448-6633
E-mail: ihq@thewnaa.org
<www.wngga.org>

WEST GLAMORGAN ARCHIVE SERVICE

Civic Centre, Oystermouth Road, Swansea, Wales SA1 3SN
Phone: +44 1792 636589
Fax: +44 1792 637130
E-mail: westglam.archives@swansea.gov.uk
<www.swansea.gov.uk/index.cfm?articleid=406>

WREXHAM ARCHIVES AND LOCAL STUDIES

Wrexham County Borough Museum and Archives, Regent Street, Wrexham, Wales LL11 1RB
Phone: +44 1978 297480
Fax: +44 1978 297461
E-mail: archives@wrexham.gov.uk
<www.wrexham.gov.uk/english/heritage/archives>

BOOKS

Beginning Welsh Research by Annie Lloyd
(Annie Lloyd)

Researching Family History in Wales by Jean
Istance and E.E. Cann (The Federation of Family
History Societies)

Second Stages in Researching Welsh Ancestry
by John and Shelia Rowlands (Genealogical
Publishing Co.)

*The Surnames of Wales: For Family Historians
and Others* by John and Shelia Rowlands
(Federation of Family History Societies)

Welsh Family History: A Guide to Research,
2nd edition, by John and Shelia Rowlands
(Federation of Family History Societies)

Welsh Surnames by T.J. Morgan and Prys
Morgan (University of Wales Press)

WEBSITES

1901 Census Online
<www.1901censusonline.com>

1911 Census Online
<www.1911census.co.uk>

Cyndi's List: Wales/Cymru
<www.cyndislist.com/uk/wls>

Flintshire
<rootsweb.ancestry.com/~wlsflnsh>

Gwent Family History Society
<www.gwentfhs.info>

Kidwelly History
<www.kidwellyhistory.co.uk>

National Welsh American Foundation
<www.britannia.com/wales/nwaf.html>

Sources for Research in Welsh Genealogy
**<www.loc.gov/rr/genealogy/bib_guid/wales.
html>**

Wales
<britannia.com/celtic/wales>

Wales Genealogy Links
<www.genealogylinks.net/uk/wales>

The WalesGenWeb Project
<www.walesgenweb.com>

CHAPTER THREE

SCOTLAND

By Nancy Hendrickson and James M. Beidler

REGIONAL GUIDE

You don't have to be a genealogy buff to recognize that Scottish heritage is tightly woven into America's cultural fabric. We're not just talking about a fondness for plaid or the popularity of golf and movies such as *Brigadoon* and *Braveheart*. With 9.2 million people claiming Scottish and Scots-Irish ancestry, Scottish-Americans are not only the United States' eighth-largest heritage group—they outnumber the 5 million Scots in Scotland nearly two-to-one.

That adds up to plentiful research opportunities for those who want to trace their Scottish family trees. When I began researching my Hume/Home family, who left Edinburgh for Spotsylvania County, Va., in 1740, I had no idea of the depth and breadth of Scottish records online. For someone who specializes in US genealogy, it was thrilling to make the jump over the pond and discover a rich heritage dating back to the 1200s. You can make that exciting leap, too.

In the Rough

Scotland's turbulent and violent history can (and does) fill volumes, going back thousands of years. Its written history, however, begins about the time the Romans pushed into Britain, and the famed Hadrian's Wall separated Caledonia (the northern part of the island, or what's now Scotland) from the Roman Empire.

From its beginnings, Scotland seemed to be a favorite target for invasion, enduring attacks from Britons, Anglo-Saxons and Vikings. As a result, Anglo-

Saxon (a variant of English) became the predominant language in Lowland Scotland, while Highlanders primarily spoke Gaelic.

Some of Scotland's most important historical events relate directly to the tug-of-war with England for control over the country. Although William Wallace defeated Edward I at the Battle of Stirling Bridge—depicted in *Braveheart*—and Robert the Bruce defeated Edward II at the Battle of Bannockburn in 1314, constant warring between the two countries continued.

Wars were fought over allegiance to England, religion and succession to the crown. Calvinist preacher John Knox led a religious "revolution," resulting in Scottish Parliament adopting the Scot's Confession in 1560. Although Protestantism spread throughout Scotland, Catholicism remained the chief religion in the Highlands. The conflict culminated in England's Elizabeth I, a Protestant, famously ordering the execution of her Catholic cousin, Mary, Queen of Scots in 1587.

In 1603, Mary's son, James VI, became James I of England and politically united the two countries. Then in 1707, James' political unification became legal: The Act of Union abolished the English and Scottish parliaments and established the Parliament of Great Britain.

Migration Patterns

Scotland's historical unrest led to several key periods of emigration and immigration, which may explain your ancestors' movements—and guide your research.

- **English Civil Wars (1642 to 1651):** This "Great Rebellion" pitted royalists, who were loyal to King Charles I, against "roundheads," the Puritan supporters of English parliament. During the "Scottish Campaign" of 1650 to 1651, English Gen. Oliver Cromwell transported thousands of Scottish soldiers to the Americas.
- **Jacobite rebellions (1715 and 1745):** Known as "The Fifteen" and "The Forty Five," these uprisings aimed to return Stuart kings to the thrones of England and Scotland. The attempts failed, but they did result in Highlanders moving to the Lowlands, and 1,600 Scots being banished to the American Colonies.
- **Lowland Clearances (1760 to 1830):** As tenant farmers were forcibly removed from their farms, tens of thousands of Scots left for Canada and the United States.
- **Highland Clearances (late 1700s to 1870s):** Highland Scots also were forcibly displaced to the lowlands and coastal areas. Some evictions were so brutal that modern historians have labeled them as a variety of ethnic cleansing. As a result, waves of Highland Scots immigrated to the Carolinas, Nova Scotia and elsewhere in Canada.
- **Scots-Irish emigration (1600s on):** During the 17th century, at least 200,000 Presbyterians migrated from Lowland Scotland to Ulster (in northern Ireland); ultimately, 2 million of their descendants—known as the Scots-Irish, or Ulster Scots—would immigrate to North America. That includes 250,000 Scots-Irish who came to the American Colonies from 1717 to 1775, settling mainly in the Carolinas, Pennsylvania and Virginia. (Read more about Ulster Scots on pages 58–59.)

Even as early as the 1790 US census, more than 6 percent of America's population came from Scottish origins, with the majority living in Virginia or North Carolina. As a group, Scottish immigrants settled primarily in the Mid-Atlantic and Southern Colonies, although many went west to the wilderness and became one of the dominant groups in backwoods Tennessee and Kentucky.

The Immigrant Ships Transcribers Guild has passenger manifests for ships that left Scottish ports **<www.immigrantships.net/departures/scotland.html>** from the mid-1700s to early 1900s.

Research Tee Off

In this land of big history, big battles and big emotions, where should you start your family search? As with all other genealogy research, the first step in trekking up your Scottish tree is talking to family members. Find out as much as you can about which ancestors lived in Scotland and when. The most important information to gather is the first name, surname and date of birth, death or marriage of one of your Scotland-born ancestors—those facts will open your door to Caledonia.

If your relatives don't know specifics, you can track down this information in US sources such as passenger lists, naturalization records and obituaries. Aids such as P. William Filby's multivolume *Passenger and Immigration Lists Index*, found at libraries, and searchable at Ancestry.com **<ancestry.com>**, are two good starting points, as is FamilySearch's **<familysearch.org>** International Genealogical Index, which includes data extracted from Scottish parish records. Scots

TIME LINE

1297	William Wallace defeats the English at Stirling Bridge.
1542–1544	King Henry VIII invades Scotland in an attempt to bring it under the Church of England.
1552	Catholic Church orders registers for baptisms and marriage banns to be kept.
1560	Scotland officially breaks from the Roman Catholic Church and organizes the Church of Scotland.
1587	Mary, Queen of Scots, executed for treason.
1600	Scotland switches from the Julian calendar to the Gregorian calendar.
1707	Act of Union binds England, Wales and Scotland as Great Britain.
1715	First Jacobite rebellion.
1745	Second Jacobite rebellion.
1759	Robert Burns, Scotland's National Poet, born near Ayr.
1764	The Old Course at St. Andrews expands from 12 to 18 golf holes.
1775	Glenturret, Scotland's oldest distillery, established.
1783	Stamp Act passed, requiring three-penny tax to record an event in the parish register.
1794	Stamp Act abolished.
1801	First national census; subsequent censuses were conducted every ten years except for 1941.
1818	Sir Walter Scott publishes Rob Roy.
1820	Parishes required to keep registers.

1829	Catholic emancipation; church records usually begin here.
1843	Free Church forms.
1855	Civil registration begins in Scotland; births, deaths and marriages recorded.
1860	First British Open golf tournament, in Prestwick.
1874	Patronage abolished.
1886	Arthur Conan Doyle writes "A Study in Scarlet," his first Sherlock Holmes story.
1929	Scotland raises minimum age for marriage to 16.
1933	First modern sighting of Loch Ness Monster.
1939	The Marriage Act allows for civil weddings.
1962	Scottish actor Sean Connery stars in *Dr. No*, the first James Bond film.
1975	County structure revised; nine regions and three island areas replace the traditional counties.
1995	Mel Gibson stars in the Oscar-winning Braveheart, the story of William Wallace.
1996	County structure again revised; Scotland reorganizes into 29 unitary districts and three island areas.
1999	New Scottish parliament opens.

Origins **<www.scotsorigins.com>** offers a free search by parish.

You'll quickly discover a plethora of Scottish genealogical guidance, databases and records online. Our choice for a jumping-off place is the national tourism agency's Ancestral Scotland **<www.ancestralscotland. com>**, an in-depth site about Scottish history and ancestry research.

Then head over to FamilySearch's wiki on Scotland **<www.familysearch.org/learn/ wiki/en/Scotland>**, which provides details on available Scottish records. Pay special attention to the Historical Geography and Maps and Gazetteers sections: Because Scottish records are kept and filed by locality, you'll need to understand the country's modern and historical administrative divisions to know where to look for your family—and to be sure a record actually describes your ancestor, not someone else of the same name.

The key jurisdiction to learn is your family's parish: Before civil registration began in 1855, churches recorded vital events (collectively, the records are called "old parish registers"). Even after that, the civil registration districts in rural areas generally coincided with those of the parishes.

Note, too, that "shires" in Scotland are roughly equivalent to counties. Scotland changed its county boundaries significantly in 1975; the map on page 51 shows the earlier counties for research purposes.

People's Choice

Scotland is one of the friendliest countries for online family tree climbers—due in large part to ScotlandsPeople **<www.scotlandspeople.gov.uk>**. This official government source for Scottish genealogical data is the motherlode: 50 million records spanning the 1500s to 1900s. Those

TARTANS

All Scots can claim a tartan—your task is figuring out which one best fits you. Start by visiting the Scottish Tartan Society's website <**www.tartans.scotland.net**>, where you can search its Scottish Tartan World Register totaling more than 2,800 patterns.

But don't be surprised if a surname search yields no results. "Only about 20 percent of Scottish surnames have a clan/family connection," says society researcher Keith Lumsden. Though people often associate tartans with clans, there are actually nine other types (all of which are included in the register): district, regimental, royal, chief, hunting, dress, trade, mourning and corporate.

So if you can't claim a clan tartan, you can wear the district tartan for the area where your ancestor was born, married or did business—pretty much any connection will do. Or you can don the regimental "Black Watch," the official government plaid that's considered universal. Other tartan types are variations of these categories—for example, "hunting" tartans use more subdued shades for camouflage and "dress" tartans contain brighter hues—so it's possible that a family or district could have multiple tartans.

include civil registrations, which started in 1855 (birth records are restricted for 100 years, marriage records for 75 years and death records for 50), old parish registers (documenting births, baptisms and marriages from the mid-1500s until 1854), census records (every ten years from 1841 to 1901), and wills and testaments covering 1513 to 1901. The site is a joint venture of Scotland's three main record agencies: the national archives, General Register Office and Court of the Lord Lyon (heraldry).

You'll have to pay to access most of the content, except for the free wills and testaments search. (Don't bother with the free surname search unless you're looking for a rare name: It tells you only how many times a surname pops up in each record group—for example, the 1841 census database includes 29,811 McDonalds.) Index searching and record viewing involves a somewhat complicated pay-per-view system: You buy 30 "page credits" for seven British pounds (about $11) good for one year. US researchers accustomed to free government websites might bristle at the fees, but it's no more expensive than ordering films from the Family History Library, and you get instant gratification. Before shelling out any money, take time to review the excellent FAQ section, which answers questions about what to expect in any set of records and what notations in record margins might indicate.

You'll also find helpful free goodies on the site. Click the Research Tools link that drops down from the Help tab to access an occupations glossary, handwriting help, medical terms and information about everyday life. I especially liked the section that chronicles daily life, whether in a humble cottage or a country mansion. Be sure to explore the Help With Searching and Getting Started areas—they're chock-full of valuable tidbits for getting the most out of the records.

Scotland's Census

A Scottish national census has been taken every ten years since 1801, with the exception of 1941. The censuses from 1841 to 1891 are available for public use.

Enumerators were instructed to list only those present in the household the night the census was taken. People who were traveling, at boarding schools or working away from home were listed where they spent the night. Here's a breakdown of the information in the Scottish censuses:

- **1801 to 1831:** These records contain only statistical information. However, some parishes compiled lists of names while gathering the census information.
- **1841:** This census was taken June 7, 1841. It lists each member of every household's name, sex, address, occupation, and whether or not they were born in the county. Note that the census takers usually rounded the ages of those over 15 down to a multiple of five years.
- **1851 and later:** From 1851 to 1931, censuses were taken between March 31 and April 9. These records list the names, ages, occupations, relationships to the head of the household, and parish and county of birth (except foreign births, which give country only) of each person.

For more information, contact:
The Registrar General Search Unit
<www.gro-scotland.gov.uk>
New Register House
3 West Register St.
Edinburgh EH1 3YT
Scotland
Tel: +44 (0) 131 334 0380

Alternative Access

Of course, ScotlandsPeople isn't the only place to document your clan. Let's take a look at three key repositories for getting the records you need. Find their contact information in the toolkit.

GENERAL REGISTER OFFICE FOR SCOTLAND: The government set up this office (GROS for short) in 1855 to record births, deaths and marriages. Now it's Scotland's main archive for all vital-events documentation—including the church records that predated civil registration (parochial registers, 1553 to 1854), as well as military vital records, such as deaths of soldiers in wars and military stations abroad. The GROS also administers Scotland's decennial censuses, and houses the records of those taken since 1841 (1901 is the most recent one open to the public). You can learn about its holdings and how to request records at **<www.gro-scotland.gov. uk/famrec>**. You'll have to supply at least the person's full name plus the date and place of the event. Records cost 8 to 23 pounds ($12 to $35) each, making ScotlandsPeople a better deal.

NATIONAL ARCHIVES OF SCOTLAND: The national archives is home to most genealogy records not kept at GROS. It holds records created by the Scottish government, businesses, landed estates, families, courts, churches and corporate bodies. Among the most important for genealogists are wills and testaments (available on ScotlandsPeople), maps, Church of Scotland and nonconformist church records, deeds and sasine records (documenting changes in land ownership), and land valuation rolls.

You'll find an excellent set of free guides detailing the archives' holdings of various record types at **<www.nas.gov.uk/guides>**. The archives also has an online catalog **<www.nas.gov. uk/onlinecatalogue>** you can search to identify ancestral records you want to get. I was fortunate to find detailed information via a search on the name *James Home*, one of my distant Scottish kin. The records detailed information about six brothers in the family who were known as the "Spears of Wedderburn," along with data on their spouses, and the land they owned.

If you can identify a document reference number in the catalog, you can request copies from the archives—see **<www.nas.gov.uk/searchrooms/copyingservices.asp>**. But the archives doesn't accept full-fledged research requests; you can either use ScotlandsPeople or hire a local researcher to hunt down documents for you.

FAMILY HISTORY LIBRARY: In terms of records access, the next-best thing to ScotlandsPeople —or the best thing, if you prefer scrolling microfilm—is the Family History Library (FHL) **<familysearch.org>**. The FHL has many Scottish birth, death, marriage, land, census, probate and military records on microfilm, which you can rent for viewing at your local Family History Center (find locations at **<familysearch.org>**).

To identify relevant films and FHL resources, start with a place search on your ancestors' town or parish, then click the subject heading of the records you want—civil registrations, church records, land and property, and so forth. Cast your net wider by doing keyword searches on place and ancestral names. (Note that FHL books don't circulate to FHCs.)

Sure, your Scottish ancestors' legacy is one of fierce battles and political tumult—but you won't face the same struggles in tracing them. With all these resources at your disposal, you'll soon be weaving your forebears' stories into your family tree.

Scots-Irish Origins

Since the Colonial period, one of America's most interesting ethnic groups has been the Scottish people who, in the 16th and 17th centuries, answered the call of leases for land in the northern counties of Ireland, known as Ulster, before immigrating en masse to America in the 18th century. Their distinct—some might even say stubborn—sense of independence has hurled them to and beyond the US frontier, and even shows up in the naming of this group.

While Americans have often called them "Scots-Irish," these fervent Protestants began adopting the term "Ulster Scots" in the mid-1800s to separate themselves from the generally Roman Catholic Irish immigrants arriving in American shores in droves.

Their two-step immigration process—first to Ulster and then to America, separated by a century or two—complicates Scots-Irish research, as do record losses and, in some cases, a simple lack of a record-keeping tradition. But despite these difficulties, you can find a bagpipe full of records and documents to track down the ancestry of these wandering, pioneering Ulster Scotsmen.

FROM SCOTLAND TO IRELAND

What led to the planting of ethnic Scots in northern Ireland begins with England's historic desire to dominate Ireland. In the 1500s, England's Tudor Dynasty made it a mission to bring Ireland under their control. The resistance was aggravated by England's participation in the Protestant Reformation juxtaposed against Ireland's continued adherence to the Catholic pope. Scotland had also embraced the Reformation, but its established Church of Scotland was Presbyterian, not Anglican.

Parts of Ireland, especially in the northern area known as Ulster, were depopulated after the earlier wars against the Tudors, and James I had a solution: Take land from Irish nobles and give it to some of his cronies, who then would invite tenant settlers called "undertakers" from the lowlands of Scotland. Some English from the England-Scotland border area also chose to settle in Ulster.

Beginning in 1609, this "plantation" of Ulster quickly grew to thousands of people. Historical Ulster contained nine counties: three (Cavan, Donegal and Monaghan) are now part of Ireland, and six (Antrim, Armagh, Down, Fermanagh, Londonderry and Tyrone) make up Northern Ireland.

FROM IRELAND TO AMERICA

Two major factors precipitated mass migration from Ulster to the American colonies in the 1710s. First, landlords sought large increases to renew the 20-year leases of many 1690s emigrants. Thousands were evicted from their lands. Second, the Presbyterians in Ulster were as politically disadvantaged as the Irish Catholics. Under British rule, only people who belonged to the Church of Ireland, the branch of the Anglican Church on the Emerald Isle, had the potential for political rights.

When added to occasional droughts in Ulster, these factors turned a trickle of Scots-Irish emigration into an open tap: Some 250,000 are thought to have come between 1717 and the beginning of the American Revolution. More than a million Scots-Irish came to America in the 19th century. After the first wave from 1717 to 1718, the Colonial era saw four more such upticks. The swells in the late 1710s and from 1725 to 1729 centered upon Pennsylvania. Philadelphia was the destination of the overwhelming majority of Scots-Irish.

As early as the 1740s, when the next great wave occurred, a number of Scots-Irish went into the Shenandoah Valley of Virginia and even into the Carolinas, where they pushed the envelope of settlement into and across the Appalachian Mountains. A limited number also came to New England. The final high tides of immigration occurred from 1754 to 1755 and 1771 to 1775.

ULSTER DOCUMENTS

Until 1922, the entire island of Ireland was one political unit; after that point, Northern Ireland remained part of the UK and the rest of the island became independent. As a consequence, some government records before 1922 will be in Irish repositories and not in Northern Ireland.

The good news is that more records survived from Ulster than from any other part of Ireland. In addition, for every record group that has been lost, there are some workarounds and substitutes. (See chapter 1 for more details on records.) Going back to the beginning of the plantation of Ulster, see the free Ulster Ancestry website **<www.ulsterancestry. com/ua-free-pages.php>** for links to records of those who took out land allotments in the early 1600s.

Of prime importance to those seeking Scots-Irish ancestry is the Public Record Office of Northern Island (PRONI) **<www.proni.gov.uk>**, which has a personal name index for in-person visitors and has placed many of its holdings online. Church congregational histories provide additional historical background. You can find an alphabetized listing of these on **<www.presbyterianhistoryireland.com>,** the website of the Presbyterian Historical Society of Ireland.

The National Library of Ireland has a detailed online catalog **<sources.nli.ie>** that can guide you to sources such as Irish manuscripts and articles in Irish periodicals. The library also has a significant collection of landed estate papers of families who owned large tracts before the 20th century, some of which will mention the tenants on those lands.

Birth, marriage and death registration began in 1864, with non-Catholic marriages starting in 1845. Where you can find them varies by the time period. The General Register Office of Ireland has master copies of Ulster vital events up to 1921. The General Register Office of Northern Ireland takes over from there, though it also has local copies of birth and death registers back to 1864.

FROM IRELAND TO SCOTLAND

The final step in Scots-Irish research is tracing your ancestors back to Scotland itself. Church registers are the primary record group for this purpose, and a variety of indexes and online sources are available. FamilySearch created the Index to the Old Parochial Registers of Scotland on microfiche; Scottish Church Records has a CD version. Both are available through Family History Centers **<familysearch.org>**. The online International Genealogical Index has abstracts of these same church records. Some records date to the mid-1500s, though a start of 1650 is more typical. Two for-pay services, Origins.net and Findmypast.co.uk, have digitized versions.

ORGANIZATIONS AND ARCHIVES

ABERDEEN UNIVERSITY LIBRARY MANUSCRIPTS AND ARCHIVE SECTION
The Sir Duncan Rice Library, University of Aberdeen, Bedford Road, Aberdeen, AB24 3AA, Scotland
Phone: +44 (0) 1224 273330
Fax: +44 (0) 1224 273956
E-mail: library@abdn.ac.uk
<www.abdn.ac.uk/library/about/special>

ASSOCIATION OF SCOTTISH GENEALOGISTS AND RESEARCHERS IN ARCHIVES
Val Wilson, Treetops, 570 Lanark Road, Edinburgh EH14 7BN, Scotland
<www.asgra.co.uk>

BRITISH ISLES FAMILY HISTORY SOCIETY—USA
2531 Sawtelle Blvd., PMB #309, Los Angeles, CA 90064
<rootsweb.ancestry.com/~bifhsusa>

COURT OF THE LORD LYON
New Register House, Edinburgh EH1 3YT, Scotland
E-mail: lyonoffice@scotland.gsi.gov.uk
<www.lyon-court.com/lordlyon>

NATIONAL LIBRARY OF SCOTLAND
Department of Manuscripts, George IV Bridge, Edinburgh EH1 1EW, Scotland
<www.nls.uk>
Phone: +44 (0)131 623 3700
Fax: +44 (0)131 623 3701

THE NATIONAL ARCHIVES
Ruskin Ave., Kew, Richmond, Surrey TW9 4DU, England
Phone: +44 (0) 20 8876 3444
<www.nationalarchives.gov.uk>

THE REGISTRAR GENERAL SEARCH UNIT
New Register House, 3 West Register St., Edinburgh EH1 3YT, Scotland
Phone: +44 (0) 131 334 0380
<www.gro-scotland.gov.uk>

SCOTTISH RECORD OFFICE
HM General Register House, 2 Princes St., Edinburgh EH1 3YY, Scotland
Phone: +44 131 314 4411
E-mail: enquiries@nas.gov.uk
<www.gro-scotland.gov.uk>

UNIVERSITY OF EDINBURGH LIBRARY
George Square, Edinburgh EH8 9LJ, Scotland
Phone: +44 (0)131 650 3409
Fax: +44 (0)131 651 5041
E-mail: IS.Helpdesk@ed.ac.uk
<www.ed.ac.uk/schools-departments/information-services/library-museum-gallery>

UNIVERSITY OF GLASGOW ARCHIVES
The University of Glasgow, 13 Thurso Street, Glasgow, G11 6PE, Scotland
Phone: +44 (0) 141 330 5515
Fax: +44 (0) 141 330 2640
E-mail: enquiries@archives.gla.ac.u
<www.gla.ac.uk/services/archives>

BOOKS

1993 National Genealogical Directory edited by Iris Louise Caley (National Genealogical Directory)

British Archives: A Guide to Archive Resources in the United Kingdom, 4th edition, by Janet Foster and Julia Sheppard (Palgrave Macmillan)

The British Isles Genealogical Register (Federation of Family History Societies)

The Clans, Septs, and Regiments of the Scottish Highlands 1934 by Frank Adam and Sir Thomas Innes (Genealogical Publishing Co.)

Collins Scottish Clan & Family Encyclopedia by George Way and Romilly Squire (HarperCollins)

Concise Scots Dictionary by Scottish National Dictionary Association (Edinburgh University Press)

A Dictionary of the Older Scottish Tongue, From the Twelfth Century to the End of the Seventeenth, multiple volumes (Oxford University Press)

Discover Your Scottish Ancestry, 2nd edition, by Graham S. Holton and Jack Winch (Edinburgh University Press)

Genealogical Research Directory by Keith A. Johnson and Malcolm R. Sainty (The Editors of The Genealogical Research Directory)

A Genealogist's Guide to Discovering Your Scottish Ancestors by Paul Milner and Linda Jonas (Betterway Books)

The Highland Clans by Sir Iain Moncrieffe of that Ilk (Random House Value Publishing)

Highland Clans and Tartans by R.W. Munro (Octopus Books)

A History of Scotland: Look Behind the Mist and Myth of Scottish History by Neil Oliver (Phoenix)

Libraries and Information Services in the United Kingdom and the Republic of Ireland 2013-2014, 38th edition (Facet Publishing)

The Original Scots Colonists of Early America, 1612-1783 by David Dobson (Genealogical Publishing Co.)

The Scots: A Genetic Journey by Alistair Moffat and James F. Wilson (Birlinn)

Scottish Christian Names: An A-Z of First Names by Leslie Alan Dunkling (Johnston & Bacon)

Scottish Family Histories Held in Scottish Libraries by Joan P.S. Ferguson (National Library of Scotland)

Scottish Family History by David Moody (Genealogical Publishing Co.)

Scottish Genealogy, 3rd edition, by Bruce Durie (The History Press)

Scottish Land-names; Their Origin and Meaning (1894) by Sir Herbert Maxwell (William Blackwood and Sons, **<archive.org/ details/scottishlandname00maxwuoft>**)

Scottish Library and Information Resources, edited by Gordon Dunsire and Brian Osborne (Scottish Library Association)

Scottish Local History: An Introductory Guide by David Moody (Genealogical Publishing Co.)

The Scottish Nation, or The Surnames, Families, Literature, Honours, and Biographical History of the People of Scotland by William Anderson (Ulan Press)

The Surnames of Scotland: Their Origin, Meaning and History by George Black (New York Public Library)

Tracing Your Ancestors in the Public Record Office, 5th edition, by Amanda Bevan (Public Record Office)

Tracing Your Scottish Ancestors: A Guide to Ancestry Research in the Scottish Record Office by the National Archives of Scotland and Cecil Sinclair (Mercat Press)

Tracing Your Scottish Ancestors: A Guide for Family Historians by Ian Maxwell (Pen and Sword)

Tracing Your Scottish Family History by Anthony Adolph (Firefly Books)

PERIODICALS
Current Periodicals in the National Library of Scotland (Edinburgh: National Library of Scotland, 1987–)

The Scots Magazine (DC Thomson, **<www.scotsmagazine.com>**, 1924–)

The Scottish Association of Family History Societies Bulletin (The Scottish Association of Family History Societies)

The Scottish Genealogist: The Quarterly Journal of the Scottish Genealogy Society (Scottish Genealogy Society, 1954–)

Scottish Local History (Scottish Local History Forum, 1960–)

WEBSITES
Alan Godfrey Maps
<www.alangodfreymaps.co.uk>

AncestralScotland
<www.ancestralscotland.com>

Ancestral Tours of Scotland
<www.scotiarootstours.co.uk>

Ar Turas: Independent Research on Scotland & the Scots
<www.ar-turas.co.uk>

BIFHS-USA National Inventory of Documentary Sources
<www.rootsweb.com/~bifhsusa/nids/nids.html>

British GENES: Scotland
<britishgenes.blogspot.com/search/label/Scotland>

CensusDiggins: Scottish Genealogy
<www.censusdiggins.com/scottish_genealogy.html>

Cyndi's List: Scotland
<www.cyndislist.com/uk/sct>

Edinburgh City Libraries: Family History Resources
<www.edinburgh.gov.uk/info/1486/researching_your_family_history>

Electric Scotland: Scottish Genealogy Research & Advice
<www.electricscotland.com/webclans/scotroot.htm>

Gathering of the Clans
<www.tartans.com>

GENUKI
<www.genuki.org.uk>

GENUKI: Scotland
<www.genuki.org.uk/big/sct>

The Highland Clearances: Stories of Scottish Ancestry **<www.theclearances.org>**

The Internet Guide to Scotland
<www.scotland-info.co.uk/bk-gene.htm>

National Archives of Scotland
<www.nas.gov.uk>

New Scottish Council Regions
<www.trp.dundee.ac.uk/data/councils/newregions.html>

Ordnance Survey Gazetteer
<www.ordnancesurvey.co.uk>

Rampant Scotland Directory of Scottish Web Sites
<www.rampantscotland.com>

ScotFind.com
<www.scotfind.com/links/Community/Genealogy>

ScotGenes
<www.scotgenes.com>

ScotlandGenWeb
<www.scotlandgenweb.org>

Scotland Royal Genealogy
<www.scotlandroyalty.org>

ScotlandsPeople
<www.scotlandspeople.gov.uk>

Scotsmart
<www.scotsmart.com/c/genealogy.html>

Scots Origins
<www.scotsorigins.com>

Scottish Ancestor
<www.scottishancestor.co.uk>

Scottish Archive Network
<www.scan.org.uk>

Scottish Association of Family History Societies
<www.safhs.org.uk>

Scottish Census Transcriptions
<www.scotlandsclans.com/census.htm>

Scottish Clans
<www.scotlandsclans.com>

Scottish DNA Project
<www.scottishdna.net>

Scottish Genealogy Help
<www.genealogypro.com/dbaptie.html>

The Scottish Genealogy Society
<www.scotsgenealogy.com>

Scottish GENES
<www.scottishancestry.blogspot.com>

Scottish Handwriting
<www.scottishhandwriting.com>

Scottish Roots
<www.scottish-roots.co.uk>

The Scottish Page
<homepages.rootsweb.ancestry.
com/~scottish>

Sources for Research in Scottish Genealogy
<www.loc.gov/rr/genealogy/bib_guid/
scotland.html>

Statistical Accounts of Scotland
<edina.ac.uk/statacc>

The Tartan Pages: Scotland's Internet
<www.tartans.scotland.net>

Ulster Ancestry
<www.ulsterancestry.com>

Undiscovered Scotland
<www.undiscoveredscotland.co.uk/uslinks/
genealogy.html>

Your Scottish Kin
<www.scottish-genealogy.co.uk>

CHAPTER FOUR

SCANDINAVIA

By Diana Crisman Smith

Though there are challenges, researching the Scandinavian countries need not be as difficult as you might think. The task is, however, very different from the familiar records and techniques used for other European research and American. There are political (or clerical) subdivisions, unfamiliar records, strange-sounding names (such as Ole Thorvaldson, Lauren Svensdatter), and—of course—new languages.

First, let's clarify "Scandinavia." Sweden and Norway are located on the Scandinavian Peninsula; Denmark is north of Germany on the Jutland Peninsula and includes a number of islands, primarily in the Baltic and North Seas. These three are the nations addressed in this article.

Some people also include Iceland, Greenland and the Faroe Islands in Scandinavia because of their historical relationships with the other countries (primarily Denmark). Others include Finland, which neighbors—but is not on—the Scandinavian Peninsula. All of these countries/territories are part of the Nordic Region but technically are not Scandinavia. An understanding of Scandinavian research and techniques will, however, transfer to many concepts in the other Nordic countries.

Here are a few hints to get you started on effectively searching your Scandinavian ancestors.

1. Search "at home" first
2. Understand those pesky patronymics

3. Utilize geographic and language aids
4. Recognize that parish records are the key
5. Always work in families

SEARCH "AT HOME" FIRST

Before you begin your research in Scandinavian records, prepare yourself with research at home. Follow the standard procedure, "start with yourself and work backwards"—this is one area where that is absolutely critical and there are no shortcuts to make that leap across the water!

When you have determined who your Scandinavian immigrant ancestor was, find out everything possible from the records here, using the standard "W" questions:

- Who was he/she? Find as much as possible about all names used.
- When was the immigration? US passenger lists and census records may be helpful.
- Where was the immigrant's prior residence (in Scandinavia)? Again, passenger lists may be helpful, as well as church records and newspapers.

Search for these details in all possible "home" resources, such as the family bible, letters from home or from other immigrant family members, naturalization documents or souvenirs from the homeland. Search through everything for hints—even photographs may have information or clues to indicate where the family originated in Scandinavia. Don't forget that family stories may contain at least a glimmer of a clue (but don't take it all for gospel without confirmation).

Note that there may be clues in the church records here leading to the church records there. Most Scandinavians were (and still are) members of the Evangelical Lutheran Church of that country (Danish Lutheran, Swedish Lutheran, etc). If there is a Lutheran Church of any "flavor" in the new community, start there. The records may contain a letter of transfer showing the former parish. There may also be a notation with a marriage or confirmation record indicating where the person was baptized, which will often name the original parish.

When researching in newspapers, obituaries are a good starting point, but don't overlook births, marriages and local-interest stories. For example, the local church might have published lists of new members received; there may be a story about visitors from "home" indicating their residence; or there might be a feature story about an immigrant family whose members have become "pillars of the community." Yes, that may mean reading the entire newspaper for all the years the family resided in the area—but it can be very worthwhile (and usually fun).

UNDERSTAND THOSE PESKY PATRONYMICS

The Scandinavian countries all used the "patronymic" system for personal names until the late 19th or early 20th century. The word patronymic comes from "father" and "name"—and it is literally a name derived from the person's father's name. The form in Scandinavia is to use the father's first (given) name and add an extension (see the sidebar).

The term "matronymic" may be encountered, and it similarly means a name derived from the mother's name. While this is not common in Scandinavia, it does occur. The illegitimate child of a Scandinavian woman might be given a matronymic name (based on the mother's first name). That is the usual reason for a child bearing a surname like Marensen (i.e., son of Maren). This is not the norm, though, since even illegitimate births generally acknowledge the name of the father, and the child is named accordingly.

Until after the Middle Ages, the people of Scandinavia did not find it necessary to use a surname—the sparse population and stability of the residents meant everyone knew Jens and Katrina (and their family) in a given town. Around the 15th or 16th century (it varied locally), surnames came into use. The normal pattern was for the nobility to first adopt fixed surnames, then the artisans, clergy, merchants and finally the general population (farmers and laborers). When the clergy initially adopted surnames, they often "Latinized" the name or used an actual Latin name. Merchants and craftsmen sometimes used German surnames or names reflecting their occupation—you may find a number of Schmidts (German for smith—such as blacksmith, tinsmith or other types of smith) in Scandinavia who never even visited Germany, for example.

To establish surnames, most of the general population adopted the patronymic system at that time. This system continued at least through the 19th century, and sometimes into the 20th century. In Denmark, the Act on Names (2006) reintroduced the use of

TIME LINE

c.770	Vikings begin sailing expeditions, eventually reaching as far as Sicily.
874	First permanent settlers arrive in Iceland.
1000	Leif Ericson discovers America.
1323	Treaty of Nöteborg gives Sweden dominance over most of Finland.
1397	Kalmar Union unites Sweden (until 1523), Denmark and Norway (including Iceland).
1536	Lutheranism arrives in Scandinavia.
1548	Written Finnish introduced with translation of the New Testament.
1617	Sweden begins its period as a great power.
1638	Colony of New Sweden founded in Delaware.
1655	New Sweden lost to the Dutch.
1660	Peace of Copenhagen establishes modern boundaries of Denmark, Sweden and Norway.
1721	Peace of Nystad ends Sweden's "Age of Greatness," ceding its Baltic provinces to Russia.
1809	Sweden loses Finland to Russia.
1814	Sweden takes Norway from Denmark.
1825	First Norwegian emigrant ship leaves Stavanger.
1835	Danish author Hans Christian Andersen publishes his first book of fairy tales.

1867–1869	"Starvation years" of crop failures and epidemics cause 60,000 Swedes to emigrate.
1876	Norwegian composer Edvard Grieg writes the music for Peer Gynt.
1893	Norwegian artist Edvard Munch paints *The Scream*.
1905	Norwegian independence from Sweden.
1917	Following the Russian Revolution, Finland gains independence.
1918	Icelandic independence from Denmark.
1969	Major discovery of North Sea oil.

patronymics as an optional method of selecting a surname for a child.

Each country mandated the end of patronymics at a different time, but adoption of fixed or heritable (or inheritable, which technically means the same thing, as confusing as that may be) surnames was not immediately universally adopted (even when required by law). These changes occurred over time, but roughly concurrently throughout Scandinavian countries.

Note that Scandinavian women did not normally adopt the surname of their husbands—the birth name was retained for life. A woman would be listed by her birth name in her own birth and marriage records (obviously), as well as birth and marriage records of her children and her death record. In the mid-1800s some women adopted the husband's surname, as in much of the rest of Europe. This was not widespread until more recently (and not necessarily now—some women still retain their birth names after marriage). One note, however: Beginning in the 19th century, upon immigration to America, Scandinavian women might have adopted the husband's surname, knowing that this was the American practice. When looking for a woman from Scandinavia, check both name possibilities.

When the change to fixed surnames became universally adopted in the late 1800s, another change took place in Norway: Women began adopting their husband's surname instead of keeping their birth names (as is often the case in North America). Thus Ane Jensdatter (daughter of Jens) who married Nils Andersen (son of Anders) could become Ane Andersen! Watch for this when looking at the parents of a child—where you might normally expect to see the parents as Nils Andersen and Ane Jensdatter, with this scenario it would be Nils Andersen and Ane Andersen. Search for their marriage record to be sure whether her father was Anders or something else (Jens, in this case) before following the wrong maternal line.

For example, the family of Niels Bertel Nielsen of Denmark came to America in 1903 (he came a year before to prepare the way). The family record consists of his wife, Karen Marie Nielsen and five Nielsen children: Lars Bertel, Dagmar Fredrica, Valdemar Theodore, Harold Holger and Elna Elise. Shortly after arriving in Iowa, all members of this family adopted an "Americanized" version of the names—Niels Bertel Nielsen became Nels or N.B. Nelson; Dagmar became Rica Nelson; Valdemar became Walter Ted Nelson; Harold was Harold Nelson; and

Time Line for Adoption of Patronymics

- In Denmark, a law was passed in 1526 requiring fixed surnames for the nobility. In 1771 an act was passed mandating universal fixed surnames in the Duchy of Schleswig (then part of Denmark); a universal law for all of Denmark was passed in 1828—but it was not immediately embraced by everyone, especially not the rural population. Additional acts were passed in 1856, 1904, 1961, 1981 and 2005. Most of the population changed over by the end of the 19th century, so the post-1900 laws set out to catch the stragglers.
- In Norway a law was enacted in 1923 requiring that all families have a single, heritable surname.
- In Sweden, the Name Adoption Act was passed in 1901, abolishing the creation of new patronymics by generation. From that time forward, everyone was required to have a family name that passed from generation to generation.

The suffixes used to create patronymics in each country are different:

Country	Son	Daughter[2,3]
Denmark	–sen	–datter
Sweden	–son	–dotter
Norway[1]	–son, –sen, –søn	–datter, –dotter

1. Note that in Norway, the extension used depended upon the ruling country: When Norway was ruled by Sweden, the Swedish extensions (-son and -dotter) were used; when it was ruled by Denmark, the Danish extensions (-sen and -datter) were used; after Norway gained independence from Sweden in 1914, the Norwegian (-søn and -dotter) were used ….. usually.

2. The endings in the chart were used through most of the 18th and 19th centuries. Late in the 19th century, just before adopting fixed surnames, many families (especially in Denmark) began using the male extension for both sons and daughters.

3. Sometimes a record will show a female's surname with "-dtr" at the end instead of spelling out the extension. That is just an abbreviation. The actual surname uses the full extension for a daughter.

Elna Elise became Elna Alice Nelson. The mother was invariably listed as Karen Marie Andersen in the Danish records, but used Karen Marie Nielsen for her passage to America, then Karen Marie (or Carrie) Nelson in Iowa. Note that this change was made *after* they arrived in America (not the changed-at-Ellis-Island story) and made them appear to be English or Swedish, not Danish. Why they did this is a story for another day.

In addition to the patronymic system, other methods were sometimes used for determining the fixed surname. Some of these are:

MILITARY SURNAME, PRIMARILY IN SWEDEN. There could be only one man in a unit with a particular name, so the next arrival with the same name was given a new surname to differentiate them. This surname was usually based on a physical attribute (bearded, red-haired, strong, trustworthy, etc.). These names sometimes prevailed after service was concluded.

FARM NAMES, PRIMARILY IN DENMARK AND PARTS OF NORWAY. This was another method to differentiate individuals (and families) of the same name in an area. The farm name was usually where the family currently resided, but it also might be carried to a new area to indicate where they had come from.

GEOGRAPHIC NAMES, PRIMARILY IN SWEDEN AND SOMETIMES NORWAY. The name usually represents some physical attribute of the land, such as Lindberg, which translates to *tree* plus *mountain*. In Denmark and sometimes Norway, a geographic surname might be the actual name of a town, usually the origin of a newcomer to an area.

UTILIZE GEOGRAPHIC AND LANGUAGE AIDS

Once you have found the clues to the Scandinavian origin of your immigrant ancestor, you need to do some homework before beginning your research. First, the geography is very important in identifying the parish, which serves as the focus of community life (since nearly everyone belongs to the same church). Even if you have found the parish name, be very careful and look for other clues to the actual physical location, since there are sometimes several parishes in different areas with the same or similar names.

Sweden

Be aware of the difference between the civil and ecclesiastical (church) jurisdictions. For genealogical research you will need to focus on the ecclesiastical jurisdictions. In Sweden, there is a rather elaborate hierarchy of organization, starting at the top with dioceses (stift) which are presided over by a bishop (biskop). Within the diocese are several rural deaneries (kontrakt) with a dean (kontraktsprost) in charge. Within the deaneries are benefices or districts (pastorat) with a rector or vicar (kyrkoherde). Within the district there are one, two or more parishes; the vicar resides in the mother parish (moderförsamling) but serves as pastor for all. The other parishes are annex parishes (annexförsamling). All of this is important because sometimes the records for the entire district will be found in the records of the mother parish, rather than in each parish.

There are approximately 2,500 parishes (söcken or församling) in modern Sweden. Each parish may contain villages (by) and farms (gård or hemman). Prior to 1862 the parishes served both civil and ecclesiastical purposes.

After 1862, two types of parishes were created: kommun for civil; församling for ecclesiastical purposes. The boundaries for the civil and ecclesiastical parish may be the same or different. Be sure to look in the ecclesiastical parish for the church records.

Norway

The structure of the Church of Norway is very similar to that of Sweden, with 1284 parishes (sogne) in 106 deaneries (prestegården), in 11 dioceses (dispedømme). As in Sweden, the parishes are the record-keeping entity for Norway. Even though Norway was ruled by Denmark for much of its history, and the records may be in Danish, be aware of the possibility of records in a mother parish, as in Sweden.

Denmark

The Danish church does not have a hierarchy as strictly defined as Sweden or Norway. The records are organized by district (herred), then by parish (sogne). As in the other Scandinavian churches, a pastor might minister to several parishes, so the records may be consolidated into one book (but usually not intermixed). If the pastor ministered to several parishes, the clerk generally served the same parishes. There is not, however, the strict concept of a "mother parish"; the consolidation of records is simply at the convenience of the pastor and clerk.

Language Aids

All of the Scandinavian languages are based on the Old Norse language, not Latin as in other parts of Europe and the Americas. However, the letters themselves are based on the Latin, with a few additions. All of the additional letters follow z in alphabetizing.

To translate Scandinavian records to English, you can also go to Google Translate **<translate.google.com>** and enter the text there to have it translate for you. This is usually close enough to figure out the intent of a passage, but the translation is not guaranteed to be accurate, especially for older documents. BabelFish **<www.babelfish.com>** is sometimes also helpful for Danish (but Swedish and Norwegian are not available at this time).

Of course, you may prefer (as I usually do) to use the "old-fashioned" way and find a good English-Danish/English-Norwegian/English-Swedish Dictionary (whichever is appropriate) and have it handy for those new terms you encounter. Note that the older the dictionary, the more likely it will have exactly the word you want.

RECOGNIZE THAT PARISH RECORDS ARE THE KEY

When researching in Scandinavia, it is important to remember that there has been a "state church" in each country, which is the official civil registration point for that country's residents—whether they are members of that church or not. These churches are all Evangelical

Lutheran Churches: the Church of Sweden; Church of Norway; Church of Denmark. Records are available for several centuries in all of these churches.
- Beginning in 1685 the Norwegian Church Ritual required each minister to keep records of christenings, betrothals and burials. Under this law, all residents were to be listed.
- In 1686 a similar law was created in Sweden requiring ministers to keep a record of the ordinances performed.
- By law, the Danish Evangelical Lutheran Church has had responsibility for recording "the beginning and end of life" for all Danish residents for hundreds of years. Records exist for most parishes before 1700, with the earliest from Copenhagen in 1619.

PARISH RECORDS

The church books in each country are somewhat similar, with sections for the major ecclesiastical events of the parishioners. The books themselves are called kyrkboken (Sweden), kirkebøker (Norway) or kirkebøger (Denmark).

PARISH RECORDS SECTIONS

Event(s)	Sweden	Denmark	Norway
Birth and Christening	född and dop	født and døbt	fødte and døpte
Confirmation	konfirmation	konfirmation	konfirmasjon
Vaccination (for smallpox)	vaccination (from 1816)	vaccination (from 1810)	vaksinasjon (from 1810)
Marriage	vigda or förbindelse	copulerede, viede or ægteskab	copulerede or viede or vigde
Banns	lysning or trolovning	lysning or forlovelse	lysingen or forlovelse
Betrothal/ Engagement	trolovning	forlovelse	forlovelse
Death and Burial	död and begravning	døde and begravelse	død and begravede
Incoming List	inflyttningsbok	tilganglister	tilganglister or in-nflyttede
Outgoing List	utflyttningsbok	afgangslister	afgangslister or uttflyttdede
Index (when used)	fösamlingsböken	register	Hovedsiden
Clerical Survey (or Household Examination Roll)	husförhörslängd	Not used	Not used

• Marriage, Banns, and Betrothals (may include one or more of these events in any church book)

The major components of the church books are:
• Birth/Baptism
• Confirmation
• Vaccination
• Marriage/Betrothal
• Death
• Incoming Lists [indicates from where transferred]
• Outgoing Lists [indicates to where transferring—sometimes "USA"]
• Clerical Survey (Sweden only) [a "minicensus" of the congregation, taken every five years intended to show the religious preparation of each family member; there is no civil census for Sweden]
• Index (sometimes used)

Once you find a record, be sure to transcribe (in the native language) and translate to your language. This will be essential to confirm it is the right person or family. Also be sure to glean all possible information from every record, including witnesses and references to other church records.

Remember that Norway was ruled by Denmark until 1814, then by Sweden from 1815 to 1905. The records, therefore, will be similar to those of Denmark (and even in Danish) until 1814. After 1815, there may be more similarity to the Swedish record, and some of the language may be Swedish. There may be later records in Norwegian, which is very similar to Danish.

Although there are other records, such as censuses and military levying rolls, land and probate records, working through the parish records thoroughly first will often yield enough.

ALWAYS WORK IN FAMILIES

Most American and European researchers are accustomed to searching for a surname. When patronymic surnames are used, the records need to be searched differently. Even with occupational, military and place surnames, these techniques should be used to confirm the right family is being investigated.

- It is even more critical in Scandinavia to work backwards from the known to the unknown—there are no shortcuts here.
- Start with the most recent person about whom you have information—for example, my grandmother was born in Denmark and came to America as a small child, so I started by finding her birth record.
- The birth record includes parents' names, with the mother's maiden name, and their

Wharf, Trondheim, Norway

SCANDINAVIAN CENSUSES

SWEDEN'S CENSUS

There are some things that researchers should keep in mind with regard to the Swedish census records. First, between 1652 and 1840, only people between the ages of 15 and 63 were listed. The earliest records often contain only the given name of the head of the household, while other family members are listed as numbers in columns. After 1841, people between the ages of 17 and 63 were recorded. After 1887, the ages were 18 to 63. Also, if your ancestor was in the military, you may not find his name because soldiers did not have to pay taxes, so only their wives and children are listed. Until 1810, noble families and their servants were also exempt from paying taxes and are usually not recorded. It's also important to remember that spellings of names and places in census records may differ from those in other records.

Once you find your family listed in a census, you should search that same location in the earlier and later census records for other family members. If you are in need of a good guide to the early census records, try Mantalsskrivningen i Sverige före 1860 (Census Records in Sweden before 1860) by Gösta Lext. (Göteborg: Göteborgs Universitet, 1968).

DENMARK'S CENSUS

In the late 18th and early 19th centuries, censuses were taken sporadically. The first Danish census of value to genealogists was taken in 1787. Beginning in 1840, information was collected every five years until 1860 and then every ten years until the end of the century. The five-year system began again in 1901.

The kind of information you will find varies from year to year, but some general guidelines will help you know what to expect from your searches. The 1787, 1801, 1834 and 1840 censuses list the name, age, sex, marital status and occupation of each member of the household, in addition to their relationships to the head of the household. Beginning with 1845, the censuses record the name, age, occupation, religious affiliation and birthplace (county and parish) of each member of the household, in addition to their relationships to the head of the household. For more information, refer to the Danish Demographic Database <ddd.dda.dk/ddd_en.htm>.

FINLAND'S CENSUS

Finnish population registration records, similar to census records, have been kept since 1634 and are called henkikirjat/mantalslängder. In addition, various taxation lists have been preserved from the 1530s until the present, though they are not as thorough. The henkikirjat/mantalslängder even precede the earliest church records, so you can use them when the time comes to look further into the past or supplement incomplete church-record information.

The age group recorded in the early henkikirjat/mantalslängder varies; here's a breakdown so you'll know what to expect while navigating these documents.

Between 1634 and 1651, only persons over the age of 12 were enumerated. Records from 1652 on included those between the ages of 15 and 63. (After 1655, heads of households over 63 were also listed.)

Also note that before 1765 (when the government started using these records to gather national statistics), those who did not have to pay taxes, such as nobility and their servants, large-estate owners, soldiers and the destitute, are often not registered in henkikirjat/mantalslängder.

A good index for these records is Luettelo henkikirjamikrofilmien käyttökopioista 1634–1808/Förteckning över brukskopior av mikrofilmer av mantalslängder 1634–1808 (Inventory of Microfilms of the 1634–1808 Censuses) Mattl Walta, ed., 2nd rev. ed. (Helsinki: Valtionarkisto, 1989).

A composite research resource unique to Finland with which you should become familiar is Suomen asutuksen yleisluettelo/Generalregistret över bosättningen i Finland (The General Register of Settlement in Finland), or SAY. Keep in mind that this register doesn't cover the entire country, but you are likely to find some valuable information about southwestern Finland, in particular.

SAY is important to genealogists because it has amassed the information in its tables from various sources from the country's Old and New Collections of Accounts (1539–1809). For each residence, you will find the name of farm owners and members of the household mentioned in original record sources, such as land records, tithing records, and tax and military rolls.

A Finnish/Swedish guide to SAY is available: Suomen asutuksen yleisluettelon opas: Generalregistret över bosättningen i Finland, en handledningen (The General Register of the Settlement in Finland: A Guide) (Helsinki: Valtion painatuskeskus, 1975).

NORWAY'S CENSUS

This Digital Archive site <**digitalarkivet.uib.no**> is in both Norwegian and English and includes several of the censuses for Norway. Unfortunately, only the 1801 and 1900 censuses are complete for the whole country.

residence. Note that in Norway the mother's name may not be her maiden name if she has taken her husband's surname.

• Search the parish records before and after the birth for a number of years to find any other children of those same parents. There may be two or more children of the same parents with the same or similar given name(s) in the records. If a child died at birth or in infancy, the parents might give the same name to the next child of that gender. In some cases, especially if the child was named to honor some other relative, a similar name might be given to a child of the other gender. For example, a child named Christen who was named to honor an uncle died just a few months after birth. The next child was a girl, but the parents decided to honor the uncle by naming the daughter Christine. (This was done particularly if the parents were nearing the end of their child-bearing years.)

- Search the marriage records in these parishes to find the parents' marriage. This record will often give the birth, christening and confirmation dates (and parishes) for both parties.
- The next step is to search for each of the parents' birth/christening, confirmation and other records in the parishes indicated by the marriage record.
- Next, look for marriages (or deaths) for all the children identified so far, and for parents of both the bride and groom of the original marriage found.
- The temptation to accept the first individual found with the full name sought is not useful in patronymic research—verification is essential to avoid a wild goose chase. There may be several people in a parish with the same name, but there will be some other detail that won't match (date or one or both parents).
- Watch for changes in surname. During the late 1800s the family may name some children with the patronymic, then fix on the surname of the father for the rest. For example, Jens Nielsen and his wife might have six children between 1870 and 1885, who are named:

  Karen Jensen [note that the –sen is used instead of the –datter]

  Niels Jensen

  Christen Jensen

  Maren Nielsen

  Jorgen Nielsen

  Jens Nielsen

  Since the parents are the same for all six children, the surname appears to have been frozen between Christen and Maren. All the children will usually continue with the name given at birth/christening throughout life. A similar situation may occur with the use of occupation, location or military names—the family may use the name during the time some children are born, but not others, so each child must be carefully analyzed to confirm that you have the right family.
- Carefully transcribe (in the original language) then translate each record. As you see the full record, other details may become clear, or you may find it is not the record you thought. Make sure to fully cite your sources as you go, as well.

ORGANIZATIONS AND ARCHIVES

NORDIC HERITAGE MUSEUM

3014 NW 67th St.
Seattle, WA 98117 USA
Phone: (206) 789-5707
<www.nordicmuseum.com>

SCANDINAVIAN-AMERICAN GENEALOGICAL SOCIETY

P.O. Box 16069
St. Paul, MN 55116 USA
Publishes *Scandinavian Saga*

BOOKS

The Scandinavian American Family Album
By Dorothy and Thomas Hoobler (New York:
Oxford University Press, 1997)

*A Student's Guide to Scandinavian American
Genealogy* By Lisa Olson Paddock and Carl
Sokolnicki Rollyson (Phoenix, Ariz.: Oryx Press,
1996)

WEBSITES

L'Anse aux Meadows National Historic Site
<whc.unesco.org/sites/4.htm>

Nordic genealogy newsgroup/mailing list
<www.rootsweb.com/~jfuller/gen_mail_
country-den.html>

Nordic Notes
<www.nordicnotes.com>

Nordic Pages
<www.markovits.com/nordic/>

Societas Heraldica Scandinavia
<www.heraldik.org/shshome2.html>

Society for the Advancement of Scandinavian
Study
<www.montana.edu/sass/resource.htm>

TravelGenie
<showcase.netins.net/web/travelgenie>

Viking Heritage Server and Database
<viking.hgo.se/>

Viking Network
<viking.no/>

SWEDEN RESOURCES

ORGANIZATIONS AND ARCHIVES

AMERICAN SWEDISH HISTORICAL MUSEUM

1900 Pattison Ave., Philadelphia, PA 19145
Phone: (215) 389-1776
<www.americanswedish.org>

AMERICAN SWEDISH INSTITUTE

2600 Park Ave. S., Minneapolis, MN 55407
Phone: (612) 871-4907
<www.americanswedishinst.org>

FEDERATION OF SWEDISH GENEALOGICAL SOCIETIES (SVERIGES SLÄKTFORSKARFÖRBUND)

Post Sveriges Släktforskarförbund,
Anderstorpsvägen 16, SE-171 54 Solna, Sweden
Phone: +46 8 440 75 50
Fax: + 46 8695 08 24
<www.genealogi.se / roots>

GENEALOGICAL SOCIETY OF SWEDEN

Allen 7-9, 172 66 Sundyberg, Sweden
Phone: +46 (8) 32 96 80
<www.genealogi.net>

GÖTEBORG EMIGRANTEN

Box 53066, 400 14 G.teborg, Sweden
Phone: +46 (31) 18 00 62
<www.goteborgs-emigranten.com>

KINSHIP CENTER
Box 331, S-651 08 Karlstad, Sweden
Phone: +46 (54) 617726
<www.emigrantregistret.s.se/frameset-en.htm>

LANDSARKIVET I GÖTEBORG
(Göteborg och Bohus, Älvsborg, Skaraborg and Värmland counties)
Box 3009, S-400 10 Göteborg, Sweden
Phone: 011-46-31-778 68 00
Fax: 011-46-31-778 68 25
<www.ra.se/gla/>

LANDSARKIVET I HÄRNÖSAND
(Gävleborg, Västernorrland, Västerbotten and Norrbotten counties)
Box 161, S-871 24 Härnösand, Sweden
Phone: 011-46-611-835 00
Fax: 011-46-611-835 28
<www.ra.se/hla/>

LANDSARKIVET I LUND
(Malmöhus, Kristianstad, Halland and Blekinge counties)
Box 2016, S-220 02 Lund, Sweden
Phone: 011-46-19 70 00
Fax: 011-46-19 70 70
<www.ra.se/lla/>

LANDSARKIVET I ÖSTERSUND
(Jämtland County)
Arkivvägen 1 S-831 31 Östersund, Sweden
Phone: 011-46-63-10 84 85
Fax: 011-46-63-12 18 24
<www.ra.se/ola/>

LANDSARKIVET I UPPSALA
(Stockholm, Uppsala, Södermanland, Örebro, Västmanland and Kopparberg counties)
Box 135, S-751 04 Uppsala, Sweden
Phone: 011-46-18-65 21 00
Fax: 011-46-18-65 21 03
<www.ra.se/ula/>

LANDSARKIVET I VADSTENA
(Östergötland, Kalmar, Jönköping and Kronoberg counties)
Box 126, S-592 00 Vadstena, Sweden
Phone: 011-46-143-130 30

Fax: 011-46-143-102 54
<www.ra.se/vala/>

LANDSARKIVET I VISBY
(Gotland County)
Box 2142, S-621 57 Visby, Sweden
Phone: 011-46-498-21 05 14
Fax: 011-46-498-21 29 55
<www.ra.se/vila/>

RIKSARKIVET (NATIONAL ARCHIVE)
Box 12541, S-102 29 Stockholm, Sweden
Phone: 011-46-8-737 63 50
Fax: 011-46-8-737 64 74
<www.ra.se/en/>

ROYAL SWEDISH EMBASSY
Watergate 600, 600 New Hampshire Ave. NW
Washington, DC 20037

SVAR (SWEDISH ARCHIVE INFORMATION)
Box 160, S-880 40 Ramsele, Sweden
Phone: 011-46-623-725 00
Fax: 011-46-623-725 55
<www.svar.ra.se>

SWEDISH AMERICAN HISTORICAL SOCIETY
3225 W. Foster Ave., Box 48, Chicago, IL 60625
Phone: (773) 583-5722
<www.swedishamericanhist.org>

SWEDISH ANCESTRY RESEARCH ASSOCIATION
Box 70603, Worcester, MA 01607
<sarassociation.tripod.com>

SWEDISH EMIGRANT INSTITUTE
Vilhelm Mobergs Gata 4, Box 201, SE
351 04 V.xj., Sweden,
Phone: +46 (470) 20120
<www.swemi.nu / eng>

SWEDISH NATIONAL ARCHIVES—MARIEBURG
Box 125 41, SE-102 29 Stockholm, Sweden
Phone: +46 (8) 737 63 50
<www.ra.se / en>

SWEDISH NATIONAL ARCHIVES— MILITARY ARCHIVES

SE-115 88 Stockholm, Sweden
Phone: +46 (8) 782 41 00
<www.ra.se/kra/english.html>

SWENSON SWEDISH IMMIGRATION RESEARCH CENTER

639 38th St., Rock Island, IL 61201
Phone: (309) 794-7204
<www.augustana.edu/swenson/genealogy. html>

CDS

24 Famous Swedish Americans and their Ancestors compiled by Sveriges Släktforskarförbund (Federation of Swedish Genealogical Societies, $34.99)

Cradled in Sweden by Carl-Erik Johansson (Everton Publishers, $31.95)

Emibas CD (Swedish Emigrant Institute, $96)

Gamla Stan CD (Stockholm City Archives, $56)

The Genealogical Guidebook & Atlas of Sweden by Finn A. Thomsen (Thomsen's, $17.50)

Kungsholmen CD (Stockholm City Archives, $74)

Swedish American Genealogist ($25 annual subscription from <www.augustana.edu/ swenson/sag.html>)

Swedish Census 1890 CD (Arkion/Federation of Swedish Genealogical Societies, $86)

Swedish Deaths 1947-2003 CD (Federation of Swedish Genealogical Societies, $75.99)

The Swedish Emigrant CD (Swedish Emigrant Institute, $180)

Swedish Genealogical Dictionary (Pladsen Sveria Press, $25 from <home.netcom.com/~v31ry>)

Swedish Passenger Arrivals in New York, 1820-1850 by Nils William Olsson (Swedish American Historical Society, out of print)

Swedish Passenger Arrivals in US Ports, 1820-1850 (Except New York) by Nils William Olsson (North Central Publishing, out of print)

Swedish Passenger Arrivals in the United States 1820-1850 by Nils William Olsson and Erik Wik (Schmidts Boktryckeri AB, $65 from <www. swedishamericanhist.org/booklist.html >)

Your Swedish Roots by Per Clemensson and Kjell Andersson (Ancestry, $24.95)

BOOKS

Cradled in Sweden By Carl-Erik Johansson (Logan, Utah: Everton Publishers, Inc., 1995)

The Emigrants By Vilhelm Moberg, translated by Gustaf Lannestock (New York: Simon & Schuster, 1951)

Hembygdsforska! Steg för steg (Guide to Local History) By Per Clemensson and Kjell Andersson (Stockholm: LTs förlag, 1990)

Riksarkivet 1618–1968 (National Archives 1618–1968) By Olof Jägerskiöld (Stockholm: P.A. Norstedt & Söner, 1968)

Släktforska! Steg för steg (Guidebook to Swedish Genealogy) By Per Clemensson and Kjell Andersson (Stockholm: LTs förlag, 1983)

Släktforskning–väg en till din egen historia (*Genealogy, The Road to Your Own History*) By Elisabeth Thorsell and Ulf Schenkmanis (Västerås: ICA-Förlaget, 1993)

Svensk slägt-kalender (*Genealogies of Swedish Families*) Lars Magnus Viktor Örnberg, ed. (Stockholm: [s.n.], 1885–1888)

Svenska ättartal (*Genealogies of Swedish City Dwellers*) Lars Magnus Viktor Örnberg, ed. (Stockholm: [s.n.], 1889–1908)

Svenska sälktkalendern (*Genealogies of Well-Known Swedish Families*) Gustaf Elgenstierna and Ulla Elgenstierna, comps. (Stockholm: Albert Bonniers förlag, 1912–1950)

Svenska släktkalendern. Ny följd (*Genealogies of Well-Known Swedish Families. Continued*) Gösta Berg, ed. (Stockholm: Albert Bonniers förlag, 1962–)

The Swedish Americans (*The Immigrant Experience*) By Allyson McGill (New York: Chelsea House, 1988)

PERIODICALS
Personhistorisk tidskrift (Journal of Personal History) Stockholm: P.A. Norstedt, 1900–.

Släkt och hävd: tidskrift (Family and Tradition) Stockholm: Genealogiska Föreningen, 1950–.

WEBSITES
Computer Genealogy Society of Sweden
<www.dis.se/denindex.htm>

Demographical Databasefor Southern Sweden
<ddss.nu/engelsk>

ET Genealogy
<www.etgenealogy.se/english.htm>

Genline
<genline.com>

FamilySearch: Vital Records Index for Scandinavia <www.familysearch.org> Click Search, then click Vital Records Index, then select Sweden.

Föreningen Släktdata
<slaktdata.org/en/start>

Indiko
<www.ddb.umu.se/windiko/windikoeng/indikohuvudsidaeng.htm>

Landsurvey
<www.lantmateriet.com>

National Atlas of Sweden
<www.sna.se/e_index.html>

Swedish-English Dictionary
<www-lexikon.nada.kth.se/skolverket/ swe-eng.shtml>

Swedish Gazetteer
<www.sna.se/gazetteer.html>

SweGGate
<rootsweb.com/~swewgw>

American Swedish Institute
<www.americanswedishinst.org>

CityGuide Sweden
<cityguide.se>

Demographic Data Base
<www.ddb.umu.se/index_eng.html>

ExploreNorth
<www.explorenorth.com/gen-swe.html>

Föreningen Släktdata
<www.slakdata.org/en/start>

Genealogy Pro: Professional Genealogists & Research Services for Sweden
<genealogypro.com/directories/Sweden.html>

Master Index to Swedish Genealogical Data Ordered by last name
<www.dcs.hull.ac.uk/public/genealogy/swedish/>

Minnesota Genealogical Society
<mngs.org>

Online Swedish-English Dictionary
<www.freedict.com/onldict/swe.html>

Rötter

The Scandinavian, Swedish, Norwegian-American page of Genealogy
<www.geocities.com/coastwater/nina_
moller_nordby.html>

Scandinavian/USA Genealogy Links

Svensk släktforskning (Swedish language only)
<www.abc.se/~m6921/geneal.html>

Sweden Genealogy Forum
<genforum.genealogy.com/sweden/>

Sweden Genealogy Mailing Lists
<members.aol.com/gfsjohnf/gen_mail_
country-swe.html>

SwedGenCo Swedish Genealogy Company
<hem.passagen.se/jonmyren/swedgenco>

Swedish 1890 Census
<www.foark.umu.se/census/Index.htm>

Swedish Ancestry Research Association (SARA)
<members.tripod.com/~SARAssociation/sara/
SARA_Home_Page.htm>

Swedish Church Records Online
<www.genline.com/databasen>

The Swedish Colonial Society

Swedish Emigrants on CD-ROM
<www.ssd.gu.se/cdprod.html>

Swedish Emigration to America
<www.americanwest.com/swedemigr/pages/
emigra.htm>

Swedish Genealogy Club
<www.libertynet.org/ashm/genealo.html>

Swedish Resources
<www.tc.umn.edu/~pmg/swedish.html>

SweGGate: Genealogical Research in Sweden
<www.rootsweb.com/~swewgw/>

The Swenson Center at Augustana College: Swedish Immigration Research Center
<www.augustana.edu/administration/
swenson/>

DENMARK RESOURCES

ORGANIZATIONS AND ARCHIVES

ARCHIVE FOR THE COUNTIES OF ÅBENRÅ, SØNDERBORG, HADERSLEV AND TØNDER: LANDSARKIVET FOR SØNDERJYLLAND

Haderslevvej 45 DK-6200 Åbenrå, Denmark
<www.sa.dk/laa/omarkiverne/default.htm>

ARCHIVE FOR THE COUNTIES OF ÅLBORG, ÅRHUS, HJØRRING, RANDERS, RIBE, RINGKØBING, SKANDERBORG, THISTED, VIBORG AND VEJLE: LANDSARKIVET FOR NØRREJYLLAND

Ll. Sct. Hansgade 5 DK-8800 Viborg, Denmark
<www.sa.dk/lav/omarkiverne/default.htm>

ARCHIVE FOR THE COUNTIES OF BORNHOLM, FREDERIKSBORG, HOLBÆK, MARIBO, KØBENHAVN AND KØBENHAVN CITY, PRÆSTØ AND SORØ: LANDSARKIVET FOR SJÆLLAND M.M.

Jagtvej 10, DK-2200 Copenhagen N, Denmark
<www.sa.dk/lak/omarkiverne/default.htm>

ARCHIVE FOR THE COUNTIES OF ODENSE AND SVENDBORG: LANDSARKIVET FOR FYN

Jernbanegade 36,DK-5000 Odense, Denmark
<www.sa.dk/lao/omarkiverne/default.htm>

COPENHAGEN'S ARCHIVE

Københavns Stadsarkiv, Rådhuset, DK 1599 Copenhagen V, Denmark

DANISH EMIGRATION ARCHIVES

Arkivstræde 1, Box 1731, DK-9100, Aalborg, Denmark
<www.emiarch.dk>

DANISH IMMIGRANT MUSEUM

2212 Washington St., Box 470, Elk Horn, IA 51531
Phone: (800) 759-9192
<dkmuseum.org>

FREDERIKSBERG KOMMUNEBIBLIOTEK (FREDRIKSBERG COMMUNITY LIBRARY)

Solbjergvej 25, DK-2000 Copenhagen, Denmark

KONGELIGE BIBLIOTEK (THE ROYAL LIBRARY)

Christians Brygge 8, DK-1219 Copenhagen K, Denmark

MILITARY ARCHIVE

Hærens Arkiv
Slotsholmgade 4, DK-1216 Copenhagen K, Denmark

MINNESOTA GENEALOGICAL SOCIETY

5768 Olson Memorial Highway, Golden Valley, MN 55422
<mngs.org>

NATIONAL ARCHIVES

Rigsarkivet
Rigsdagsgården 9, DK-1218 Copenhagen K Denmark
<www.sa.dk/ra/engelsk/default.htm>

UNIVERSITY LIBRARIES

Universitetsbibliotekets
1 Af (Div.), Fiolstræde 1, DK-1171 Copenhagen, Denmark

UNIVERSITETSBIBLIOTEKETS 2 AF (DIV.)

Nørre Alle 49, DK-2200 Copenhagen, Denmark

BOOKS

Definitely Danish By Julie McDonald (Iowa City, Iowa: Penfield Press, 1993)

Find dine rødder (Find Your Roots) By Hans H. Worsøe (Viborg: Politikens Forlag A/S, 1987)

Genealogical Guidebook and Atlas of Denmark By Frank Smith and Finn A. Thomsen (Salt Lake City, Utah: Thomsen's Genealogical Center, 1969)

Min slægt, Hvordan-Hvornår-Hvorfor? (My Lineage, How-When-Why) By Suno Scharling (København: Aschehoug Dansk Forlag A/S, 1989)

Searching for Your Danish Ancestors By the MGS Danish Interest Group. To order, write to: Park Genealogical Books, Dept. WWW, Box 130968, Roseville MN 55113 **<www.parkbooks.com>**

Tante Johanne: Letters of a Danish Immigrant Family, 1887–1910 By John W. Nielsen (Blair, Neb.: Lur Publications, 1996)

PERIODICALS

Fortid og Nutid (The Past and the Present) 1914–. Published by the Dansk historisk Fællesforening, Rigsarkivet, Rigsdagsgarden 9, 1218 Copenhagen K, Denmark.

Hvem Forsker Hvad (Who's Researching What) 1969–. Published by the Samfundet for Dansk Genealogi og Personalhistorie, Christian Xs Vej 27, 8260 Viby J, Denmark.

Personalhistorisk Tidskrift (Periodical and Serial of Personal History) 1880–. Published by the Samfundet for Dansk-Norsk Genealogi og personalhistorie. After 1930, published by Samfundet for Dansk Genealogi og Personal-historie.

WEBSITES

Danish Demographic Database
<ddd.sa.dk/DDD_EN.HTM>

Danish Emigration Archives
<www.emiarch.dk/home.php3?l=en>

Danish-English Online Dictionary
<www.freedict.com/onldict/dan.html>

Danish Genealogy Links
<www.rootsweb.com/~mnstloui/danlnk.htm>

Danish Immigrant Museum
<www.dkmuseum.org/DenmarkDanish GenealogyTracingFindingAncestors Archives.html>

Denmark Genealogy Mailing Lists
<www.rootsweb.com/~jfuller/gen_mail_ country-den.html>

DIS-Danmark
<www.dis-danmark.dk/forenuk.htm>

Facts About Genealogical Research in Denmark
<www.genealogi.dk/factwors.htm>

Genealogy Resource Index for Denmark (GRID)
<www.genealogyindex.dk>

Genealogy Today: Danish Surnames
<www.genealogytoday.com/names/origins/ danish.html>

History of Denmark
<www.um.dk/english/danmark/ danmarksbog/kap6/6.asp>

The Society for Danish Genealogy and Biography
<www.genealogi.dk/index_us.htm>

ORGANIZATIONS AND ARCHIVES

ÅLANDS LANDSKAPSARKIV
(Ahvenanmaa [Åland] County)
PB 60, 22101 Mariehamn, Finland
Phone: 011-358-18-253 44
Fax: 011-358-18-191 55

FINNISH-AMERICAN HISTORICAL ARCHIVES, SUOMI COLLEGE
601 Quincy St., Hancock, MI 49930

GENEALOGICAL SOCIETY OF FINLAND
Liisankatu 16A, FIN-00170, Helsinki, Finland
<www.genealogia.fi/indexe.htm>

HÄMEENLINNAN MAAKUNTA-ARKISTO
(Häme and Uusimaa counties)
13100 Hämeenlinna, Finland
Phone: 011-358-3-653 3801
Fax: 011-358-3-653 3810
<www.narc.fi/ma/hma/index.html>

IMMIGRATION HISTORY RESEARCH CENTER, UNIVERSITY OF MINNESOTA
826 Berry St., St. Paul, MN 55114

INSTITUTE OF MIGRATION EMIGRANT REGISTER
Piispankatu 3, 20500 Turku, Finland
<www.utu.fi/erill/instmigr/eng/e_rekist.htm>

JOENSUUN MAAKUNTA-ARKISTO
(Pohjois-Karjala County)
PL 146, 80101 Joensuu, Finland
Phone: 011-358-13-251 4602
Fax: 011-358-13-251 4606
<www.narc.fi/ma/joma/index.htm>

JYVÄSKYLÄN MAAKUNTA-ARKISTO
(Keski-Suomi County)
40100 Jyväskylä, Finland
Phone: 011-358-14-617 592
Fax: 011-358-14-610 651
<www.narc.fi/ma/jyma/index.html>

MIKKELIN MAAKUNTA-ARKISTO
(Kymi, Mikkeli and Kuopio counties; the former Viipuri county; and the parishes of Salla and Petsamo, which were ceded to the USSR in 1944)
PL 2, 50101 Mikkeli, Finland
Phone: 011-358-15-321 310
Fax: 011-358-15-321 3157
<www.narc.fi/ma/mma/mmapsivu.htm>

MILITARY ARCHIVES
(before 1810)
Krigsarkivet
S-115 88 Stockholm, Sweden
Phone: 011-46-8-782 41 00
Fax: 011-46-8-782 69 76
<www.ra.se/kra>

MILITARY ARCHIVES
(most begin in 1812)
Sota-arkisto
PL 266, 00170 Helsinki, Finland
Phone: 011-358-9-161 6362
Fax: 011-358-9-161 6371

NATIONAL ARCHIVES OF FINLAND
Kansallisarkisto
PL 258, 00171 Helsinki, Finland
Phone: 011-358-9-228 521
Fax: 011-358-9-176 302
<www.narc.fi> (Finnish)
<www.narc.fi/sve/index.html> (Swedish)

OULUN MAAKUNTA-ARKISTO
(Lappi and Oulu counties)
PL 31, 90101 Oulu, Finland
Phone: 011-358-8-311 7066
Fax: 011-358-8-311 7068
<www.narc.fi/ma/oma/oulu1.htm>

SWEDISH-LANGUAGE NEWSPAPER ARCHIVE
Brages Urklippsverk, Kaserngatan 28, 00130 Helsingfors, Finland

TURUN MAAKUNTA-ARKISTO (TURKU-PORI COUNTY)
PL 383, 20101 Turku, Finland
Phone: 011-358-2-2760 818
Fax: 011-358-2-2760 810
<www.narc.fi/ma/tma/index.htm>

UNIVERSITY OF HELSINKI LIBRARY
Helsingin yliopiston kirjasto
Unioninkatu 36
00170 Helsinki, Finland
<renki.helsinki.fi/hyk/kirjasto/kokoelma/
arkistot.html>

VAASAN MAAKUNTA-ARKISTO
(Vaasa County [see also Jyväsklän
maakunta-arkisto])
PL 240, 65101 Vaasa, Finland
Phone: 011-358-6-317 3912
Fax: 011-358-6-312 0392
<www.narc.fi/ma/vma/finhtml/index.htm>

BOOKS
*The Fabulous Family Holomolaiset: A
Minnesota Finnish Family's Oral Tradition* by
Patricia Eilola (North Star Press)

Finns in Wisconsin by Mark Knipping
(Wisconsin Historical Society Press)

Finnish Genealogical Research
By Timothy Laitila Vincent and Rick Tapio (New
Brighton, Minn.: Finnish America, 1994)
Finnish Touches: Recipes & Traditions (Penfield
Books)

Hometown Folks: A Finnish-American Saga by
Gerald F. Carlson (North Star Press)

Guide to the Military Archives of Finland
(Helsinki: The Military Archives, 1977)

Guide to the Public Archives of Finland
(Helsinki: National Archives, 1980)

Hometown Folks: A Finnish-American Saga By
Gerald F. Carlson (St. Cloud, Minn.: North Star
Press, 1997)

Kansallisarkisto, asiakkaan opas
(The National Archives: A Guide) (Helsinki:
Kansallisarkisto, 1994)

Krigsarkivet: en handledning
(Guide to the Military Archives)
(Helsingfors: Statens tryckericentral, 1977)

Maakunta-arkistojen opas (Guide to
the Provincial Archives)(Helsinki: Valtion
painatuskeskus, 1976)

Riksarkivet, en handledning (The National
Archives: A Guide) (Helsingfors: Riksarkivet,
1995)

Släktforskning, praktisk handbok för Finland
(Genealogical Research, Practical Handbook for
Finland) By Alf Brenner (Helsingfors: Söderström
& Co., 1947)

Sota-arkiston opas (Guide to the Military
Archives)(Helsinki: Valtion painatuskeskus, 1974)

Sukututkijan tietokirja (Reference Book for
Genealogists) (Sirkka Karskela. Suomi: Finnroots,
1983)

*Suomen arkistojen opas: Arkiven i Finland, en
handledning* (Guide to Archives Repositories in
Finland) (Helsinki: Valtion painatuskeskus, 1975)

*Valtionarkiston yleisluettelo—Översiktskatalog
för Riksarkivet*
(Inventory for the National Archives) 4 vols.
(Helsiniki: Valtioneuvoston kirjapaino, 1956–73)

PERIODICALS
*Genos: Suomen Sukututkimusseuran
aikakauskirja/Genos: tidskrift utgiven av
Genealogiska Samfundet i Finland* (Genealogy:
Periodical Published by the Genealogical Society
in Finland) Helsinki: 1930–.

Sukutieto: datateknik (Computer Technique)
Helsinki: Sukutietotekniikka ry, 1982–.

Sukuviesti: sukumme eilen ja tänään, sukuyhteisöjen yhteyslehti (Genealogical News: Our Family Yesterday and Today, Newsletter for the United Genealogical Societies) Espoo: SYT, 1978–.

WEBSITES

Beginner's Guide to Finnish Family History Research
<members.aol.com/dssaari/guide.htm>

Cyndi's List: Finland
<cyndislist.com/finland.htm>

DISBYT database: Pre-1909 people search
<frigg.abc.se/~disbyt/finland/english/index.html>

Encyclopedia of Genealogy: Finnish Genealogy
<www.eogen.com/finnishgenealogy>

English-Finnish Dictionary
<www.fincd.com>

Family History Finland
<www.open.org/rumcd/genweb/finn.html>

FamilySearch: Finland Research Outline
<www.familysearch.org/eng/search/rg/guide/finland.asp>

Finfo
<virtual.finland.fi>

Finland's Family History Association
<www.digiarkisto.org/sshy/index_eng.htm>

Finland Festivals
<www.festivals.fi/english/keskioikea.lasso>

Finland Genealogy Forum
<genforum.genealogy.com/finland/>

Finland Genealogy Mailing Lists
<www.rootsweb.com/~jfuller/gen_mail_country-fin.html>

Finngen Mailing List
<www.tbaytel.net/bmartin/finngen.htm>

Finnish-American Historical Society of the West
<www.finamhsw.com>

Finnish Genealogy Group
<feefhs.org/fi/frgfinmn.html>

Finnish Genealogy Links (Suomalaisia Sukututkimus Linkkeja)
<www.engr.uvic.ca/~syli/geneo/links.html>

Finland Genealogy Resources
<feefhs.org/links/finland.html>

FinlandGenWeb
<rootsweb.ancestry.com/~finwgw>

Finnish Grammar
<www.uta.fi/~km56049/finnish>

Finnish Institute of Migration
<www.migrationinstitute.fi/index_e.php>

Genealogical Society of Finland
<www.genealogia.org>

Google Translate
<translate.google.com>

Genealogical Society of Finland
<www.genealogia.fi/indexe.htm>

Helsinki City Library
<www.lib.hel.fi/english>

History of Finland
<www.pp.clinet.fi/~pkr01/historia/history.html>

HisKi Project
<hiski.genealogia.fi/historia/indexe.htm>

Institute of Migration
<www.utu.fi/erill/instmigr/art/finngeneal.htm>

Minnesota Finnish Pages
<www.minnesotafinnish.org>

National Archives Service of Finland
<www.arkisto.fi>

National Land Survey of Finland
<www.maanmittauslaitos.fi/en>

National Land Survey of Finland
<www.maanmittauslaitos.fi>

Online Finnish-English Dictionary
<www.freedict.com/onldict/fin.html>

RootsWeb's guide to tracing Finnish family trees
**<www.rootsweb.com/~rwguide/lesson23.
htm#Finns>**

ORGANIZATIONS AND ARCHIVES

BERGEN OFFENTLIGE BIBLIOTEK (PUBLIC LIBRARY-BERGEN)
Strømgaten 6, 5015 Bergen, Norway
Phone: 47 55 56 85 60
Fax: 47 55 56 85 70

BIBLIOTEK FOR HUMANIA OG SAMFUNDSVITENSKAP (UNIVERSITY LIBRARY)
Postboks 1009 Blindern, 0315 Oslo, Norway
Phone: 47 22 85 91 02
<www.ub.uio.no/unsl>

DEICKMANSKE BIBLIOTEK (PUBLIC LIBRARY-OSLO)
Henrik Ibsensgate 1, N-0179 Oslo 1, Norway
Phone: 47 22 03 29 00
Fax: 47 22 11 33 89
E-mail: deichman@deich. folkebibl.no
<www.deich.folkebibl.no>

EVANGELICAL LUTHERAN CHURCH IN AMERICA ARCHIVES
8765 West Higgins Road, Chicago, IL 60631
Visit by appointment only:
321 Bonnie Lane, Elk Grove Village, IL 60007
Phone: (847) 690-9410

GENEALOGY SOCIETY OF NORWAY (DIS-NORGE)
PB 6601, St. Olavs plass, NO-0129 Oslo, Norway
<www.disnorge.no/eng>

NORDIC HERITAGE MUSEUM
3014 NW 67th, Seattle WA, 98117
Phone: (206) 789-5707
<www.nordicmuseum.com>

NORWEGIAN-AMERICAN HISTORICAL ASSOCIATION
1510 St. Olaf Ave., Northfield, MN 55057
Phone: (507) 646-3221
<www.naha.stolaf.edu/home.htm>

NORWEGIAN EMIGRANT MUSEUM
Åkershagan, 2312 Ottestad, Norway
Phone: 47 62 57 48 50
<www.museumsnett.no/emigrantmuseum>

NORWEGIAN EMIGRATION CENTER
Strandkaien 31, N-4005 Stavanger, Norway
<www.emigrationcenter.com>

NORWEGIAN HISTORICAL DATA CENTRE, UNIVERSITY OF TRØMSO
N-9037 Tromso, Norway
<www.rhd.uit.no/indexeng.html>

OSLO LIBRARY
Deichmanske Bibliotek
Henrik Ibsensgate 1, N-0179 Oslo 1, Norway
Phone: 47 22 03 29 00
<www.deichmanske-bibliotek.oslo.kommune.no/english>

RIKSARKIVET (NATIONAL ARCHIVE)
Folke Bernadottes vei 21
Postboks 4013, Ullevål stadion
N-0806, Oslo, Norway
Phone: 47 22 02 26 00
Fax: 47 22 23 74 89
E-mail: ra@riksarkivet.dep.
<www.riksarkivet.no/english>

SONS OF NORWAY
1455 W. Lake St.
Minneapolis, MN 55408
Phone: (612) 827-3611
<www.sofn.com>

UNIVERSITY LIBRARY (SIMILAR TO LIBRARY OF CONGRESS)
Bibliotek for humania og samfundsvitenskap
Postboks 1009 Blindern, 0315 Oslo, Norway
Phone: 47 22 85 91 02
<www.ub.uio.no/english/>

VESTERHEIM GENEALOGICAL CENTER & NAESETH LIBRARY
415 W. Main St., Madison, WI 53703
Phone: (608) 255-2224
<vesterheim.org/genealogy/index.php>

VESTERHEIM NORWEGIAN-AMERICAN MUSEUM

523 W. Water Street, Box 379, Decorah, IA 52101
(563) 382-9681
<vesterheim.org/index.php>

DIGITAL ARCHIVES
<digitalarkivet.uib.no>

Norway has eight regional archives, grouped by counties, which hold church, land and court records:

STATSARKIVET I OSLO (ØSTFOLD, AKERSHUS AND OSLO COUNTIES)

Folke Bernadottes vei 21, Postboks 4015 Ulleval stadion, N-0806 Oslo, Norway
Phone: 47 22 02 26 00

STATSARKIVET I KONGSBERG (BUSKERUD, VESTFOLD AND TELEMARK COUNTIES)

Frogsvei 44, N-3611 Kongsberg
Norway
Phone: 47 32 86 99 00

STATSARKIVET I HAMAR (OPPLAND AND HEDEMARK COUNTIES)

Lille Strandgate 3, N-2304 Hamar, Norway
Phone: 47 62 52 36 42

STATSARKIVET I KRISTIANSAND (AUST-AGDER AND VEST-AGDER COUNTIES)

Marthas vei 1, Serviceboks 402, 4604 Kristiansand, N-4613 Kristiansand, Norway
Phone: 47 38 14 55 00

STATSARKIVET I STAVANGER (ROGALAND COUNTY)

Bergjelandsgt.30, N -4012 Stavanger, Norway
Phone: 47 51 50 12 60

STATSARKIVET I BERGEN (HORDALAND, BERGEN AND SOGN OG FJORDANE COUNTIES)

Arstadveien 22, N-5009 Bergen
Norway
Phone: 47 55 31 5070

STATSARKIVET I TRONDHEIM (MØRE OG ROMSDAL, SØR-TRONDELAG, NORD-TRONDELAG AND NORDLAND COUNTIES)

Høgskoleveien 12, Postboks 2825 Elgesreter, N-7432 Trondheim, Norway
Phone: 47 73 88 45 00

STATSARKIVET I TROMSØ (TROMS AND FINNMARK COUNTIES AND SPITSBERGEN)

N-9293 Tromsø, Norway
Phone: 47 77 67 66 11

BOOKS

Norsk Biografisk Leksikon (Norwegian Biographical Encyclopedia) by Edv. Bull, Anders Krogvig, Gerhard Gran, et al, 19 volumes (out of print, FHL book 948.1 D36n, computer number 0215638)

Scandinavian Biographical Index (out of print, FHL book 948 D32s, computer number 0731014)

Norway to America: A History of the Migration by Ingrid Semmingsen (University of Minnesota Press, $16.95)

The Promise of America: A History of the Norwegian-American People by Odd Sverre Lovoll (University of Minnesota Press, $24.95)

Aslak Bolts jordebok (Aslak Bolt's Land Book) by Jon Gunnar Jørgensen (Oslo: Riksarkivet, 1997)

Giants in the Earth: A Saga of the Prairie by Ole Rølvaag (New York: Harper & Row, 1964)

Norway to America: A History of the Migration by Ingrid Semmingsen (Minneapolis: University of Minnesota Press, 1978)

The Promise of America: A History of the Norwegian-American People by Odd Sverre Lovoll (Minneapolis: University of Minnesota Press, 1999)

PERIODICALS

Norsk Slektshistorisk Tidsskrift (Periodical of Norwegian Family History)

Oslo: Norsk Slektshistorisk Forening, 1928–.

WEBSITES

Ancestors from Norway
<homepages.rootsweb.com/~norway>

The Documentation Project
<www.dokpro.uio.no/engelsk>

Culture Net Norway
<www.culturenet.no/links.php?kat=2021>

Cyndi's List: Norway
<www.cyndislist.com/norway.htm>

Emigration Ship Index
<www.norwayheritage.com/ships>

Genealogy/Slekt in Troms Norway
<www.troms-slekt.com>

Genealogy Society of Norway-DIS
<www.disnorge.no>

genealogyPro
<genealogypro.com/directories/Norway.html>

GenealogySpot: Norway
<www.genealogyspot.com/country/norway.htm>

History of Norway
<odin.dep.no/odin/engelsk/norway/history>

How to Trace Your Ancestors in Norway
<odin.dep.no/odinarkiv/norsk/dep/ud/1996/eng/032005-990804/index-dok000-b-n-a.html>

National Archives of Norway Digital Archive
<digitalarkivet.uib.no>

Norge.no
<english.norge.no/andrelenker>

Norway Family
<www.norwayfamily.com>

Norway Genealogy
<home.online.no/~oekaas/Ny%20web/indexeng.htm>

Norway Genealogy Forum
<genforum.genealogy.com/norway>

Norway Genealogy Mailing Lists
<www.rootsweb.com/~jfuller/gen_mail_country-nor.html>

Norway Genealogy: WorldGenWeb
<www.rootsweb.com/~wgnorway>

Norway Heritage Passenger and Ships Lists
<www.norwayheritage.com/ships>

Norway—The Official Site in the US
<www.norway.org>

Norway Online Information
<www.norway.org>

The Norway Post: Genealogy/Roots
<www.norwaypost.no/default.asp?folder_id=72>

Norwegian-American Bygdelagenes Fellesraad
<www.fellesraad.com>

Norwegian American Genealogy Center & Naeseth Library
<www.nagcnl.org>

Norwegian Genealogy Resources on the Internet
<www.hfaa.org/bygdelag/links.shtml>

Norwegian-American Homepage
<www.lawzone.com/half-nor/nor-am.htm>

Online Norwegian-English Dictionary
<www.freedict.com/onldict/nor.html>

Odin (government site)
<odin.dep.no/odin/english/bn.html>

The Promise of America (Norwegian National Library)
<www.nb.no/emigrasjon/emigration>

Research Outline: Norway
<www.familysearch.org/Eng/Search/RG/ frameset_rhelps.asp> (click on "N" and scroll down)

Slekt, Genealogy
<home.online.no/~cfscheel/genindex.htm>

Sogn og Fjordane County Migration Database
<www.sffarkiv.no/sffeng.htm>

Uffda: Genealogical Links to Norway
<www.fromnorway.net/uffda_norwegian_ directory/geneol.htm>

US Embassy Norway
<www.usa.no/norway/genealogy.html>

CHAPTER FIVE

FRANCE

By Nancy Hendrickson and Maureen A. Taylor

REGIONAL GUIDE

Despite our countries' political differences (freedom fries, anyone?), France holds a certain romance for Americans—the Eiffel Tower and Champs-Élysées, the sun-drenched lavender fields of Provence, the glamorous Riviera, haute couture, rich chocolate confections and world-renowned wines … *ooh la la*!

For Americans with French ancestry, that *je ne sais quoi* makes genealogy all the more alluring. Just imagine the history and culture your forebears witnessed. Lucky for you, the process of tracing your French roots isn't literally indescribable: Follow the five research steps we've outlined, and say *bonjour* to your family tree.

Brush Up on Background

How well do you know your French history? Part of Gaul (which covered most of western Europe) in ancient times, France has been home to a jumble of ethnic groups, including Celts, Germans, Romans and Greeks.

Julius Caesar brought Roman culture and the Latin language when he conquered Gaul in 59 BC. In the third and fourth centuries, a Germanic tribe called the Franks captured some of the region, and it later became part of Charlemagne's Carolingian Empire. The country now called France was a monarchy from then until the French Revolution in 1789, after which a general named Napoleon Bonaparte became premier consul of the new French Republic. He

crowned himself emperor of France in 1804 and reigned until 1815, when the monarchy was restored under Louis XVIII. A second republic and a second empire later, today's France has a bicameral legislature, a president and prime minister.

During the 17th through 19th centuries, France was a religious battleground torn apart by warring elements of the predominantly Catholic population and its much smaller Protestant flock. Although laws called for tolerance, Protestant emigration siphoned off talented craftsmen such as weavers and silversmiths. One of the latter, Apollos Rivoire, anglicized his name to Paul Revere; his namesake son became the famous American revolutionary.

Though such turbulent episodes spurred some immigration to America, the French didn't come en masse like other ethnic groups did—they arrived in trickles rather than floods. Samuel de Champlain formed North America's first permanent French colony in 1608 at Quebec. If you paid attention in grade school, you may recall Jacque Marquette and Louis Joliet's 1673 exploration up the Mississippi River and the 1682 expedition with René Robert Cavelier, sieur de La Salle at the helm. La Salle claimed the Mississippi basin for France and named it Louisiana.

La Nouvelle France was based in Canada, with a string of settlements (St. Louis, Natchez, New Orleans) along the Mississippi River. Protestants fleeing persecution in France were banned from New France; many went to the British Colonies. By the American Revolution, New France had an estimated population of 80,000, compared to 1.5 million in Britain's 13 Colonies.

The French settled Quebec and Acadia (mostly Canada's Maritime Provinces) early on, but in the 1750s and 1760s, the British expelled Acadians who wouldn't pledge allegiance to the Crown. This ousting sent several thousand back to France and south to the British Colonies and Louisiana (then in Spanish hands). Following several French-English-Spanish hullabaloos, the United States bought Louisiana in 1803.

During the French Revolution, from 1789 to 1799, thousands of political refugees left for the United States—enough that top destinations New York, Charleston and Philadelphia had French-language newspapers. Another immigration wave arose during the Franco-Prussian War of 1870-1871, when France lost its Alsace-Lorraine region. Many in this group settled in New York, New Orleans and Chicago.

The post-Civil War era saw an increase in French Canadian immigration to the United States, most frequently into the Northeastern states of Massachusetts, Vermont, Maine and Rhode Island. The 1930 census revealed that more than 135,000 US residents were French natives. The total French immigration from 1820 onward weighs in at about 750,000, a minimal number compared with immigration from elsewhere in Europe—but quite important if that figure counts your ancestor.

Take Care of Translations

My own introduction to French genealogy came via a Huguenot (Protestant) ancestor who left France after Louis XIV revoked the Edict of Nantes (see the time line at right), and settled for a

time in the "Low Countries," the approximate area of the Netherlands. Then he moved to England, whence he sailed to the New World, traveled down the East Coast and, apparently disliking one stop after another, wound his way back up to Pennsylvania.

I quickly discovered France has excellent records, particularly civil registrations and church records. Civil records are in French, but the format is easy to follow and you should be able to read them with a good French dictionary and knowledge of basic terms (refer to the genealogy glossary on page 262). Try the free online dictionary at **<artfl-project.uchicago.edu>** and translation tool **<translate.google.com>**. Church records also are in French.

Other records, such as military, notary and land documents, can be more difficult to interpret. This is a good time to find someone who can translate them for you. For recommendations, ask around at your genealogical society, a local college or your nearest Family History Center (see **<familysearch.org>** for locations' contact information).

When requesting French records by mail, use the letter-writing guides on the Family History Library's (FHL) FamilySearch website **<www.familysearch.org/learn/wiki/en/France_Letter_Writing_Guide>**.

You may need to translate some dates, too. France used the French Republican Calendar from 1793 to 1805 (an 1871 attempt to reinstate it failed). It gave every month the same number of days and dubbed months and days of the week after poetic tree and plant names. Find a date converter online at **<www.fourmilab.ch/documents/calendar>**

TIME LINE

1534	Jacques Cartier begins French exploration of North America.
1539	Date and hour of birth first appear in French baptismal registers. French replaces Latin as official language.
1541	Protestantism attracts converts in France.
1559	Protestant pastors start keeping baptisms and marriage registers for their congregation. Many of these are later destroyed during Protestant persecutions.
1579	Death and marriage records are filed for the first time.
1632	French settle Quebec and Acadia in Canada.
1685	Revocation of the Edict of Nantes makes Protestantism illegal, causing Huguenots to flee France.
1698	Dom Pérignon creates champagne.
1722	First wave of settlers begins moving from Alsace-Lorraine to colonies in the Banat, Austria-Hungary.
1755	Acadians exiled to Louisiana from Canada.
1764	First wave of settlers begins moving from Alsace-Lorraine to colonies in Russia and the Ukraine.
1784	The Montgolfier brothers pioneer hot-air ballooning at Versailles.
1789–1791	French Revolution topples the monarchy. Half a million refugees flee.
1792	Beginning of civil registration in France.

1793-1805 ◆	Revolutionary Calendar replaces Gregorian.
1804 ◆	Napoleon crowns himself emperor.
1848 ◆	Monarchy again overthrown; Napoleon's nephew named president.
1857 ◆	Gustave Flaubert writes *Madame Bovary*.
1874 ◆	Impressionist painters stage their first exhibition, in Paris.
1885 ◆	The Statue of Liberty arrives in New York from France.
1889 ◆	Eiffel Tower constructed.
1903 ◆	First Tour de France bicycle race.
1914 ◆	Germany declares war on France.
1915 ◆	Number of immigrants returning to France exceeds number arriving in the United States.
1918 ◆	By the end of World War I, 1.3 million Frenchmen are dead.
1940 ◆	French Jews flee; German troops enter Paris.
1943 ◆	Jacques Cousteau invents the Aqua-Lung, the original scuba gear.
1944 ◆	Paris is liberated from German occupation.
1958 ◆	Fifth Republic established with Charles DeGaulle as president.
1962 ◆	Algeria gains independence from France after eight years of war
1990 ◆	France linked to Britain by the Channel Tunnel.
2002 ◆	The euro replaces the franc, France's currency since 1360.

(scroll down for the French Republican Calendar).

Find the Place of Birth

Knowing your ancestor's place of birth is critical, since most French records are kept at the department level—roughly equivalent to a US county clerk's office. France has 100 departments (including some for former colonies), each administered by a prefect (*prefet*). Find departments and the towns (*communes*) in their jurisdictions at **<www.francegenweb. org/mairesgenweb>**; note some departments, especially around Paris, have undergone boundary changes.

Not sure what French town your family came from? Begin researching at home. Look for your ancestor's town name or immigration date in family Bibles, letters, naturalization papers and obituaries. If you're not the keeper of the family goodies, contact your most knowledgeable relative. Even if you have no documentation, a village name might be part of a family story or legend.

Next, try to track down your ancestor (or members of allied families, who may be traveling companions) on a passenger list. The Immigrant Ships Transcribers Guild **<immigrantships.net>** has French manifests from as early as 1820; most are for ships that departed from French ports such as Le Havre and Marseilles. Also check Ellis Island's free database **<ellisisland.org>** of 22 million names of passengers and crew who entered that port between 1892 and 1924.

The FHL in Salt Lake City has several microfilms, microfiches and books that could be helpful in tracking place of origin, including:

- *Les Combattants Français de la Guerre Américaine, 1778–1783* (microfilms 0547088 and 0962689) lists about 46,000 French soldiers who fought in the American Revolution.
- *L'Emigration des Alsaciens et des Lorrains du XVIIIe au XXe Siècle* by Norman Laybourn Strasbourg (Association des Publications près les Universités de Strasbourg, fiche numbers 6001613-4 and 6001614-6) is a microfiche of a French-language book naming immigrants from Alsace-Lorraine.
- *The Acadians in France, 1762–1776* by Milton P. Rieder is a book of names, arranged by town, of Acadians—whom Britain had expelled from Canada—living in France from 1762 to 1776.

To find other records that might document your ancestor's emigration, run a keyword search of the FHL catalog on terms such as *france immigration*. You can rent FHL films and fiche through your local FHC, but the library's books don't circulate. Instead, search WorldCat **<worldcat.org>** to locate books in closer-to-home libraries or those offering interlibrary loan.

Seek Microfilmed Records

Once you know your family's place of origin, you're ready to delve into French records—but you can start right here at home, through FamilySearch. Start by exploring the site's French genealogy guides **<www.familysearch.org/learn/wiki/en/France>**. You'll also find outlines with search strategies for various records; for instance, click French Church Records Marriage 1564-1791 for instructions on how to find and read a marriage record, and document your results.

Next, check the FHL catalog for microfilmed records by running a place search on your ancestor's town or parish. Click a topic, such as church records, then select a title to see details on places and years covered. For example, a search of Verlans (in the department of Haute-Saône) returns a listing under Census and Civil Registration. The FHL has microfilms of the 1841, 1851 to 1856, 1866 to 1876, and 1886 to 1906 censuses. Microfilm also exists for civil registrations from 1793 to 1902.

Here's what you should know about the French records you'll start with.

CIVIL REGISTRATION: Government authorities have kept birth, marriage and death records (*naissances, mariages, décès*) since 1792. Unfortunately, there's no national index to them. Civil registers are at the city or village "town hall" (*mairie*), which is somewhat like a US city court. Privacy laws prevent most access to birth and marriage records for the past 100 years; however, genealogists can obtain a certificate with proof of direct descent. Death records aren't confidential.

Once a record is 100 years old, it's transferred to the *archives départmentales*, or departmental archives. If the FHL doesn't have vital records for your ancestor's town, request them by writing to the archives—link to addresses from **<www.genealogy.tm.fr/archives/archives.htm>**.

HUGUENOT HISTORY

Beginning in 1562, Protestants and Catholics waged a series of wars throughout France. That year, a group of Huguenots—also known as French Calvinists—left to settle Fort Caroline in Florida. The colony was short-lived: An attack on nearby St. Augustine backfired, and the Spanish wiped out Fort Caroline in 1565.

In 1572, trying to end the conflict in France, the Catholic Catherine de Medici (queen consort of France's King Henry II) arranged for her daughter, Marguerite de Valois, to marry the Protestant Henry of Navarre, the future Henry IV. Catholics didn't approve of the Aug. 18 union. Six days later, during the Feast of St. Bartholomew, a massacre of Huguenots began in Paris and spread across France. Many Huguenot leaders, in Paris for the celebration, were killed. The exact number of fatalities is unknown—anywhere from 10,000 to 100,000 Huguenots died.

In 1598, Henry IV issued the Edict of Nantes granting Huguenots the civil rights of their Catholic countrymen. But in 1685, his grandson Louis XIV renounced the edict and declared Protestantism illegal, ordering Huguenot churches destroyed and schools closed. The bloody fighting didn't resume, though many Huguenots fled France.

It's unlikely these immigrants went directly to the United States. Begin searching in the Protestant countries of Great Britain, Prussia, the Netherlands and Switzerland. Once in the United States, a Huguenot might have reported his origins as his last residence prior to departure, not his original French village.

Protestants were barred from settling in French territories in North America. Many headed for the Dutch colony of New Netherland (later New York and New Jersey) and for the British Colonies, primarily Pennsylvania, South Carolina and Virginia. There, they frequently merged with other Protestant denominations.

Birth records often include the date and place of registration; date and place of birth; parents' names and ages; as well as the name, age and occupation of the informant. Some birth records also give the parents' birthplaces. The records sometimes bear margin notes that might indicate other records you should search. And fortunately, married women in France use their maiden names on records.

Marriage records include the bride's and groom's names, addresses and occupations; the marriage date and place; parents' names; and occupations of at least two witnesses. The records also note previous marriages or children born prior to the marriage. The couple had to be married by civil authorities before marrying in the church, so note the civil and church ceremonies may have taken place in different locations.

Deaths were registered in the towns where they occurred. Information on death records varies with the era. Early papers might state only the name, date and place of death; later records can include the birthplace and parents' names, as well as names, ages and occupations of witnesses.

Abbey of Senanque, Gordes, Provence

PARISH REGISTERS: After civil registrations, turn to parish records (*registres paroissiaux*). Because Catholicism was a national religion, you can do almost all your pre-1792 research in church records. A 1539 royal decree required priests to record baptisms; their duties eventually included tracking marriages and burials, too. A later decree required that records be kept in duplicate, but compliance wasn't routine until 1736. Churches continued to record baptisms, marriages and deaths after 1792, and these records aren't subject to the 100-year confidentiality law.

Most baptismal records are from the mid-1600s on; a few date to the 1300s. Baptism records typically include the date of baptism; names of the child, parents and godparents; and the family's residence. Church death records note the place and date of death, and names of the deceased and his parents or spouse. In church marriage records, you'll find the date; place of origin; names of the bride, groom, parents and witnesses; and at times, the relationship of the witnesses to the couple. Records for brides and grooms who were close relatives may indicate permission or dispensation (*dispense*) was needed for *consanguinité*. You probably can track down the common ancestor because the record will reveal the degree of relationship.

The FHL has microfilmed many French parish records. Keep in mind the records aren't indexed, so you'll need to know the name of your ancestor's parish, as well as the approximate date of the record, to order the right film. To identify parishes your family might've belonged to, the FHL recommends using the gazetteer *Bottin des Communes* (Éditions Bottin), available at libraries in print and through LexisNexis (a database offered by some libraries). If the FHL doesn't have microfilmed records from your ancestors' parish, try the departmental archives or write to the parish office.

What about finding records for Protestants in this Catholic nation? Those registers are in departmental archives, the Protestant Historical Society in Paris (*Société d'Histoire du Protestantisme Français*), or the national archives (*archives nationales*). See the resources on the page 105 for contact information.

Open It Up to Other Records

Now that you've gotten your feet wet, it's time to look for the following records, which are a little more difficult to access and use (*sacre bleu!*). You'll probably need to send a request letter to France, but check the FHL online catalog first.

MILITARY RECORDS, some dating from the 1600s, are at the Army and Navy Historical Services at the Château de Vincennes in Vincennes **<en.chateau-vincennes.fr/rubrique. php?ID=1003632>**. Departmental archives hold local conscription records; the FHL has microfilmed few of these records. The government began keeping lists of soldiers organized by regiment and date of origin of the group in 1716. Unindexed military censuses were compiled yearly and list men 19 and 20 years old. Military records are challenging unless you're fluent in French. They're not indexed, and they're grouped by year, then alphabetically. You may want to consider hiring a French genealogy expert for help; search for a pro at **<www.apgen.org>**. You'll have to provide the man's birth year and the department that recorded his birth.

NOTARIAL RECORDS (*actes notariés*) are some of the best sources of French genealogical information, but they're also difficult to locate unless you know the name of the notary and where he lived. These officials recorded legal events such as marriage contracts, wills, property divisions, guardianships and household inventories. Theirs are the oldest type of record kept in France.

Archived chronologically under the name of each notary, notarial documents older than 125 years are usually—but not always—located in the departmental archives. Try to determine the name of the notary in the area your ancestor lived from the departmental archives so that you can check those documents first. Families typically used the same notary for several generations, but not necessarily the one closest to them geographically.

Notarial records are mostly unindexed, though you may find lists of indexed records in local genealogical society publications. French notarial papers are only in France, so you may need to hire a professional genealogist there to assist you. Similar materials for French Canada are on microfilm, however, available through the Family History Library.

LAND AND PROPERTY RECORDS are in the national archives, *mairies* or departmental archives. The FHL hasn't microfilmed them. Property-transfer documents prepared by notaries are among notary records (see above).

CENSUSES began in 1772, but until 1836, they almost always show the number of people living in a household, not the names. Thereafter, censuses were taken every five years plus 1872 and 1916. French national censuses, held in departmental archives, are not on microfilm and are not indexed. They are therefore rarely used for genealogical research. Unlike the US, Canadian or British censuses, they cannot be easily searched to locate families. Church and civil records are better sources.

EMIGRATION DOCUMENTS are one last resource you should search for. Published indexes to different types of emigration materials exist, but depend on where in France your ancestors lived, the specific group they left with and the time period. For instance, very few 19th-century passenger lists from the major port of Le Havre still exist. Whatever passenger lists still exist for France are unindexed but usually contain the name, age, occupation, place of origin and sometimes birthplace.

FRENCH NAMING PRACTICES

Some confusing French naming practices can complicate your research. Prenoms or Christian names can be multiple and nicknames can be used instead of given names. Check both the birth certificates and baptismal records for name verification. Be prepared for surprises. In one Bessette family, for example, all the sisters have the same first name with different middle names; all their lives, however, they've been known by still other, unrecorded names—Loretta, Rita and Alice. So remember: With given names, keep good notes and never make assumptions.

French surnames follow the same rules as in other cultures, but with some additions. For example, French Canadian settlers often added an additional surname, or *dit* name, to further distinguish themselves. This means you may have to identify and search for information under several different surnames. Confused? The American French Genealogical Society offers a list of common French Canadian surnames and variations, including *dit* names, at **<www.afgs.org/ditnames/index1.html>**. There are also cases of double surnames in families from the mountainous areas of France.

You can also search French surname maps at websites including **<http://www.genealogie.com/nom-de-famille/>**, **<www.familleunie.fr/cartes>** and **<www.geopatronyme.com>**.

In the absence of French emigration lists, try American records. The availability and completeness of US passenger arrival lists depends on the time period; you'll find these in the US National Archives and in the Family History Library. In the case of French Canadians, many immigrants left family in Canada and frequently traveled back and forth to the United States. They would have left multiple entries in border crossing lists, which are also located at the National Archives.

Your French family heritage is part of the grand tapestry of European history. Once you discover that little village that your *arrière-grand-père* called home, you've won half the battle. *Bonne chance*!

Gargoyle overlooking Paris

CENSUS

French national censuses have not been transferred to microfilm, are not indexed, and are, therefore, rarely used for genealogical research. Unlike the US, Canadian, or British censuses, they cannot be easily searched to locate families. Church and civil records are better sources.

RESOURCES

ORGANIZATIONS AND ARCHIVES

ACADIAN CULTURAL SOCIETY
Box 2304, Fitchburg, MA 01420

AMERICAN-CANADIAN GENEALOGICAL SOCIETY
Box 6478, Manchester, NH 03108
Phone: (603) 622-1554
E-mail: acgs@acgs.org
<www.acgs.org>

AMERICAN FRENCH GENEALOGICAL SOCIETY
Box 830, Woonsocket, RI 02895-0870
Phone: (401) 765-6141
Fax : (401) 597-6290
E-mail: database@afgs.org
<www.afgs.org>

ARCHIVES DES AFFAIRES ÉTRANGÈRES (FOREIGN AFFAIRS ARCHIVES)
3, rue Suzanne-Masson, 93126 La Courneuve Cedex, France
Phone: +33 1 43 17 42 46
Fax: +33 1 43 17 48 44
E-mail: lecture.Archives@diplomatie.gouv.fr
<lannuaire.service-public.fr/services_
nationaux/administration-centrale-ou-
ministere_172025.html>

ARCHIVES MILITAIRES (MILITARY ARCHIVES)
Avenue de Paris, Vincennes, Val-de-Marne (94), France
Phone: +33 (0)1 41 93 22 57
<www.servicehistorique.defense.gouv.
fr/?lang=en>

ARCHIVES NATIONALES (NATIONAL ARCHIVES)
11, rue des 4 Fils, 75003 Paris, France
Phone: +33 01 40 27 64 19
Fax: +33 01 40 27 66 28
<www.archivesnationales.culture.gouv.fr/
chan/chan/index.html>

BIBLIOTHÈQUE GÉNÉALOGIQUE ET D'HISTOIRE SOCIAL
Z.A. Grand Marais, 3 digue d'Alfortville, 94034 Creteil Cedex, France
Phone: +33 01 42 33 58 21
E-mail: bibgen@bibgen.org
<www.bibgen.org>

BIBLIOTHÈQUE NATIONALE (NATIONAL LIBRARY)
Quai François-Mauriac, 75706 Paris Cedex 13, France
Phone: +33 (0)1 53 79 59 59
<www.bnf.fr>

BIBLIOTHÈQUE PUBLIQUE D'INFORMATION (LIBRARY OF PUBLIC INFORMATION)
Centre Georges Pompidou, rue Saint-Martin, 75197 Paris Cedex 04, France
Phone: +33 (0)1 44 78 12 75
Fax: +33 (0)1 44 78 12 15
<www.bpi.fr/en>

CENTRE HISTORIQUE DES ARCHIVES NATIONALES (HISTORICAL CENTER OF THE NATIONAL ARCHIVES OF FRANCE)
Records room: 60, rue des Francs-Bourgeois, 75141 Paris 03, France
Phone: +33 (1) 40 27 64 19
<www.archivesnationales.culture.gouv.fr>

FRENCH HERITAGE SOCIETY
14 E. 60th St., Suite 605, New York, NY 10022
Phone: (212) 759-6846
Fax: (212) 759-9632
E-mail: fhs@frenchheritagesociety.org
<www.frenchheritagesociety.org>

THE HUGUENOT SOCIETY OF AMERICA
20 W. 44th St., Suite 510, New York, NY 10036
Phone: (212) 755-0592
Fax: (212) 317-0676
E-mail: hugsoc@verizon.net
<www.huguenotsocietyofamerica.org>

HUGUENOT SOCIETY OF GREAT BRITAIN AND IRELAND
Box 444, Ruislip, Middlesex HA4 4GU England
Phone: +44 020 7679 2046
E-mail: library@huguenotsociety.org.uk
<huguenotsociety.org.uk>

LES ARCHIVES D'OUTRE-MER (OVERSEAS ARCHIVES)
29 Chemin du Moulin, de Testas, 13090 Aix en Provence, France
Phone: + 33 (0) 4 42 93 38 50
Fax: + 33 (0) 4 42 93 38 89
E-mail: anom.aix@culture.gouv.fr
<www.archivesnationales.culture.gouv.fr/anom/fr>

NATIONAL HUGUENOT SOCIETY
7340 Blanco Road, Suite 104, San Antonio, TX 78216-4970
Phone: (210) 366-9995
<www.huguenot.netnation.com>

BIBLIOTHÈQUE NATIONALE DE FRANCE (NATIONAL LIBRARY OF FRANCE)
François-Mitterrand Library, Quai François-Mauriac, 75706, Paris 13, France
Phone: +33 (0) 53 79 82 22,
<www.bnf.fr>

SOCIÉTÉ D'HISTOIRE DU PROTESTANTISME FRANÇAIS (PROTESTANT HISTORICAL SOCIETY)
54 Rue des Saints-Peres, 75007, Paris, France
Phone: +33 (1) 45 48 62 07
Fax: +33 (1) 45 44 94 87
<www.shpf.fr>

U.C.G.L. (GENEALOGICAL SOCIETY OF LORRAINE)
14 rue du Cheval Blanc, MJC Lillebonne, 54000 Nancy, France
Phone: +33 03 83 32 43 88
<www.genealogie-lorraine.fr/infos>

BOOKS

Ancestral Research in France: The Simple Guide to Tracing Your Family History Through French Records by Patrick Pontet (self-published)

Annuaire international des archives (International Directory of Archives) International Council on Archives. (Saur)

Beginning Franco-American Genealogy by Rev. Dennis M. Boudreau (American-French Genealogical Society)

Early Louisiana Settlers CD (Genealogical Publishing Co.)

État des inventaires des archives départementales, communales et hospitalières au 1er janvier 1983 (Report on archive inventories of departments, communities, and hospitals), 2 volumes, France, Direction des Archives (Archives nationales)

Fiches op de registers, collectie La Rochelle, 1602–1685 (Card index of Huguenots of La Rochelle, Charente-Maritime, France, 1602–1685) Bibliothèque Wallonne, Leiden. (Genealogical Society of Utah)

Fiches op de registers, collectie Montauban, 1647–1682 (Card index of Huguenots of Montauban, Tarn-et-Garonne, France, 1647–1682) Bibliothèque Wallonne, Leiden. (Genealogical Society of Utah)

Fiches op de Waalse register, 1500–1828 (Card index of Huguenots, 1500–1828)Bibliothèque Wallonne, Leiden. (Genealogical Society of Utah)

The French Canadian Heritage in New England by Gerard J. Brault (University Press of New England)

French Canadian Sources: A Guide for Genealogists by Patricia Kenney Geyh (Ancestry)

A Genealogist's Guide to Discovering Your Immigrant & Ethnic Ancestors by Sharon DeBartolo Carmack (Betterway Books)

Genealogy: An Introduction to Continental Concepts by Pierre Durye (Polyanthos)
A Great and Noble Scheme: The Tragic Story of the Expulsion of the French Acadians from Their American Homeland by John Mack Faragher (W.W. Norton)

Guide to Quebec Catholic Parishes and Published Parish Marriage Records by Jeanne Sauve White (Clearfield Co.)

Guide des recherches sur l'histoire des familles (Family history research guide) by Gildas Bernard (Archives Nationales)

Huguenot Genealogies: A Selected Preliminary List, 16 volumes, by Arthur Louis Finnell (Clearfield Co.)

Huguenot Settlers in America, 1600s-1900s CD (Genealogical Publishing Co.)
In Search of Your European Roots by Angus Baxter (Genealogical Publishing Co.)

Immigrants to America from France and Western Switzerland, 1859–1866 by Clifford Neal Smith (Westland Publications)

In Search of Your Canadian Roots: Tracing Your Family Tree in Canada, 3rd edition, by Angus Baxter (McClelland & Stewart)

La généalogie: histoire et pratique (Genealogy: History and Practice) by Joseph Valynseele (Larousse)

Les familles Protestantes en France (XVIe siècle-1792) (French Protestant families from the 16th century to 1792) France. Archives nationales. (Archives Nationales)

The New Orleans French, 1720–1733: A Collection of Marriage Records Relating to the First Colonists of the Louisiana Province by Winston De Ville (Genealogical Publishing Co.)

Nouveau guide de généalogie (New guide to genealogy) by Robert Aublet (Ouest-France)

Recensement des dépouillements systématiques réalisés en France pour faciliter les recherches généalogiques (Inventory of the systematic extraction made in France to help genealogical researchers) (Bibliothèque généalogique)

Répertoire de généalogies françaises imprimées (French genealogical bibliography), 3 volumes, by Étienne Arnaud (Berger-Levrault)

PERIODICALS

Acadian Genealogy Exchange (Janet Jehn, Acadian Genealogy Exchange, 1972–. English text. It includes Acadian/Cajun families throughout the world.)

Bulletin de la Société de l'Histoire du Protestantisme Français (Bulletin of the Society for the History of French Protestantism, Société de l'histoire du Protestantisme Français [Society for the History of French Protestantism], 1852–)

Cahiers du Centre de Généalogie Protestante (Notices of the Center for Protestant Genealogy, Société de l'histoire du Protestantisme Français [Society for the History of French Protestantism], 1978–)

Cercle de Généalogie Juive (Jewish Genealogical Society, Cercle de Généalogie Juive, 1985–)

Gé[néalogie] Magazine (Genealogy Magazine, Editions Christian, 1982–)

Geschichtsblätter des Deutschen Hugenotten-Vereins Sickte (History sheets of the German Huguenot Society Sickte, Deutschen Hugenotten-Vereins [German Huguenot Society], 1892–, German text)

Héraldique et généalogie (Heraldry and genealogy, Héraldique et Généalogie, 1969–)

Je me souviens (I remember, American French Genealogical Society, 1978–, English text)

La revue française de généalogie (French Genealogical Review, La Revue, 1979–)

Les Voyageurs (The Voyagers, German-Acadian Coast Historical and Genealogical Society, 1980–, English text)

Lifelines (Northern New York American Canadian Genealogical Society, 1984–, English text)

WEBSITES

1755: The French and Indian War
<web.syr.edu/~laroux>

Acadian Genealogy Exchange
<www.acadiangenexch.com>

American-French Genealogical Society
<www.afgs.org>

Bibliothèque Nationale de France
<www.bnf.fr>

Cyndi's List: France
<www.cyndislist.com/france>

Cyndi's List: Huguenot
<cyndislist.com/huguenot.htm>

FamilySearch: French Letter-Writing Guide
<www.familysearch.org/learn/wiki/en/France_Letter_Writing_Guide>

France.com
<www.france.com>

France Genealogy Forum
<genforum.genealogy.com/france>

France Genealogy Links
<www.genealogylinks.net/europe/france>

France GenWeb
<www.francegenweb.org>

France Mailing Lists
<rootsweb.ancestry.com/~jfuller/gen_mail_country-fra.html>

Franco-Gene
<www.francogene.com>

French Government Tourist Office
<www.francetourism.com>

French Heraldry
<www.heraldica.org/topics/france>

French Heritage DNA Project
<www.frenchdna.org>

French Migration Resource Center
<www.frenchmigration.com>

Geneactes
<www.geneactes.org>

GeneaGuide
<www.geneaguide.com>

Genealogia.com
<www.genealogia.com>

Genealogie & Histoire en France
<www.gefrance.com>

Genealogy: Acadian and French Canadian Style
<ourworld.compuserve.com/homepages/lwjones>

GeneaLor: Genealogy in Lorraine
<genealor.net>

Geneanet
<www.geneanet.org>

Guide Practique de Genealogie en France (A Practical Guide to French Genealogy)
<www.genealogy.tm.fr>

The Habitant: Acadian and French Canadian Genealogy
<habitant.org>

Le Centre de Genealogie Francophone d'Amerique (The Center of Genealogy for French-speaking Americans)
<www.genealogie.org/accueil.htm>

Les Pages Jaunes (French Yellow Pages)
<www.pagesjaunes.fr>

Library of Congress Portals to the World: France
<loc.gov/rr/international/european/france/fr.html>

List of the Departmental Archives
<www.genealogy.tm.fr/archives/archives.htm>

National Archives of Canada
<www.archives.ca>

RootsWeb's Guide to Tracing Family Trees, Lesson 24
<rootsweb.ancestry.com/~rwguide/lesson24.htm>

Theriault Acadian Family
<www.terriau.org>

YourDictionary.com
<www.yourdictionary.com/languages/romance.html#french>

CHAPTER SIX

BENELUX REGION

By Rhonda R. McClure and Sunny Jane Morton

Millions of people can trace their ancestry to the Benelux region; most of them find their connection to the Netherlands. The countries of Belgium, the Netherlands and the Duchy of Luxembourg formed an economic union in 1948, and they were also known as the Low Countries. The duchy of Luxembourg is bordered on the east by Germany, on the south by France, and on the west and north by Belgium. Belgium, in addition to the eastern section of the country that borders Luxembourg, is also bordered on the east by Germany. France borders Belgium on the south. The North Sea borders it on the west, and the Netherlands is on its northern border. The Netherlands has the longest coastline, which constitutes its western and northern borders. Germany borders to the east.

THE NETHERLANDS

The Netherlands is a low-lying land where levees and water-pumping windmills have worked for 500 years to keep the sea at bay. Flooding from the fierce North Sea has been a constant threat, to which the Dutch have responded by becoming some of the world's best hydraulic engineers.

Now the Dutch have a new flood on their hands—but this one's good. Far from stemming the tide, technology is generating a deluge of Dutch genealogical records that have now become accessible by the millions. Of course, the age

of the internet is making all genealogical records more accessible—what's so different about Dutch digitization?

The long-standing difficulty of Netherlands research is that its records—even national data—are kept on a local level. If you didn't know what town your forebears hailed from, it was difficult to find them with no centralized place to search.

But the genealogical waters have converged, so to speak. Databases such as WieWasWie **<www.wiewaswie.nl>** now allow you to search millions of vital records from the Netherlands and even from Dutch colonies. Previously obscure sources have floated to the surface: provincial and local records, historical images and documents, maps, oral histories and more have been digitized for easy netting online.

If you haven't searched for your *Nederlander* forebears lately, take another look. They might be just clicks away.

Lay of the Land

The lowdown on this low country's geography, history and people will be helpful once you start exploring records. Some Dutch boundaries aren't what they used to be, and language and provincial differences may give you pause. ("Frisian? Flemish? I thought my ancestors were Dutch!") Your ancestors may have married in a church to which they didn't belong and changed their surnames every generation.

The Kingdom of the Netherlands (literally, "lowlands") lies on the North Sea in the northwestern corner of Europe. Home to 16.4 million people, the Netherlands is roughly twice the size of New Jersey, and a quarter of it lies below sea level. The country has 12 provinces, but the two most populous—North and South Holland—include the national capital (Amsterdam), the governmental seat (The Hague) and the largest port in the world (Rotterdam). Perhaps because the Hollands existed as a single province until the 1840s, the Netherlands is still commonly (and mistakenly) referred to as "Holland."

The remaining provinces are less populated but may well be home to your ancestors. They are Zeeland, Groningen, Drenthe, Overijssel, Flevoland, Utrecht, Gelderland, Noord-Brabant, Friesland and Limburg. (*Noord* means north; *zuid* means south).

Tides of History

The Netherlands has a long history of relationship issues with its neighbors—and not just those next door, Germany and Belgium. In the 1500s, Holy Roman Emperor and King of Spain Charles V ruled the Dutch territory. His insistence on all things Catholic prompted William of Orange to lead a Protestant rebellion in 1568, and in 1579, the Netherlands declared its independence.

A golden age followed in the 1600s. The Netherlands dominated on the sea, in financial markets and even in the art world. Amsterdam quadrupled in population and became a major port. The Dutch East and West India Companies expanded Dutch influence globally—including to the New Netherlands in North America.

Eventually the Dutch spread themselves too thin, and their influence waned abroad and at home. The French occupied the weakened country in the early 1800s; Napoleon set up a puppet government with his brother at the helm. When Europe reorganized itself under the Congress of Vienna, the United Kingdom of the Netherlands was born. The Netherlands regained independence and received the consolation prizes of Belgium and Luxembourg. (Belgium escaped Dutch rule in 1830; Luxembourg broke off in 1839.)

The Netherlands remained neutral and free during World War I but wasn't so lucky during World War II. During a five-year occupation by Nazi Germany, nearly 280,000 Nederlanders died, and a third of the victims were Jews. (Anne Frank wrote her famous diary in Amsterdam.) The country was physically and economically devastated, and the Dutch left by the boatful for many destinations, including the United States.

Cultural Waters

As early as 1500, the Dutch were a distinct group descended from Germanic tribes, particularly the Franks, who used a version of the patronymic naming system. But plenty of mixing and mingling happened with neighboring cultures and religions.

Patronymics were frequently used as surnames or middle names in the Netherlands through the 1700s, though many families had adopted permanent surnames by then. The

Timeline

10th-11th c.	Belgium is made up of 17 counties, including Luxembourg.
1548	Belgium under the Habsburg dynasty.
1556	Belgium becomes part of the Spanish Netherlands, under the kings of the Spanish monarchy.
1606	Dutch Baroque-era artist and engraver Rembrandt van Rijn is born.
1703–1706	French occupy Belgium; the French remain in Luxembourg until 1714.
1713	As a consequence of the War of the Spanish Succession, the Spanish Netherlands passes to the Archdukes of Austria (Austrian Netherlands).
Jan. 1790	United Belgian (or Netherlands) States are formed, but Luxembourg remains under Austrian rule.
Dec. 1790	Austrian rule is restored.
1792–1794	Belgium occupied again by France.
1795	Belgian territory is divided into nine departments, which quickly become annexed by France.
1797	Austria officially cedes Belgium to France.
1814	Belgian territory separated from France, Government General of Belgium established.
1815	Incorporation of the Belgian lands and Liège into the Kingdom of the Netherlands.
1830	The Provisional Government of Belgium proclaims independence from the Netherlands.

1831	Congress proclaims Louis-Charles-Philippe-Raphaël d'Orléans, duc de Nemours, son of King Louis-Philippe of the French, to be king; his father refuses. Leopold Georg Christian Friedrich, Prinz von Sachsen-Coburg und Gotha is then chosen as king.
1878	King Leopold II of Belgium makes plans for colonization of Congo.
1898	Dutch graphic artist M.C. Escher, known for his visual puzzles, is born.
1908	Reacting to outcry over atrocities committed against Congolese, the Belgian parliament annexes Congo Free State, renaming it Belgian Congo.
1914–1918	Germany invades and occupies first Luxembourg and then Belgium.
1925–1942	Henri de Baillet-Latour served as the first Belgian president of the International Olympic Committee.
1940–1944	Germany occupies Belgium and rules together with the Nord and Pas de Calais departments of France.
1944	Allied occupation.
1963–1965	First Belgian-Dutch Antarctic expedition.
2001	Palestinian leader Yasser Arafat and Shimon Peres, the Israeli Foreign Minister, meet for peace talks at the European Union conference in Brussels.
2003	Justine Henin-Hardenne became the first Belgian to win a Grand Slam tennis title after a stunning 6-0 6-4 win over Belgian compatriot Kim Clijsters.

patronymic was derived from the father's first name: Peder's son would be surnamed Pedersen. Other suffixes include *-zoon* (son) and *-dochter* (daughter), which sometimes show up abbreviated as *-sz* and *-dr* at the end of a surname. The use of patronymics officially ended with the Civil Register of 1811, when the occupying French government forced everyone to take a permanent surname.

You may also encounter the Frisians and the Flemish. The Frisians come from Friesland (*Fryslân*), a far northern Dutch province that boasts its own language (Frisian) and a provincial pride rivaling that of Texas. Friesland corresponds roughly to a historical region known as West Friesland, which might pop up in your research. (Your Frisian forebears may also hail from neighboring Germany.)

The Flemish find roots in the old County of Flanders, a historical region now divided among the Netherlands, Belgium and France. There's plenty of cultural holdover in this area: Dutch is still the native language of about 60 percent of Belgians. Many Belgians identify as Flemish and speak Flemish, also called Belgian Dutch or *tussentaal*—meaning "in-between language."

Religion was another cultural definer in old Netherlands. Until the 1500s, Roman Catholicism dominated, but from 1588 until 1795, the Dutch Reformed Church was the state religion. Many religious minorities lived in the Netherlands: Jews, Huguenots and Walloons (French and Belgian Protestant refugees), Mennonites (also known as Anabaptists), Lutherans, and members of the Remonstrant Brotherhood, a Belgian offshoot of the Dutch Reformed Church.

Immigrant Waves

Dutch immigration to the United States waxed and waned. Three high-water marks were the 17th-century commercial expansion, the immigration free-for-all of the 19th and early 20th centuries, and an influx following World War II.

In the early to mid-1600s, the Netherlands' colonization efforts included a region along the Hudson and Delaware River valleys in what's now New York state. New Netherland came to include a Dutch outpost on Manhattan Island known as New Amsterdam.

New Netherland grew slowly, by modern standards. Its settlers were merchants drawn by commercial opportunities, and the "tired and poor": religious refugees, the rural poor, orphans and the unemployed.

About 40 years into its history, New Netherland had a population of about 7,000 Dutch (and 3,000 others). When England conquered the region in 1664, New Netherland became New England; New Amsterdam became New York. But the Dutch colonists remained—and multiplied. Their descendents followed rivers and newly blazed trails west through New York and Pennsylvania, and south through New Jersey to Maryland. By the 1790 census, 100,000 Americans claimed Dutch ancestry; 80 percent of them still lived within 50 miles of New York City.

If your ancestor was one of those early settlers, you might find him or her in the North America Chronology (*Noord-Amerika Chronologie*), a 5,000-card index to Amsterdam notarial records on people who left for New Netherland between 1598 and 1750. Microfilm copies are accessible at the New York State Library in Albany **<www.nysl.nysed.gov>** and the New York (City) Public Library **<www.nypl.org/research/chss/lhg/genea.html>**.

Dutch immigration picked up again in the 19th century. A quarter-million working-class families, mostly from rural areas, entered the United States in the mid-1800s. It began with a trickle of families and individuals in the 1830s, lured by the promise of prosperity. By the mid-1840s, the Dutch were arriving en masse—entire neighborhoods and congregations. They came in response to a potato crop failure, in religious dissent from the Dutch Reformed Church (particularly Jews, Roman Catholics and Seceders), and inspired by the example of neighboring German group migrations. Many of these Dutch communities put down their US roots inland, in Holland, Mich., Pella, Iowa and Wisconsin's Fox River Valley.

For these latecomers, you can check the National Archives' US passenger-arrival lists at Ancestry.com **<ancestry.com>** and on microfilm at libraries. Digital Resources Netherlands and Belgium has passenger records back to 1620 (search under "Passenger Lists"). The Family History Library has microfilmed some of them; search by province of departure. Published lists for incoming Dutchmen include *Ship Passenger Lists, New York and New Jersey, 1600–1825* by Carl Boyer (self-published) and the two-volume set *Dutch Immigrants in US Ship Passenger Manifests, 1820–1880* by Robert P. Swierenga (Scholarly Resources).

The Netherlands also kept emigration lists from 1845 to 1877. They include the emigrant's name, age, occupation, religion, town of last residence, reason for leaving, destination and number of traveling companions. After 1877, some provinces continued to keep their own rolls. Lists were kept at the place of departure; the most common jump-offs to the United States were Rotterdam, Amsterdam and Antwerp. Check the records from these cities for emigration records filed by your ancestors.

In the ensuing years that followed, Dutch generally immigrated during times of US prosperity and peace (1880s; 1903 to 1914; 1920s) and didn't when America suffered economic depression and war (1860s to 1870s, 1890s, World War I, 1930s, World War II). A strong Dutch presence remains today in the upper Midwest, southern and central California, northwestern Iowa, New York and northern New Jersey.

Stream of Vital Stats

Though the Dutch have always kept good records, their decentralized files made research tricky—but that's changed in the last few years. Dutch records are increasingly available for remote searching online.

The civil register—that is, the government-generated records of Dutch births, marriages and deaths—dates back to 1795 in the south and 1811 in the north. Birth records list the children's and parents' names, birth date and often the parents' address. Marriage records reveal the brides' and grooms' names, ages, previous widow(er) status, and often birthplaces and professions, as well as the parents' names and birthplaces. Death records provide the deceased's name and exact death date, and sometimes the age, birthplace, address and names of the deceased's parents and/or spouse. These records had been kept locally in more than 1,000 municipalities until the 1930s.

A joint initiative by a number of archives in the Netherlands resulted in Genlias, a genealogical treasure trove with more than 13.5 million vital records. Genlias was a major breakthrough for Dutch research, but in 2012 it was shut down and replaced with WieWasWie, which was still only available in Dutch as of mid-2013 and did not hold all the original Genlias records.

Some city and provincial websites post their own civil register data, such as the cities of Delft **<www.archief.delft.nl>** and Rotterdam **<www.gemeentearchief.rotterdam.nl>** (change the language to English, then hover over Archives and Collections in the left menu to click on Family Tree). You can find more city and provincial websites at Archiefnet **<www.archiefnet. nl>**. You'll also find civil register data at Digital Resources Netherlands and Belgium **<www. geneaknowhow.net/digi/resources.html>**.

If you find a website in a language you don't understand, look for the word English or a British flag to click on. Or go to **<translate.google.com>** and type in the site's URL. Brush up on your Dutch with our genealogy glossary on page 262.

When online searches fail, head to a Family History Center (FHC) near you (find locations at **<familysearch.org>**). The Family History Library (FHL) **<familysearch.org>** has microfilmed nearly 100 percent of available civil vital records, and you can borrow those microfilms at your local FHC. Enter a town in the Place Search field in the online FHL catalog; results will appear under Civil Registration.

Flood of Records

The civil register is a great place to start, but you can round out your research in many other Dutch records. Generally, original records are at municipal, provincial or church archives. Some records are available in Family-Search's databases, and Ancestry.com claims more than a million entries from the Netherlands. You'll also find strong collections of microfilmed and published resources of most of the types mentioned below in the FHL catalog (search by town or province plus relevant keyword) and the Central Bureau for Genealogy in the Netherlands **<www.cbg.nl>**.

Civil records before 1811 of marriages, births and deaths exist in many Dutch municipalities. Civil marriages were also called court marriages and were especially common for people who weren't Dutch Reformed. The records can contain bride's and groom's names, widow(er) status, birthplace and residence, earlier spouses, marriage dates, and sometimes parents' and witnesses' names. Contact municipal archives directly with research requests (find contact information at **<www.archiefnet.nl>**). The FHL has many of these as well.

Church records are most important for pre-civil register days. Catholic record-keeping picked up around 1563, then the Dutch Reformed Church did most of the vital record-keeping from the 1570s until around 1800, even for "nonconformists" (nonchurch members). These include births, baptisms, confirmations, marriages, membership records, deaths and burials. Parish boundaries weren't the same as civil boundaries, so check neighboring parishes for stray ancestors. The FHL has an excellent microfilm collection of church records before 1811, but fewer after 1811.

Notarial records include marriage contracts, probate records, wills, taxes, property registration and powers of attorney. These records are particularly useful for pre-1811 searches, sorting out family relationships and recurring names, finding mothers and other close relatives, and learning property values and occupations. More than 30,000 volumes of pre-1811 notarial records exist. They can be laborious to search, but some are indexed and searchable online through Digital Resources Netherlands and Belgium. The FHL has many of these on microfilm; search on Netherlands notarial records.

Death duties files declared the heirs of an estate and were created to collect inheritance taxes. Use these records to trace generations and confirm family relationships. They're kept in local archives, but you'll find a few in Digital Resources Netherlands and Belgium.

Cemetery records most often consist of the transcriptions of gravestone and monument inscriptions. Many are available online through Digital Resources Netherlands and Belgium,

Online Begraafplaatsen **<www.online-begraafplaatsen.nl>** and subscription sites World Vital Records **<www.worldvitalrecords.com>** and Ancestry.com.

Dutch census data is not widely consulted for genealogical purposes because the civil register is more useful. The first national census occurred with the inception of the civil register in 1811. National censuses happened every 10 years from 1829 to 1929 and again in 1947, 1960 and 1971; a few provincial and special-population censuses (citizens and "able-bodied men") may also be useful. The most complete entries provide family relationships, ages and birth years, birthplaces, marital status and religion. Find copies of the census in the FHL catalog by searching on census and the locality's name.

Address-based registrations began after the 1849 census to record changes in a household, such as births, marriages, deaths and moves. Data could include a person's birthplace and date, death date, marriage information, relationship to head of household, religion, tax class, previous address, move-in date, move-out date and new address.

You can confirm emigration with these records: an emigrant's last entry should list the new address as another country. In 1920, the address-based system changed to a family record that moved with the family, which in turn converted to personal record cards. Find address-based registrations through municipal and regional archives; some are posted on Digital Resources Netherlands and Belgium.

Personal record cards were kept on every Dutch inhabitant from 1938 to 1994 (a more abbreviated, automated Personal Record List has been kept since then). You can request genealogical information (including parents' and children's names, and sometimes their birthplaces and birth dates) from cards of deceased persons by mail through the Central Bureau for Genealogy.

Beyond the Data Deluge

To fully understand your low-country forebears, you'll want to do more than just find their names in databases and registers. Flesh out your Dutch family history with these helpful resources:

- **Images:** A picture is worth a thousand words, so page through het Geheugen van Nederland (Memory of the Netherlands) **<www.geheugenvannederland.nl>**, a large collection of cultural and historical images. Though the collection is strongest from the photography age forward, you'll also find old drawings, paintings and historical maps to help you visualize your ancestor's world.
- **Historical documents:** Check subscription websites for city directories, historical newspapers and archival documents from areas Dutch immigrants settled. Try searching on your family's hometown. If you have roots in the US Northeast, explore the websites of the New Netherland Institute **<www.nnp.org>**; it preserves and shares historical documents of New Netherland.

- **Personal histories:** Even if you can't find your ancestors' personal stories, the stories of neighbors, co-workers and fellow immigrants can shed light on their experiences. The Joint Archives of Holland **<jointarchives.org>** at Hope College in Holland, Mich., maintains an archive that includes dozens of oral histories from Dutch women, furnace company workers, retired Reformed Church officers, post-WWII immigrants and others. *Dutch Touches* by Carol Van Klompenburg and Dorothy Crum (Penfield Press) contains stories and recipes from Dutch-Americans in traditionally Dutch communities such as Pella, Iowa, and South Holland, Ill.

If you aren't a devoted Dutchophile already, your research will likely turn you into one. The Netherlands has a pull all its own: Those mesmerizing windmills, wide Dutch smiles, gorgeous art and architectural treasures, and the ghosts of those seafaring people whose descendants continue to navigate the sea.

After all your attempts to find your forebears without going to the Netherlands, you may still find yourself booking a flight on KLM. There's nothing like going straight to the sources—provincial archives, the Central Bureau for Genealogy or the doorstep of your great-grandfather's apartment building in Rotterdam. But do all the research you can from home first. That way, you can spend your dream vacation in the Netherlands finding unique genealogical treasures, connecting with distant relatives and exploring the land your ancestors loved and left behind.

BELGIUM

As a kingdom, Belgium has no history before 1830. But as individual territories, the ten counties and duchies from which Belgium derived its present land, the accounts are long and varied. From 57 B.C. until it became its own country in 1830, Belgium was at various points under the rule of the Romans, the Franks, France, the Hapsburg Empire, Spain, Austria and the Netherlands. It was only after the revolt that began in 1830 that it was recognized as a separate entity, the Kingdom of Belgium. From 1555 to 1700 it was considered the Spanish Netherlands, and from 1700 to 1795 it was known as the Austrian Netherlands.

In addition to these different names, there are the ten individual counties and duchies that you will find yourself turning to as your research in Belgium progresses beyond 1830. They are:
- the County of Flanders (now found in the Netherlands, Belgium and France)
- le Tournaisis (now entirely in Belgium)
- the County of Hainaut (now found in Belgium and France)
- the Duchy of Brabant (now in Belgium and the Netherlands)
- the County of Namur (now in Belgium and France)
- the Prince-Bishopric of Liège (now in the Netherlands, Belgium and France)
- Bouillon (now entirely in Belgium)
- the Duchy of Luxembourg (now found in Belgium, Germany, France and the Grand Duchy of Luxembourg)

Houses in Ghent, Belgium

- the Duchy of Limburg (now found in Belgium, the Netherlands and Germany)
- the Duchy of Juliers (now found in Belgium, the Netherlands and Germany)

With such a varied history and the close proximity of so many countries, it is not surprising to find that the present-day population of Belgium is 52 percent Flemish and 32 percent Walloon. The Flemish, while not actually speaking Dutch, speak a German derivative that is almost indistinguishable from Dutch. The Walloons speak French. When working in the records of Belgium, you can expect to find these two languages, along with possibly some German in areas along the eastern border. While the language may be divided, the religion is almost entirely Roman Catholic.

Even though Belgium is one of the smallest countries in Europe, you will find that if you do not know the town of origin of your ancestors, you're in a stalemate. There are too many towns to search individually.

Most Belgians emigrated through the port of Antwerp and went to places as varied as the United States, Brazil, Guatemala, England, Algeria and Portugal. Belgian immigrants tended to look for rural communities in which to settle. They were trying to leave industrialization behind and hoping to find fertile farmland upon which to reestablish their homes and communities.

When trying to find the town of origin, be creative in your record searching. Look for biographical sources, including obituaries and published directories for different professions. You may find that there are some native-language newspapers that were published, especially in the

1800s, that may help you. Passenger lists will not give you the place of birth until the 1900s, though naturalization records may. Death records, unfortunately, usually only indicate that the person was born in Belgium. But if your ancestor referred to him or herself specifically as Flemish or a Walloon, that will help narrow your search to a degree.

LUXEMBOURG

One of the smallest countries in the world today, encompassing only 999 square miles of land, Luxembourg is also a relatively young country if you look only at the time it has been an independent duchy. However, the history of the country traces back to the 10th century. Throughout that history, Luxembourg has been occupied by the French, has been a member of the German Confederation, and was held in a sort of limbo in the 1830s when the small nation was to have been divided between Belgium and the Netherlands. That was settled in 1839, when a larger portion of the country became the province of Luxembourg in Belgium and the remaining area became the independent state. Of course, it wasn't long before it found itself again in the forefront, when Napoleon III saw the duchy as his way to offset Prussia's growing influence. It was not until May of 1867, when the European powers gathered in London, that Prussia was forced to withdraw and the duchy's neutrality was established.

Over a period of 50 years beginning around 1840, some 72,000 Luxembourgers immigrated to the United States and France. Those emigrants who opted for a new life in France were mostly craftsmen who toured the country in order to learn and improve their craft before returning home. On the other hand, those who left for the United States tended not to return to Luxembourg. The Institut Grand-Ducal in Luxembourg asserts that if you consider the population of Luxembourg during that period (fluctuating between 175,000 and 213,000), you can deduce that the duchy lost one out of every five inhabitants to the United States.

Unlike in the Netherlands, emigration from Luxembourg was largely a result of devastating famines, although several other factors contributed including demographic pressure, the unavailability of land, high taxes, political discrimination of the lower classes (only the rich had the right to vote) and a military draft.

The migration patterns reflect a strong family and village bond, as people emigrated and settled collectively. Be aware that certain settlements of immigrants from Luxembourg have corresponding specific villages and areas in the homeland.

Determining that your ancestor was from Luxembourg may at first have you thinking you were descended from an immigrant from one of the many other countries geographically close to the duchy. Many of those who came from what is now recognized as the Duchy of Luxembourg were sometimes identified as Belgian, Dutch, French, German or Prussian. This is a direct result of the political changes during the 1800s, when Luxembourg was shuffled from one country to another. The problem is you may be trying to find a place of birth in a country from which your Luxembourger was mistakenly thought to have come.

BELGIUM RESOURCES

ORGANIZATIONS AND ARCHIVES

ARCHIVES GÉNÉRALES DE L'ÉTAT
2-6 rue de Ruysbroeck, 1000 Bruxelles, Belgium
Phone: +32 02 513 76 80
<arch.arch.be/index.php?lang=en_GB>

OFFICE GENEALOGIQUE ET HERALDIQUE DE BELGIQUE (GENEALOGY AND HERALDRY OFFICE OF BELGIUM)
Maison communale de Woluwe St Pierre, Av. Charles Thielemans 2, B-1150 Bruxelles, Belgium
Phone: + 32 (0) 2 772 50 27
<oghb.be>

BOOKS
Etymological Dictionary of the Surnames in Belgium and North France, 2 volumes, by Dr. Frans DeBrabandere (Uitgegeven door het Gemeentekrediet, Brussel)

Searching for Flemish (Belgian) Ancestors by Jozef J. Goethals (Clearfield)

PERIODICALS
Belgian Laces (The Belgian Researchers)

WEBSITES
Archives Générales de l'État
<arch.arch.be/index.php?lang=en_GB>

Belgian cities and villages web index
<www.a-z.be/steden.html>

Belgium Genealogy Forum
<genforum.genealogy.com/belgium>

The Belgium-Roots Project
<belgium.rootsweb.ancestry.com>

Cyndi's List: Belgium
<www.cyndislist.com/belgium>

Family Explorer Benelux
<freepages.genealogy.rootsweb.ancestry.com/~jberteloot>

Genealogie
<genealogie.start.be>

LUXEMBOURG RESOURCES

ORGANIZATIONS AND ARCHIVES

ARCHIVES NATIONALES DE LUXEMBOURG
Plateau du Saint Esprit, BP 6, 2010 Luxembourg
Phone: +352 2478 66 60
Fax : +352 47 46 92
E-mail: archives.nationales@an.etat.lu
<www.anlux.lu/multi/fr>

LUXEMBOURG TOURIST OFFICE IN LONDON
Sicilian House, 7 Sicilian Ave, London WC1A 2QR, England
Phone: +44 020 7434 2800
<www.visitluxembourg.com/en>

BOOKS
Familienchronik der Gemeinden Remerschen und Bürmeringen (All the inhabitants of Remerschen, Schengen, Wintringen/Wintrange [1668–1900], Buermeringen/Burmerange, Elvingen/Elvange and Emeringen/Emerange [1800–1900]) by Prosper Kayser and Roger Kayser (Institut Grand-Ducal, Section de linguistique, d'ethnologie et d'onomastique)

Familienchronik der Gemeinde Wellenstein (All the inhabitants of Wellenstein, Bech-Kleinmacher and Schwebsingen/Schwebsange 1688–1999) by Prosper Kayser and Roger Kayser (Institut Grand-Ducal, Section de linguistique, d'ethnologie et d'onomastique)

Familienchronik der Stadt Remich (All the inhabitants of Remich 1688–1900) by Prosper Kayser and Roger Kayser (Institut Grand-Ducal, Section de linguistique, d'ethnologie et d'onomastique)

WEBSITES

Cyndi's List: Luxembourg
<**www.cyndislist.com/luxembourg**>

Discussion group for genealogical research in Luxembourg
<**fr.groups.yahoo.com/group/ GDLuxembourg**>

FamiLux Luxembourg-American Genealogy
<**www.familux.org**>

Institut Grand-Ducal
<**www.igd-leo.lu**>

KindredTrails
<**www.kindredtrails.com/luxembourg.html**>

Luxembourg GenWeb
<**www.rootsweb.com/~luxwgw**>

Luxembourg on My Mind
<**faustogardini.com/ luxembourg-on-my-mind**>

Luxembourg Surname Navigator
<**www.geneaservice.nl/navigator/ luxembourg**>

Researching Luxembourg Genealogy
<**luxembourggenealogy.blogspot.com**>

ORGANIZATIONS AND ARCHIVES

CENTRAAL BUREAU VOOR GENEALOGIE (CENTRAL OFFICE FOR GENEALOGY)
Prins Willem-Alexanderhof 22, 2595 BE Den Haag, The Netherlands
Phone: +31 070 31 50 500
Fax: +31 070 34 78 394
<**www.cbg.nl**>

CENTRAAL REGISTER VAN PARTICULIERE ARCHIEVEN (CENTRAL REGISTER OF PUBLIC ARCHIVES)
Prins Willem-Alexanderhof 30, 2595 BE The Hague, The Netherlands
Phone: +31 0703 31 55 73
Fax: +31 0703 31 54 99
E-mail: info@nationaalarchief.nl

KONINKLIJK NEDERLANDS GENOOTSCHAP VOOR GESLACHT—EN WAPENKUNDE (THE ROYAL DUTCH SOCIETY FOR GENEALOGY AND HERALDRY)
Prins Willem-Alexanderhof 24, Postbus 85630, 2508 CH The Hague, The Netherlands
<**www.knggw.nl**>

NATIONAAL ARCHIEF (NATIONAL ARCHIVES)
Box 90520, 2509 LM The Hague, The Netherlands
Phone: +31 70 331 5400
Fax: +31 70 331 5499
E-mail: info@nationaalarchief.nl
<**en.nationaalarchief.nl**>

NEDERLANDSE GENEALOGISCHE VERENIGING (DUTCH GENEALOGICAL SOCIETY)
NGV, Box 26, 1380 AA Weesp, The Netherlands
E-mail: info@ngv.nl
<**www.ngv.nl**>

BOOKS

Church and Civil Records of Amsterdam, the Netherlands, before 1811 (Genealogical Society of The Church of Jesus Christ of Latter-day Saints)

Dutch roots. Finding your ancestors in the Netherlands by Rob van Drie (Centraal Bureau voor Genealogie)

Handleiding voor Genealogisch Onderzoek in Nederland (Handbook for Genealogical Research in the Netherlands), 2nd edition, edited by J.C. Okkema (Fibula-Van Dishoeck)

Handleiding voor Stamboomonderzoek (Handbook for Ancestral Research) by Roelof Vennik (Donker)

Names, Names & More Names: Locating Your Dutch Ancestors in Colonial America by Arthur C.M. Kelly (Ancestry.com)

PERIODICALS

De Nederlandsche Leeuw: Maandblad van het Koninklijk Nederlandsch Genootschap voor Geslacht– en Wapenkunde (The Dutch Lion: Journal of the Royal Dutch Society for Genealogy and Heraldry, Koninklijk Nederlands Genootschap voor Geslacht–en Wapenkunde, 1883–).

Genealogie: Kwartaalblad van het Centraal Bureau voor Genealogie (Genealogy: Quarterly of the Central Office for Genealogy, 1995–)

Gens Nostra: Maandblad van de Nederlandsche Genealogische Vereeniging (Our Ancestry: Monthly Journal of the Netherlands Genealogical Society, Nederlandse Genealogische Vereniging, 1945–)

Ons Voorgeslacht (Our Ancestry, South Holland chapter of the Dutch Genealogical Society)

Ons Waardeel (Our Valuable Volume, a journal for genealogy in Drenthe and Groningen)

Van Zeeuwse Stam (Of Zeeland Origin, a journal of the Zeeland chapter of the Dutch Genealogical Society)

Veluwse Geslachten (Families from the Veluwe, a regional journal for Gelderland)

WEBSITES

Archieven.nl
<www.archieven.nl>

Archiefnet
<www.archiefnet.nl>

Cyndi's List: Netherlands
<www.cyndislist.com/netherlands>

Digital Resources Netherlands and Belgium
<www.geneaknowhow.net/digi/resources.html>.

DutchGenWeb
<www.rootsweb.ancestry.com/~nldwgw>

Trace Your Dutch Roots
<blog.traceyourdutchroots.com>

WatWasWaar
<watwaswaar.nl>

WieWasWie
<www.wiewaswie.nl>

Yvette's Dutch Genealogy Homepage
<www.dutchgenealogy.nl>

ZeeuwenGezocht
<www.zeeuwengezocht.nl/en>

Ghent, Belgium canal

CHAPTER SEVEN

GERMANIC REGION

By James M. Beidler

GERMANY

In this era of globalization, it's easy to think of ourselves as citizens of the world. If you turn the clock back a century, though, you'll see people took a much more regional view. Italians considered themselves Sicilians, Sardinians, Tuscans or Venetians. Regional loyalties in America helped start the Civil War. And the people we now call Germans referred to themselves as anything but.

In those days, you had Prussians and Bavarians, Palatines and Hessians, Saxons and Swabians—who all spoke various dialects of German and were united only in their dislike for each other. "In Europe as well as America, immigrants who came from Prussia didn't like the immigrants from Bavaria, and the Bavarians didn't like the Prussians," says German genealogy scholar John T. Humphrey. "And immigrants from Swabia in southern Germany did not like either one."

Because finding a German immigrant's village of origin is so crucial to genealogical research, this more provincial view can be helpful in narrowing the search from "Germany" to a more-manageable area. But territorial shifts can create difficulties in matching up the names of current and former entities to which the villages belonged.

How this evolved is the stuff of many volumes, but in short, Germany's history is unlike that of England, France or Spain, where the king's central authority eclipsed feudal nobles' power by the 1600s. Germany, on the other hand, remained a collection of several hundred independent states until unification in 1871.

This patchwork political landscape is good and bad for genealogists. Before the 1870s, record-keeping was inconsistent from one German state to another—and availability is spotty. But if you can pinpoint an immigrant's origin in a particular German state, your ancestral search will be *kein Problem*.

Moving from Micro to Macro

Over the centuries, some local dynasties became extinct and others married into new amalgamations of territories. Until a reorganization in the early 1800s, the average German "microstate" had a mere 2,500 people, and boundaries changed constantly. Following the Protestant Reformation in the 16th and 17th centuries, each state was supposed to adopt its ruler's religion, but this often wasn't uniformly enforced.

One big German word spelled the end for a lot of little states in 1803: *Reichsdeputation-shauptschluss*—the final high decision of the Imperial Diet of the Holy Roman Empire. It eliminated the microstates and secularized the ecclesiastical states that had been under the power of Roman Catholic bishops and archbishops. This reduced the number of German states from several hundred to just 39 in 1815.

The climate had become ripe for such a consolidation during the 1700s, when most nobles freed their serfs—but kept the right to tax and receive a portion of the farmers' crops as a feudal obligation. "The German nobility changed its attitude from being like the overseer—as they were when the common people were serfs—to more of a landlord with tenants," says Kenneth Heger, a German history specialist and administrator with the National Archives and Records Administration (NARA). "This was a change in outlook from running a really big farm to wanting to have a lavish palace built."

The rulers of the remaining 39 states—who suddenly had much larger territories—began looking at the bigger picture of what we now call infrastructure: Roads, for example, had been poor because many microstates were small enough to traverse in a day. Farms, too, were generally small and inefficient. The nobles of the microstates willingly gave up their sovereignty because "they didn't lose their personally owned lands and contracts for service—many ended up with more clout as part of a larger state and a seat in the upper house of that state's legislature," Heger says. And the aftereffects—better road systems, more miles of railroads and the need for fewer farmers in the 1800s—helped spur massive emigration from German states in the 1800s.

You can follow the splits and mergers of the German microstates through the centuries in Gerhard Koelber's *Historische Lexikon*.

Reviewing the Records

Certain genealogical guidelines apply to all German states. For one, church records are the most helpful resource no matter the region or time period in which you're looking, and many of them have been microfilmed by the Family History Library (FHL). You can see what's available by searching the catalog at **<familysearch.org>**, then order microfilm at your local Family History Center. Note that the FHL catalogs records according to the political divisions of the German Empire of 1871, not today's jurisdictions.

That means church records from areas across modern Germany get filed as Prussian (not just the specifically named provinces of East and West Prussia). See FamilySearch's German page at **<www.familysearch.org/learn/wiki/en/Germany>**.

If you need church records the FHL hasn't filmed, try searching for Protestant (or *Evangelisch* in German) denominations at **<www.ekd.de/english>**. Consult Address Book for Germanic Genealogy and Ancestors in German Archives for information on Roman Catholic archives.

The German system of vital records, in place since 1876, has become even more useful since the loosening of privacy laws. *Das Personenstandsrechtsreformgesetz*—the Civil Registration Reform Act—allows anyone to access records; previously, only direct-line descendants could. New time lines make records available after 110 years for births, 80 years for marriages and 30 years for deaths.

Surveying the States

But to get to that point, you need to know where to look—and that's where an understanding of the old German states comes in. Knowing the regional particulars can aid your genealogical problem solving. To get you started, here's a breakdown of the major historical states, along with a little background, records coverage, immigration trends and

TIME LINE

300–500	The invasion of nomadic Asian Huns causes Eastern European tribes, such as the Goths, Saxons, Franks and Alemans, to move.
800	Charlemagne is crowned emperor of the Holy Roman Empire, an area that included France, Switzerland, roughly half of modern-day Germany and parts of Austria.
1291	The Old Swiss Confederacy is founded.
1517	Martin Luther posts his 95 theses, sparking the Protestant Reformation.
1545	The Catholic Church in Germany begins to record all marriages, births and deaths.
1618–1648	Germanic lands are ravaged by the Thirty Years' War. Many records and documents are destroyed.
1653	A tax revolt spurs the Swiss Peasant War of 1653.
1670s & 1680s	The French repeatedly attack the Palatinate region of Germany.
1708–1709	The Rhine freezes solid during a very harsh winter in the Palatinate, causing many to emigrate.
1798	Switzerland is "liberated" by France, which renames the country the Helvetic Republic.
1803	Switzerland again becomes a confederacy.
1815	The Congress of Vienna establishes the borders of Switzerland and the territory's neutrality.

1848	Some 8,000 political refugees, known as "Forty-Eighters," flee Germany when the Frankfurt constitution fails.
1852	The Butcher's Guild in Frankfurt introduces the frankfurter.
1867	The dual monarchy of Austria-Hungary is established.
1871	Germany becomes a nation-state under Bismarck.
1881	Anti-Catholic atmosphere and the decline of cottage industries causes German emigration to the United States to peak.
1914	Archduke Franz Ferdinand, the heir to the Austrian throne, is assassinated, starting World War I.
1919	Germany and Austria become federal republics.
1929	Germany is hit hard by the Great Depression.
1934	Hitler pronounces himself Führer.
1938	Germany annexes Austria.
1945	Germany is divided during into West Germany and East Germany, as is Berlin.
1948	After the Soviets blockade West Berlin, the massive Berlin Airlift supplies the city of 2 million people by air for more than a year.
1989	Fall of the Berlin Wall sets Germany on a course to reunification in 1990.
2002	Switzerland joins the United Nations.
2005	Joseph Ratzinger of Bavaria becomes Pope Benedict XVI.

other peculiarities. When you search the FHL catalog, the entries reflect the German state names given in parentheses here.

PRUSSIA (PREUSSEN): First and foremost among the bygone German states is one that doesn't appear on the map at all today. Prussia's rulers were from the Hohenzollern family, which inherited Brandenburg (the area surrounding Berlin) and later the Eastern European area called Prussia. Prussia became a kingdom in 1701 and was the largest component of the German Empire from 1871 to 1918.

The Prussia of the 1800s was so large, in fact, that pinpointing the origins of a person identified as "Prussian" in American records can be tricky—the kingdom encompassed Pomerania, Mecklenburg, Hannover, Westphalia and the Rhineland, among other territories. So don't be thrown for a loop if you encounter an ancestor who seems to have been born in multiple regions. He or she might just have been reacting to those changes and reporting a birthplace by its then-current ownership rather than what it was called when he or she was born.

PALATINATE (PFALZ): This southwestern area was the center of German immigration to America in the 1700s. For much of its history, the Palatinate was tied to the rulers of Bavaria, which leads to confusion because there's a separate area in Bavaria called the Upper Palatinate, or Oberpfalz. In addition to many microfilmed church records, the FHL also has 18th-century tax lists from Palatine villages, some of which contain notations about emigrants. A copy of a card file of emigrants is available at the Pennsylvania German Cultural Heritage Center at Kutztown University **<sites. google.com/site/pagermanchc>**.

WÜRTTEMBERG: This longtime grand duchy—elevated to a kingdom in the 1800s—supplied transplants to America in both the 18th- and 19th-century immigration waves. If your ancestors came during the 1800s, you can search more than 60,000 exit records in the Wuerttemberg Emigration Index on Ancestry.com **<ancestry.com>**. These records are also available in book and CD format. The index gives an immigrant's name, birth date and place, residence at time of application, application date and an FHL microfilm number for the original source material—which could include birth certificates, family records, military releases and renunciations of citizenship rights.

HESSE (HESSEN): Virtually everyone's heard of the Hessians, the soldiers hired out by their rulers to fight for the British in the Revolutionary War. In reality, only about half of the German mercenary soldiers came from the state of Hesse-Kassel; German princes from Brunswick, Waldeck, Ansbach-Bayreuth and Anhalt-Zerbst also sold troops. About 5,000 of the 30,000 soldiers stayed in North America; many simply joined the local German populations. The Johannes Schwalm Historical Association **<www.jsha.org>** studies these soldiers and their descendants.

OSTFRIESLAND AND SCHLESWIG-HOLSTEIN: These two northern areas (Ostfriesland borders the Netherlands, and Schleswig-Holstein adjoins Denmark) are distinctive because Germans here used Scandinavian-style patronymic naming systems as late as the mid-1800s. This method turns the quest for ancestors' names on its head. Normally, we can assume we know the surname but not the first name of the individual's father. Patronymic surnames reveal the father's first name. For example, Henrich Petersen is the son of Peter Karlsen, who is the son of Karl Petersen. The American/Schleswig-Holstein Heritage Society **<www.ashhs.org>** in Iowa has a 32,000-name database available to its members.

SAXONY AND THURINGIA (SACHSEN AND THÜRINGEN): The first question to ask is "Which one?" Thuringia was an exception to the 19th-century consolidation; it made up a dozen of the 39 German states in the early 1800s. Even today, three of the 16 modern German states have Saxony in their names—Lower Saxony, Saxony-Anhalt and Saxony. The *Arbeitsgemeinschaft für Mitteldeutsche Familienforschung* (Working Group for Central German Family Research) is the leading organization for these areas; the group publishes records and has an archive in Leipzig.

BADEN: Now united with Württemberg, Baden was divided into two or more states for much of its history. It became an enlarged grand duchy in 1771 when the countryside united with the city of Baden (also called Baden-Baden). Ancestry.com has a Baden emigration index similar to Württemberg's, though Baden's doesn't begin until 1866. If your ancestor departed in the 1700s, you may find emigration records in Werner Hacker's *Eighteenth Century Register of Emigrants from Southwest Germany to America and Other Countries.*

BAVARIA (BAYERN): Bavaria weathered centuries of inter-German wars and less-than-stable rulers (Mad King Ludwig, anyone?). As an example of how deep a regard Bavarians have for their history, they still refer to ethnic divisions in the state in terms of tribes: The Old Bavarians (*Altbayern*) occupy the eastern half of the modern state, while the Franks (*Franken*) occupy the northern districts, and the southwestern Swabians (*Schwaben*) became part of Bavaria only in the early 19th century. Germany's largest state in terms of geography is also its most Roman Catholic area, but substantial numbers of Protestants reside in the Franconian areas. You can find more information at **<wiki-en.genealogy.net/bavaria>**.

Conquering the Challenges

There's no doubt that Germany's political history requires some study. Add that to the challenge of needing to learn some German words—as well as deciphering archaic scripts and typefaces—and it's clear you've got your work cut out for you. But for each test of your research skills, the famous Teutonic thoroughness yields a solution. Remember, too, if you do a Google **<google.com>** search for a German-language website, you'll have the option to "Translate this page" when your search results come up.

Once you have a village name—or some reasonable facsimile thereof—you're ready to consult *Meyers Orts- und Verkehrs-Lexikon des Deutschen Reiches*, a 1912 geographical and commercial gazetteer that's the No. 1 source for information about places in Germany. The gazetteer identifies a community's state, transportation and communication services, population, churches and more. Learn more about using *Meyers Orts-* on page 131.

SWITZERLAND

The area that's now Switzerland was in the Roman Empire in ancient times and part of Charlemagne's Frankish Empire in the late 8th and early 9th centuries. Then the emerging crazy quilt of states that made up the Holy Roman Empire included today's Swiss territory for several hundred years. Late in the 13th century, three mountainous forest cantons declared independence and formed the Swiss Confederation, which took its name from one of the three, Schwyz.

More cantons (political equivalents to American states) joined them over the centuries until Switzerland's current boundaries were reached in 1815, when the Congress of Vienna reshaped Europe after the defeat of Napoleon I. Switzerland was declared politically nonaligned, a neutrality that was respected in both World Wars. Some 6 million Americans have Swiss ancestry, with a large majority stemming from the German-speaking cantons of Bern and Zurich. French predominates in six of the 26 cantons. There's one Italian-speaking canton, and about 6 percent of the population speaks Romansch, a Latin-based Romance language and the fourth of Switzerland's national tongues.

Cantons are divided into municipal communities known as communes (similar to a village or parish). The first thing to remember with Swiss research is that "rights of citizenship"—

Heimatberechtigung in German—are based on the commune. These citizenship rights often stayed with a family that left the commune, which means that the original commune kept records (including baptisms, marriages and deaths) for people no longer residing in that commune. It's estimated today that some 80 percent of Swiss people have citizenship in a commune other than the one in which they live.

Emigration from Swiss cantons took several forms. Some Swiss came directly to

MAKING DATES

This handy chart will help you sort out the months in German genealogy records.

English	German	Old-Style Abbreviation	New-Style Abbreviation
January	Januar	I	
February	Februar	II	
March	März	III	
April	April	IV	
May	Mai	V	
June	Juni	VI	
July	Juli	VII	
August	August	VIII	
September	September	7ber, VIIber	IX
October	Oktober	8ber, VIIIber	X
November	November	9ber, IXber	XI
December	Dezember	10ber, Xber	XII

America beginning around 1700. But a fairly large number were "two-steppers" who originally left Switzerland to repopulate areas along the Rhine River—particularly Alsace and the Palatinate—that were devastated after the Thirty Years War ended in 1648. In another two to three generations, more warfare soured many of these newcomers on life in the Rhine Valley, and they followed reports of economic opportunity to America.

SURNAME REGISTERS: To overcome the difference between residence and citizenship, use the Swiss surname registry, called the *Familiennamenbuch der Schweiz* in German. For each surname, these compilations list communes where people with that surname lived. If you're researching less-common surnames, you may be able to pinpoint just a few communes to search. One catch is that if a surname became "extinct" in a commune (for instance, every family of that name emigrated), you won't find it listed for that commune.

The third edition of this surname registry was published in 1989 as three volumes in each of the four official Swiss languages plus English. It's out of print but available in major genealogical libraries and online at **<hls-dhs-dss.ch/famn>**. A similar compilation, *Familiennamenverzeichnis der schweizer Bürger bis 1861*, is on CD.

CHURCH RECORDS: The most important Swiss records are parish registers of baptisms, confirmations, communions, marriages and burials. Baptismal records ordinarily contain the names of the child, parents and godparents (who often were relatives), as well as dates of birth and baptism. Records of confirmation, a rite usually performed in the early teen years, list the name and age of the individual and his or her father's name. Communion records, usually ordered by family group,

MEYERS ORTS-, STEP BY STEP

The seminal handbook for tracking down German villages goes by the title *Meyers Orts- und Verkehrs-Lexikon des Deutschen Reiches*. (Is it any wonder genealogists call it *Meyers Orts-* for short?) You'll find this resource on Ancestry.com **<ancestry.com>**, but it takes a little help to use effectively. Here's a 1-2-3 from the folks at the Mid-Atlantic Germanic Society:

1. On the Ancestry.com home page, go to the link for Card Catalog.
2. Enter the words *Meyers* under Database Title and click Search.
3. Click on the search result Meyers Gazetteer of the German Empire.
4. In the Location search box, enter the town's name. Don't check the "exact matches only" box.
5. If you don't get any hits or you wind up on the wrong page, go back to the Location search box and enter at least the first three letters of the town name followed by an asterisk (*).
6. Search the results for the town or one that sounds similar to the spelling you have, and call up the page from *Meyers Orts-* by clicking View Record, then View Original Image.
7. If you discover several towns with the same name, look for the one or two that are in the correct German state.
8. See Wendy K. Uncapher's *How to Read and Understand Meyers Orts-* (Origins) to interpret what you find.

are the equivalent of church membership lists. Marriage records give the names of the couple, as well as their residences, but don't often name their fathers. Burials give the name of the deceased, dates of death and burial, and age notation—sometimes in years, months and days; other times as an estimate such as "about 40 years old."

These rich record books, which also sometimes include "family registers" of sacraments for those related to each married couple, typically begin around 1550 for churches that turned Protestant (called Reformed or Evangelical Reformed) in the Reformation. Most Roman Catholic registers begin about 1600. Many Anabaptists (predecessors of today's Amish and Mennonites) also lived in Switzerland, but they were often persecuted and didn't keep documentation that might identify members. Still, some Anabaptists show up in Protestant or Catholic church registers, which were used for civil purposes. The FHL **<familysearch.org>** has microfilmed a large number of parish registers. To find your ancestors' parish, search the online catalog by place and type in the name of the commune. An increasing number of registers are digitized and accessible on the free FamilySearch.org. You should also refer to FamilySearch's Switzerland page at **<www.familysearch.org/learn/wiki/en/Switzerland>**.

CIVIL REGISTRATIONS: These vital records, as well as family certificates (which document one couple's vital events in addition to naming their parents and children) are helpful if you're doing 19th- and 20th-century Swiss research. Standardized registration of vital records began in 1876, though a handful of cantons began to document vital events earlier. The FHL has microfilmed a small group of these. Those not on microfilm are in civil registrar's offices in the communes. The records are technically available only to Swiss citizens for 120 years, though enforcement varies by canton.

CENSUSES: For the most part, these were taken irregularly by some communes and cantons in the first half of the 19th century. Those head counts are available, either on FHL microfilm (such as a 1764 census for the city of Bern) or through the archives of communes or cantons. Unfortunately, surviving census records from 1850 onward are merely statistical.

AUSTRIA

Like Switzerland, most of today's Austria was in the ancient Roman Empire. It later was an eastern outpost of Charlemagne's empire, which earned it the name *Österreich* (German for "eastern borderland"). Until the late 1200s, the area remained a backwater on the border between German-speaking peoples to the west, and Hungarians and Slavs on the east. Then Rudolf of Hapsburg, lord of territories in southwest Germany and what became Switzerland, acquired the duchies that make up present-day Austria. His ambition culminated in wearing the crown of the Holy Roman Empire.

After Rudolf, the Hapsburg lineage fractured until Emperor Maximilian reunited it in the late 1400s. His grandsons ruled territories including Spain, the Low Countries, much of Italy, Bohemia, Austria and Hungary. The Hapsburg heirs to Austria, Hungary and Bohemia continued as Holy Roman Emperors until the empire was dissolved in 1806. The family ruled until its end on the losing side of World War I. Under its tenure, Hungarians revolted and in 1867, became equal partners in the entity rechristened Austria-Hungary. Post-WWI Austria was a small, almost exclusively German-speaking state as Austria-Hungary was carved up into what's now Hungary, the Czech Republic, Slovakia, Slovenia, Croatia and Bosnia. Hungary administered part of Burgenland, now one of Austria's federal states, until the empire broke up.

American records such as censuses and naturalizations may show Austria as the nation of origin and Austrian as the nationality for the many non-German-speaking minorities in the Austrian empire. References to language will help you pinpoint their origins—for example, look outside of today's Austria for those listing a Slavic language as mother tongue in historical records. But many German-speaking enclaves peppered the eastern edge of Austria-Hungary and its successor states until the end of World War II. The tip-off is that most German-speaking folks in these enclaves were Protestant instead of Catholic, as in the Austrian heartland. For more information on these enclaves of German speakers who lived outside of Germany, see page 138–139.

You'll find as many contrasts between Swiss and Austrian genealogy as between, well, Switzerland and Austria as nations. Although Austria's population (historically and today) has been larger than Switzerland's, Americans descended from immigrants who originated within today's Austrian boundaries number only in the thousands—compared to the millions with

Swiss ancestry. Still, Austria's former prominence on the European stage makes its records more important than those numbers might otherwise indicate.

CHURCH RECORDS: Austria today is primarily Roman Catholic. Holy Roman Emperors were considered "defenders of the faith" and until the 16th century, most were crowned by the pope. This put the Hapsburgs on the Catholic side in the religious wars of the 1500s and 1600s. A substantial number of Protestants lived within the boundaries of Hapsburg territories after the Reformation, but waves of expulsions took place until the emperor decreed a law of toleration in 1781. Before this Patent of Tolerance, Protestants may be in Catholic records. Some Protestant records—primarily Lutheran—may exist after that date.

Unfortunately, the FHL has microfilmed relatively few of Austria's Roman Catholic parish registers. A substantial number are still housed in the original parishes, making requests for research in these records hit-or-miss. Many Catholic dioceses have archives with websites; look for their addresses on the Catholic Pages of Austria website **<www.rc.net/austria>**. Notable exceptions to this dearth of access are the St. Pölten and Vienna dioceses, which have digitized their church records and posted them free online at **<www.matricula-online.eu>**.

Austria, especially its capital of Vienna, was home to many Jews before World War II. JewishGen has an online primer on tracing Jews from this area available at **<www.jewishgen.org/austriaczech/ausguide.htm>**. Learn more about Jewish genealogy in Chapter 14.

MILITARY RECORDS: A large volume of military records from Austria's empire period helps make up for the hard-to-access church records. The FHL has literally thousands of rolls of microfilm of these records, because most men owed at least some military service. The records cover men from the districts now part of Austria, not other parts of the empire. In most cases, you'll need to know your ancestor's regiment and when he served to find him in the records. To help you determine the regiment, use the FHL's microfilmed typescript of Otto Kasperkowitz's *Location Index for Recruitment into the Imperial and Royal Austrian Army and Navy Troops*. This index shows the locations in which regiments, battalions and other units had permission to recruit. The major categories of military records include:

- *Grundbuchblätter* (personnel sheets) cover enlisted soldiers, starting with those born as early as 1780. Information about the soldiers includes name, birth year, birthplace, religion, occupation, regiments and dates of service. These records are arranged alphabetically by surname within each Austrian state and cover more than 600 rolls of microfilm.
- *Musterlisten und Standestabellen* (muster rolls and formation tables) cover soldiers from 1740 to 1820 on more than 5,000 rolls of microfilm. They're arranged by regiment (except for rolls of officers, which are alphabetical) and give the same information as the personnel sheets, plus names of children and marital status.
- *Grundbücher und Stellungslisten* (personnel books and formation lists) cover soldiers and officers from 1820 to 1869. They have information similar to muster rolls and like those rolls, are arranged by regiment. The FHL has almost 3,000 rolls of film for these

records. See FamilySearch's Austria page **<www.familysearch.org/learn/wiki/en/Austria>**.

- *Dienstbeschreibungen* (service records) apply only to the 10 percent of military men who were officers but give much more detail on each man's service. They're organized alphabetically on nearly 3,500 rolls of film.
- *Militärkirchenbücher* (military church records) were kept for military units and garrisons. They include baptisms, marriages and burials on nearly 600 rolls of film and are arranged by regiment.
- Seigniorial records: FamilySearch's digitization initiative is making available these registers of court records kept by feudal lords in Austria. The records include marriage contracts, inventories of estates and transfers of feudal land leases from one generation to another—giving many family relationships.

SHORT STUFF

Your ancestor may appear in genealogical records by his given or middle name, or by a shortened form of the name. These are some common German names and nicknames:

Full Name	Nickname
Johann or Johannes	Hans
Friedrich	Fritz
Heinrich	Heinz
Wilhelm	Willy
Josef	Sepp
Nicolaus	Klaus
Catharina	Trina
Elisabeth(a)	Lisa, Betty
Margaretha	Gretl, Greta
Dorothea	Dora
Carolina	Lina
Magdalena	Lena, Helena
Johanna	Hanna

Surmounting Language Barriers

To research most Austrian or Swiss handwritten church records, you'll want some knowledge of German cursive script and vocabulary. Even printed materials from the first half of the 20th century are in a Gothic font that presents a number of quirks to modern researchers. But don't let the script or the font keep you from attempting this research. Use the resources listed in the Toolkit and remember that Google will translate most German-language websites into English.

Delving beyond beers and bratwurst to yodeling and Edelweiss brings up the larger question of "what is 'German' research?" For most people, German ancestry ends up being an ethnicity defined more by language than by national borders, because they'll likely have amongst those forebears a "German" who never set foot within the boundaries of a nation called Germany. Knowing the peculiarities of Swiss and Austrian research will prepare you for finding these folks.

GERMANS OUTSIDE GERMANY

Following is an overview of the major ethnic German groups; we've also pointed out important records, websites, published histories and genealogical societies for each.

DEUTSCHBALTEN (BALTIC GERMANS)

- **Origin:** Throughout Germany
- **Destination:** The Baltic Sea's eastern shore in three main areas: Estland, roughly the northern half of present-day Estonia, Livland in southern Estonia and northern Latvia, and Kurland (Courland in English), the southern half of present-day Latvia
- **Migration history:** Baltic Germans settled their land in the late 1100s. They founded an association of knights that became affiliated with the Teutonic Catholic order in 1236 and morphed into an aristocracy that owned much of the Baltic states. Though Estonia and Latvia became provinces of the Russian Empire in the 1700s, the German-speaking aristocracy remained until after WWI. Some Deutschbalten left, mainly for America and Germany; most stayed until 1939, when nearly all the 70,000-plus German-speaking residents were sent to Poland and later to Germany.
- **Records:** The FHL has church records of major towns; most start in the mid-1600s or early 1700s.

BUKOVINANS

- **Origin:** Swabians came from the southwestern German states of the Palatinate, Württemberg and the Rhineland; Sudeten Germans, from the Bohemian Forest area; and Zipsers, from the district of Zips in what's now Slovakia.
- **Destination:** part of Bukovina, in Romania since World War I
- **Migration history:** After Bukovina became an Austrian province in 1775, the government encouraged ethnic Germans to settle there. More Sudeten Germans followed during the early 1800s. A late-19th-century population explosion spurred migration primarily to Canada, but also the United States and Brazil. The Soviet Union and Romania divided Bukovina after World War I, and in 1940, nearly all the Germans in Bukovina left for Germany proper.
- **Records:** Fortunately, the migrants took along their Roman Catholic and Lutheran church records, which the FHL has microfilmed. Some date to original German settlement.

KARPATENDEUTSCHE (CARPATHIAN GERMANS)

- **Origin:** Several areas of Germany—see migration history below
- **Destination:** The northern arc of the Carpathian Mountains (now in Slovakia and subject at the time to Hungary), including four areas: Pressburg (the German name for Bratislava), central Slovakia in the Hauerland, the Zips and the Carpatho-Ukraine (now called Transcarpathia)
- **Migration history:** As early as the 12th century, a Bavarian bishop with extensive landholdings in Tyrol encouraged his subjects from the town of Eisacktal in South Tyrol to populate the village of Eisdorf in the Zips district. Germans who spoke a Bavarian-Franconian dialect went to Hauerland and Pressburg; those from the northwestern Lower Rhineland and Flanders ended up in the Zips. After 1860, Zipser German peasants and craftsmen immigrated to the United States en masse, most notably to Philadelphia,

though more than 150,000 Carpathian Germans still lived in Europe before World War II. The war left 6,000 to 15,000 in Slovakia and 3,000 in Ukraine. Descendants of this group reside mainly in Germany, Austria, the United States and Canada.

• **Records:** Eisdorf and Menhard are among the few villages with church records on FHL microfilm.

DONAUSCHWABEN (DANUBE SWABIANS)

• **Origin:** Many came from the Swabian region centered around Stuttgart; others were miners and craftsmen from Styria (part of modern-day Austria), Austrian military and civilian administrators and office workers, and people from Carpathian areas and the Baden microstate of Durlach.

• **Destination:** Enclaves along the Danube River in what are now Hungary, Romania and Serbia

• **Migration history:** The first of this large group to migrate were about 15,000 to an area known as the Banat, now in southwestern Romania, between 1718 and 1737. Ottoman raids and a bout with bubonic plague killed many of these settlers. The second colonization wave, from 1744 to 1772, consisted of 75,000 people and resulted in German-dominated towns throughout what's now southern Hungary, Croatia and Serbia in regions called Batschka, Sathmar and Slavonia. A third wave added another 60,000 colonists during the 1780s. Most set out from the German city of Ulm and passed through Vienna and Budapest. Before World War II, nearly half a million German speakers lived in the Banat. After the war, Hungary and Serbia expelled many of them. Meanwhile, 100,000 Donauschwaben left Romania ahead of the Russian army; some who stayed were sent to labor camps in Ukraine. Upon release, many left for Germany or Austria and later moved to the United States, Canada, Australia, France, Argentina, Brazil and Venezuela.

• **Records:** Museums and ethnic clubs keep the Donauschwaben memory alive, and you can find numerous records of their journey. Records include *Ansiedlerakten* (settler documents) dating from 1686 to 1855. These records give settlers' names, number of children, places of origin and other info recorded as they passed through Vienna. Many settlers and their descendants were conscripted into the Austro-Hungarian army, so check FHL microfilm of Austrian military records.

GOTTSCHEER

• **Origin:** German states of Carinthia, Tyrol, Salzburg, Brixen and Freising

• **Destination:** Gottschee, part of the Austrian duchy of Carniola (now in Slovenia)

• **Migration history:** This group first settled vacant forest land in the 1300s. During World War II, the Nazis relocated them nearby; after the war, the Gottscheer were again expelled, this time to the United States, Germany, Austria, Canada and Australia. Most of the 20,000 to 30,000 Gottscheer and their descendants in America arrived after the expulsions, but some came as early as 1870. Many live in large cities such as New York, Cleveland, Chicago and Milwaukee (and Toronto, Kitchener and Vancouver in Canada) as well as Upper St. Clair Township in Allegheny County, Pa.

• **Records:** Roman Catholic church records dating to the 1700s are on FHL microfilm.

SIEBENBÜRGER SACHSEN (TRANSYLVANIAN SAXONS)

• **Origin:** The Rhineland and the Mosel River region, the Eifel and Luxembourg

- **Destination:** What was then Hungary, now the northern part of Romania
- **Migration history:** The area these ethnic Germans settled also goes by Transylvania—the same place Dracula made famous. Don't confuse them with the Carpathian Germans. In the 1100s, Hungary's king invited the Transylvanian Saxons to farm and gave them autonomy to establish their own laws and justice system. Their enclave swelled to some 500 settlements, including the cities Hermannstadt (now called by its Romanian name, Sibiu), Kronstadt (Brasov) and Schäßburg (Sighisoara). Many Transylvanian Saxons immigrated to America beginning in the 1880s, clustering around steel factories in cities such as Youngstown and Cleveland, Ohio, and Sharon and New Castle, Pa. All but a few thousand left after WWI, when Romania absorbed the area. The majority—some 200,000—of post-WWII emigrants from here have returned to Germany. An estimated 30,000 to 40,000 Americans are their descendants, mostly from migration during the 1880s.
- **Records:** The FHL has church records for many Transylvanian villages, but most date only from the early 1800s. Collections for some towns cover only registers of Austrian military families. You'll also find the Conscriptio Czirakyana feudal land tenancy census of 1819 to 1820.

VOLGA GERMANS AND GERMANS FROM RUSSIA

- **Origin:** Throughout Germany
- **Destination:** Near the Volga River in southern European Russia
- **Migration history:** These colonies were the most prominent of the German-speaking enclaves established in the Russian Empire during the 18th and early 19th centuries. Starting in 1763, about 30,000 colonists founded "closed cities" on the Russian steppe; they remained until Communist Russia banished them to Kazakhstan and Siberia in 1941. You'll find histories of several colonies, maps, photos and more at **<www.volgagermans. net>**. Other groups—collectively called Germans from Russia—include isolated southern Russian settlements founded in the late 1760s; Hutterites, who first moved in 1770, and Mennonites, who began settlement by 1789; German towns in the Bessarabian and Black Sea regions starting in the early 1800s; and mid-19th century arrivals in Volhynia, Crimea and the Caucasus. About 1.8 million Germans lived in Russia at the end of the 19th century. Thousands of Mennonites began leaving for the Americas in the 1870s to avoid compulsory Russian military service. Stalin expelled Volgans as the German army advanced during World War II. The descendants of German-speaking Russian emigrants live all over the world, including Canada, the United States, Germany, Argentina and Brazil.
- **Records:** You can purchase Russian census lists covering various years from the mid-1700s through the mid-1800s from the American Historical Society of Germans from Russia **<www.ahsgr.org>**. Church records are mostly unavailable, but Lutheran Germans expelled from Bessarabia during World War II saved their church records; they're on FHL microfilm.

ORGANIZATIONS AND ARCHIVES

AMERICAN HISTORICAL SOCIETY OF GERMANS FROM RUSSIA

631 D St., Lincoln, NE 68502
Phone: (402) 474-3363
<www.ahsgr.org>

ARBEITSGEMEINSCHAFT FÜR MITTELDEUTSCHE FAMILIENFORSCHUNG (WORKING GROUP FOR CENTRAL GERMAN FAMILY RESEARCH)

Schloßgartenstr. 14, 86695 Nordendorf, Germany
Phone: +49 08273 9983318
E-mail: vorstand@amf-verein.de
<www.amf-verein.de>

ARBEITSGEMEINSCHAFT OSTDEUTSCHER FAMILIENFORSCHER (WORKING GROUP FOR EAST GERMAN FAMILY RESEARCHERS)

Wacholderweg 25, 06849 Dessau-Roßlau, Germany
E-mail: kontakt@agoff.de
<www.agoff.de>

ARBEITSGEMEINSCHAFT PFÄLZISCH-RHEINISCHE FAMILIENKUNDE (RHEINLAND-PFALZ FAMILY HISTORY WORKING GROUP)

Rottstr. 17 (Stadtarchiv), 67061 Ludwigshafen/Rhein, Germany
<www.genealogienetz.de/reg/RHE-PFA/rhein-p.html>

ARCHIVES DÉPARTEMENTALES DU BAS-RHIN

6 rue Philippe Dollinger, 67100 Strasbourg, France
<archives.bas-rhin.fr>

ARCHIVES DÉPARTEMENTALES DU HAUT-RHIN

Cité administrative, 3 rue Fleischhauer, 68026 Colmar Cedex 3, France
Phone: +33 03 89 21 97 00
E-mail: archives@cg68.fr
<www.archives.cg68.fr>

ARCHIVES DÉPARTEMENTALES DE LA MOSELLE

1 allée du château, 57070 St. Julien-les-Metz, France
Phone: +33 03 87 78 05 00
E-mail: archives@cg57.fr
<www.archives57.com>

AUSTRIAN STATE ARCHIVES, FAMILY RESEARCH

Nottendorfergasse 2, A-1030 Vienna, Austria
Phone: + 43 1 79540 0
E-mail: webmaster@oesta.gv.at
<www.oesta.gv.at/site/5170/default.aspx>

BUKOVINA SOCIETY OF THE AMERICAS

Box 81, Ellis, KS 67637
<www.feefhs.org/members/bukovina/bukovina.html>

DANUBE CULTURAL SOCIETY OF SOUTHEASTERN WISCONSIN

E-mail: danubeculturalsociety@yahoo.com
<www.danubeculturalsociety.com>

DEUTSCHE ZENTRALSTELLE FÜR GENEALOGIE (GERMAN CENTER FOR GENEALOGY)

Sächsisches Staatsarchiv Leipzig, Schongauerstr. 1, 04109 Leipzig, Germany
Phone: +49 0341 255 5500
Fax: +49 0341 255 5555
E-mail: poststelle-l@sta.smi.sachsen.de
<www.archiv.sachsen.de/6319.htm>

FEDERATION OF EAST EUROPEAN FAMILY HISTORY SOCIETIES

Box 321, Springville, UT 84663

GENEALOGIE ZENTRUM WORB
Paradiesweg 5, CH-3076 Worb, Switzerland
E-mail: lewisrohrbach@hotmail.com
<www.swissgenealogy.com>

GENERALLANDESARCHIV KARLSRUHE
Nördliche Hildapromenade 2
76133 Karlsruhe Germany
Phone: +49 0721 926 2206
Fax: +49 0721 926 2231
E-mail: glakarlsruhe@la-bw.de
<www.landesarchiv-bw.de/web/49673>

GERMAN RESEARCH ASSOCIATION
Box 711600, San Diego, CA 92171-1600
<feefhs.org/members/gra/frg-gra.html>

GERMANIC GENEALOGY SOCIETY
Box 16312, St. Paul, MN 55116
<www.ggsmn.org>

GOTTSCHEER HERITAGE AND GENEALOGY ASSOCIATION
Box 725, Louisville, CO 80027
<www.gottschee.org>

HESSISCHE FAMILIENGESCHICHTLICHE VEREINIGUNG (HESSEN GENEALOGICAL ORGANIZATION)
Staatsarchiv, Karolinenplatz 3, 69289 Darmstadt, Germany
Phone: +49 6151 165960
E-mail: hfv@haus-der-geschichte.com
<www.genealogy.net/vereine/HFV/english. html>

HOMELAND ASSOCIATION FOR CARPATHIAN GERMANS IN GERMANY (KARPATENDEUTSCHE LANDSMANNSCHAFT)
Haus der Heimat, Schloss-strasse 92/II, D-70176 Stuttgart, Germany
Phone: +49 0711 62 62 62
Fax: +49 0711 62 01 437
E-mail: landsmannschaft@karpatenpost.de
<www.karpatendeutsche.de>

IMMIGRANT GENEALOGICAL SOCIETY
Box 7369, Burbank, CA 91510-7369
Phone: (818) 848-3122
Fax: (818) 716-6300
<www.immigrantgensoc.org>

(INSTITUT FÜR DONAUSCHWABISCHE GESCHICHTE UND LANDESKUNDE) INSTITUTE FOR DANUBE-SWABIAN HISTORY AND REGIONAL STUDIES
Mohlstrasse 18, D-72074 Tubingen, Germany
Phone: +49 07071 9992 502
Fax: +49 07071 9992 501
E-mail: susanne.munz@idgl.bwl.de
<www.idglbw.de>

LANDESARCHIV
Prinzenpalais, Gottorfstr. 6, D-24837 Schleswig, Germany
Phone: +49 04621 861800
Fax: +49 04621 861801
E-mail: landesarchiv@la.landsh.de
<www.archive.schleswig-holstein.de>

LANDESHAUPTARCHIV KOBLENZ
Box 20 10 47, 56010 Koblenz, Germany
Phone: +49 0261 9129-0
Fax: +49 0261 9129-112
E-mail: post@landeshauptarchiv.de
<www.landeshauptarchiv.de>

NATIONAL ARCHIVES OF THE FEDERAL REPUBLIC OF GERMANY (SINCE 1945)
Potsdamer Straße 1, 56075 Koblenz
Phone: +49 0261 505 0
Fax: +49 0261 505 226
E-mail: koblenz@bundesarchiv.de
<www.bundesarchiv.de>

NATIONAL LIBRARY OF AUSTRIA
Josefsplatz 1, Postfach 308, 1015 Vienna, Austria
Phone: +43 1 534 10
Fax: +43 1 534 10-280
E-mail: onb@onb.ac.at
<www.onb.ac.at>

PALATINES TO AMERICA
Box 141260, Columbus, OH 43214
Phone: (614) 267-4700
<www.palam.org>

SOCIETY FOR GERMAN GENEALOGY IN EASTERN EUROPE

Box 905 Station M, Calgary, Alberta T2P 2J6, Canada
<www.sggee.org>

SWISS NATIONAL ARCHIVES

Archivstrasse 24, CH-3003 Bern, Switzerland
Phone: +41 31 322 89 89
Fax: +41 31 322 78 23
<www.bar.admin.ch>

SWISS NATIONAL LIBRARY

Hallwylstrasse 15, CH-3003 Bern, Switzerland
Phone: +41 31 322 89 35
Fax: +41 31 322 84 08
E-mail: info@nb.admin.ch
<www.nb.admin.ch>

VEREIN FÜR FAMILIEN- UND WAPPENKUNDE IN WÜRTTEMBERG U. BADEN (ORGANIZATION FOR FAMILY AND HERALDRY WÜRTTEMBERG AND BADEN)

Postfach 10 54 41, 70047 Stuttgart, Germany
E-mail: wappen@wlb-stuttgart.de
**<www.genealogienetz.de/vereine/VFWKWB/
VFWKWB.html>**

WESTDEUTSCHE GESELLSCHAFT FÜR FAMILIENKUNDE (WEST GERMAN SOCIETY FOR FAMILY HISTORY)

Unter Gottes Gnaden 34, 50859 Koln-Widdersdorf, Germany
Phone: +49 0221 508488
Fax: +49 0221 9502505
E-mail: info@wgff.net
<www.wgff.net>

BOOKS

Address Book for Germanic Genealogy, 6th edition, by Ernst Thode (Genealogical Publishing)

Bibliography of Swiss Genealogies by Mario von Moos (Picton Press)

Deutsches Geschlechterbuch (German lineage book) 194+ volumes (C.A. Starke)

Encyclopedia of German-American Genealogical Research by Clifford Neal Smith and Anna Piszczan-Czaja Smith (Clearfield)

Even More Palatine Families, 3 volumes, by Henry Z. Jones Jr. and Lewis Bunker Rohrbach (Picton Press)

Finding Your German Ancestors: A Practical Guide for Genealogists by John T. Humphrey (Pennsylvania Genealogy Books)

Genealogical Guide to German Ancestors from East Germany and Eastern Europe by Arbeitsgemeinschaft ostdeutscher Familienforscher (Degener)

A Genealogical Handbook of German Research by Larry O. Jensen (Jensen)

A Genealogist's Guide to Discovering Your Germanic Ancestors by S. Chris Anderson and Ernest Thode (Betterway Books)

German Church Books: Beyond the Basics by Kenneth Lee Smith (Picton Press)

German-English Genealogical Dictionary by Ernest Thode (Genealogical Publishing Co.)

German Genealogical Research by George K. Schweitzer (Schweitzer)

German Towns in Slovakia and Upper Hungary by Duncan Gardiner (Family Historian)

Germanic Genealogy: A Guide to Worldwide Sources and Migration Patterns by Edward R. Brandt (Germanic Genealogy Society)

Historical Atlas of Central Europe by Paul Robert Magocsi (University of Washington Press)

If I Can, You Can: Decipher Germanic Records by Edna M. Bentz (self-published)

In Search of Your German Roots by Angus Baxter (Genealogical Publishing Co.)

Introductory Guide to Swiss Genealogical Research by Lewis Bunker Rohrbach (Swiss American Historical Society)

Österreichisch-Ungarisches Orts-Lexikon (Austro-Hungarian Empire Gazetteer) by Hans Mayerhofer (Carl Fromme)

Stammfolgen-Verzeichnisse für das genealogische Handbuch des Adels und das deutsche Geschlechterbuch (Index of the genealogical handbook of nobility and the German lineage books) (C.A. Starke)

The Swiss Emigration Book by Cornelia Schrader-Muggenthaler (Closson Press)

Taschenbuch für Familiengeschichtsforschung (Pocketbook for family history research) by Wolfgang Ribbe and Eckart Henning (Degener)

Tracing Romania's Heterogeneous German Minority from Its Origins to the Diaspora by Jacob Steigerwald (Translation and Interpretation Services)

WEBSITES

Ahnenforschung
<ahnenforschung.net>

Archives in Germany
<home.bawue.de/~hanacek/info/earchive. htm>

Austria Genealogy Forum
<genforum.genealogy.com/austria>

Austria GenWeb
<rootsweb.ancestry.com/~autwgw>

Austrian Family History
<www.austrianfamilyhistory.org>

Austrian Genealogy
<rootsweb.ancestry.com/~autwgw/agsfr. htm>

Austrian telephone book
<www.herold.at/telefonbuch>

Carpathian German Home Page <carpathiangerman.com>

Catholic Churches in Germany
<www.kath.de>

Catholic Pages of Austria
<www.rc.net/austria>

Cyndi's List: Austria
<cyndislist.com/austria>

Cyndi's List: Germany
<cyndislist.com/germany>

Cyndi's List: Switzerland
<cyndislist.com/switzerland>

Deutsch-Balten Gesellschaft
<www.deutschbalten.de>

Donauschwaben Research Exchange
<www.banaters.com/dre/nogo.asp>

East European Genealogical Society
<www.eegsociety.org>

Familiennamenbuch der Schweiz
<www.hls-dhs-dss.ch/famn>

Federation of East European Family History Societies
<www.feefhs.org/links/germany.html>

German Genealogy Databases
<searchgenealogy.net/Germany.html>

German Genealogy Forum
<genforum.genealogy.com/germany>

German Genealogy Home Page
<www.genealogienetz.de>

Germanic Genealogy: The German Way
<www.german-way.com/gene.html>

GermanRoots
<www.germanroots.com>

Germany GenWeb
<rootsweb.ancestry.com/~wggerman>

Kartenmeister
<www.kartenmeister.com>

LEO German-English Dictionary
<dict.leo.org>

Odessa: German-Russian Digital Genealogical Library
<www.odessa3.org>

Script Tutorial
<www.mun.ca/rels/morav/script.html>

Society for German Genealogy in Eastern Europe
<www.sggee.org>

Stammbaum: Journal of Jewish-Germanic Genealogy
<feefhs.org/links/Germany/stam>

Swiss American Historical Society
<www.swissamericanhistory.org>

Swiss Anabaptist Genealogical Association
<saga.ncweb.com>

Swiss Genealogy on the Internet
<kunden.eye.ch/swissgen>

Swiss Society of Genealogical Studies
<www.sgffweb.ch>

SwitzerlandGenWeb
<rootsweb.ancestry.com/~chewgw>

The German Genealogy Group
<www.germangenealogygroup.com>

Volga Germans
<www.volgagermans.net>

CHAPTER EIGHT

POLAND

By Cecile Wendt Jensen with Sunny Jane Morton

REGIONAL GUIDE

If you have Polish roots, you're a member of the largest Slavic group in the United States. You also share the legacy of Polonia, a diaspora that built new communities abroad while the Polish homeland suffered more than a century of foreign occupation.

Today Poland is a country again, but Polonia became permanent for millions of its former citizens. Ten million Polish progeny are Americans, and many of them have begun looking backward at their families' pathways from Poland.

The stories they encounter vary widely. Some find comforting images of a grandmother in her Detroit kitchen, preparing pierogi for her autoworker husband. Others discover a WWI soldier uncle's longing for an independent Poland. Still others, grim but grateful, record their survival of the Holocaust and the names of loved ones lost.

Whatever brought your Polish ancestors here, you can retrace their pathways home. Polonian communities in the United States proudly record their heritage, and increasingly accessible Polish records can tell you more about lives lived under Russian, German or Austrian rule. Here's how to start your own virtual journey back to the Old Country.

Pieces of Polonia

Poles began coming to the United States in large numbers in the 1880s, along with many other immigrants looking for a better life. Nearly 100,000 arrived in the 1890s, over a quarter-million in the 1920s and another 50,000 in the 1960s. They came largely for jobs advertised by industry recruiters and to escape harsh governmental policies at home.

Polish immigrants flocked to Michigan, Wisconsin and Connecticut, but also to other Great Lakes and northeastern states, and even Florida, Texas, Arizona and California (see the map at **<en.wikipedia.org/wiki/File:Polonia_USA.png>**). Polish-American neighborhoods grew, with their own religious parishes and schools, benevolent societies and newspapers. Chicago, Detroit, Pittsburgh, Milwaukee, Buffalo and Cleveland all claimed pieces of Polonia.

These new heartlands can be excellent sources for material on your relatives' Polish-American experience. Polish genealogical groups in these areas preserve records and ethnic identity. See the Polish Genealogical Society of America (PGSA) site **<www.pgsa.org/refdesk. php#Societies>** for links to such organizations. Local histories capture stories and images, such as those in *Chicago's Polish Downtown* by Victoria Granacki (Arcadia Publishing) and the Wisconsin Historical Society's online article "Fifty Years of Polish Settlement in Portage County [WI], 1857–1907" **<www.wisconsinhistory.org/turningpoints/search.asp?id=1347>**. A Google search on *Polish* and your ancestors' US hometown or state will turn up publications and organizations relevant to your search.

Determining Your Destination

You're traveling your ancestor's route in reverse: Your final destination is the exact village from which their pathway from Poland originates. Look to these US sources.

CENSUSES: US census records can pinpoint your immigrant ancestors' year of arrival (starting with the 1900 census), help identify a birthplace (beginning in 1850) and report citizenship status (starting in 1900). Parents' birthplace is requested beginning in 1880. Subscription site Ancestry.com **<ancestry.com>** has indexes and images of the entire US census (see if your library offers the free Ancestry Library Edition) and Archives.com is adding them. Many censuses are on the free FamilySearch.org **<familysearch.org>**.

NATURALIZATION PAPERS: Post-1906 citizenship papers may give an applicant's last foreign address and birthplace (married women and children didn't need their own paperwork until after 1922). Order these records from the US Citizenship and Immigration Service **<www.uscis. gov/genealogy>**; some are on National Archives **<archives.gov>** and Family History Library (FHL) microfilm. Pre-1906 records, which may reveal only the country of origin, could be in county, state or US district courts. Consult *The Family Tree Sourcebook* for information on how to request naturalization records for each state or county. Ancestry.com and Fold3 **<fold3.com>** have some naturalizations made in federal courts.

SOCIAL SECURITY APPLICATIONS: SS-5 forms start in 1936 for people who registered with the Social Security Administration and may show a town of birth. You can search the Social Security Death Index on several sites, including FamilySearch.org and Ancestry.com. Most names are for deaths after 1961. Request a copy of the SS-5 by mail or online for a fee; see **<www.ssa.gov/foia/request.html>**.

DRAFT REGISTRATIONS: WWI and WWII draft cards, which even nonnaturalized immigrants had to fill out, request a birthplace in detail—town, state and nation. (Also look for clues in draft registrations of your ancestor's brothers, cousins, uncles and parents.) Digitized draft cards are on Ancestry.com for both wars. FamilySearch.org has an index for World War II and has begun to post images. You can order $5 copies of WWI draft registrations at **<eservices.archives.gov/orderonline>**; click on Order Reproductions. For the same price, order WWII draft registrations from the National Personnel Record Center by mail; see **<archives.gov/st-louis/archival-programs/other-records/selective-service.html>**.

PASSENGER LISTS: Ship manifests can give an ancestor's hometown, though you may find just the country or last port of call. It'll help your search to know the arrival year or ship name, plus your ancestor's proper Polish name (see box, left), which may be different from the name in US records. Ancestry.com has post-1820 US passenger manifests. Search Port of New York records from 1892 to 1924 at **<www.ellisisland.org>**. Also

TIME LINE

966	Duke Mieszko I, Poland's first recorded leader, converts to Christianity
1241	A Mongol army raids Poland
1320	Polish state is reunified
1364	The Academy of Krakow, now called the Jagiellonian University, founded by Casimir the Great
1388	Jadwiga, Poland's Sovereign, marries Wladyslaw Jagiello, the Grand Duke of Lithuania, uniting Poland and Lithuania under one crown.
1493	The bicameral Polish Parliament is first convened.
1543	Nicolaus Copernicus proposes that the earth revolves around the sun.
1573	The *Sejm* guarantees religious equality.
1655–1660	Sweden invades Poland with the help of the Tartars and Cossacks from the East. Poland's population of 10 million is reduced to 6 million by wars, famine and the bubonic plague.
1772	The first partition of Poland by Russia, Prussia and Austria.
1791	The Constitution of the Third of May.
1793	The second partition of Poland: More Polish territory is annexed by Russia and Prussia.
1795	The Third Partition divides the rest of Poland, which officially does not exist for the next 123 years.

1870s	Russia attempts to eradicate Polish culture, making Russian the official language of the Russian partition. Prussia does the same in their portion of Poland, attempting to Germanicize Poles. Under the Austrian partition, Galician Poles are allowed to retain some autonomy.
1918	Poland regains independence after World War I. It is recognized under the terms of Versailles Treaty. Marshal Jozef Pilsudski becomes President.
1939	Hitler attacks Poland from the west on Sept. 1, and World War II starts. On Sept. 17, the Soviet Union invades Poland from the east. A partition of Poland follows on Sept. 28.
1943	The Warsaw Ghetto Uprising.
1978	Karol Wojtyla, the Archbishop of Krakow, is elected Pope. Taking the name John Paul II, he is the first non-Italian pope in nearly 500 years.
1980	Strikes and riots ensue as the economy crumbles. Workers are allowed to organize into an independent trade union, called Solidarnosc, or Solidarity.
1990	The first fully free election is won by Lech Walesa.
1997	Poland's National Assembly adopts a new Constitution.
1999	Poland becomes a member of NATO, the North Atlantic Treaty Organization.
1999	Poland becomes a member of the European Union.

check indexes at **<immigrantships.net>** and **<www.theshipslist.com>**.

OTHER US RECORDS: Church records, vital records and newspaper announcements of births, marriages and deaths may mention a hometown or relatives whose origins you can research. Local histories also may mention villages from which many local immigrants arrived.

Polish Places

Once you've identified your ancestors' town, plot its location in modern Poland. That's not as easy as it sounds: Poland is made up of 16 provinces (*voivodeships*), 379 counties (*powiaty*) and more than 2,000 municipalities (*gminas*, some of which are large enough to have concurrent *powiat* status). Records on individuals are generally kept by municipalities. Because records may be in several languages and you'll be communicating with Polish records custodians, you need two important traveling tools: maps and translating devices.

MAPS: First, identify your ancestral town on a historical map and then confirm its modern location. You can use online maps; **<english.mapywig.org>,** the Wojskowy Instytut Geograficzny (Military Geographical Institute) is a go-to source for pre-WWII Poland. Between 1919 and 1939, this organization published geographic materials that are now online, along with a Polish-English map vocabulary list. You can order copies free of charge via the Library of Congress' Ask the Librarian program **<loc.gov./rr/askalib>** (click on Geography & Map). Request a specific map (or the village name, longitude and latitude) along with the map key.

Old Town in Warsaw

If your ancestor lived in a predominantly Jewish village (*shtetl*), turn to the ShtetlSeeker **<www.jewishgen.org/Communities>**, a village-seeking tool that uses a Soundex system tailored to Central and Eastern European languages. You'll also find links to modern maps.

Marco Polo Polska Atlas Drogowy (Road Atlas of Poland) is an excellent modern map series. As a companion tool, you'll want the First Edition Index to this map, published by Genealogy Unlimited **<www.genealogyunlimited.com>**. It references more than 90,000 place names that correspond to cataloging by voivodeship for FHL microfilms of Poland.

You also can access a modern city finder at **<mapa.szukacz.pl>**. Even if you don't read Polish, you can do a place search in the field labeled *Miejscowość*, then hit *Pokaż* (find). Results will appear as circles on a map (the name might correspond to more than one location). See a guide to using this site and other invaluable place-finders in *Sto Lat: A Modern Guide to Polish Genealogy* by Cecile Wendt Jensen **<www.mipolonia.net>**. Find a helpful directory of regional Polish resources at **<www.rootsweb.ancestry.com/~polwgw/polandgen.html>**.

TRANSLATION TOOLS: Before 1918, genealogical records may be written in Polish, German, Russian or Latin. In Russian Poland, Polish was used in vital records from 1808 to 1868; Russian took over until 1917. In German Poland, you'll see German or Latin records, with a sprinkling of Polish. Austrian Poland primarily relied on Latin, but you'll come across German and some in Polish.

Market Square, Krakow

For help reading Polish records, consult *A Translation Guide to the 19-Century Polish-Language Civil Registration Documents* by Judith R. Frazin (Jewish Genealogical Society of Illinois), free in Google Books (see *Family Tree Magazine*'s Google Library **<snipurl.com/ftm-google-library>**). Also see Jonathan D. Shea's *Russian Language Documents from Russian Poland: A Translation Manual for Genealogists* (Genealogy Unlimited). You'll find translation tips at the Society for Germany Genealogy in Eastern Europe website **<www.sggee.org/research/translation_aids>** and in the FamilySearch Research Wiki **<wiki.familysearch.org>** (enter the language and word list in the search box).

Letter-writing guides will be vital if you need to write to Polish archives (don't expect archivists to read English). The Polish Genealogy Project **<polishgeno.com/?page_id=33>** website posts helpful links to letter-writing guides (including FamilySearch's) as well as tips for understanding records an archives sends back (or why your request isn't successful).

Homing in on Homeland Records

With these tools in hand, you're ready to delve into Polish records. Start your search with these record groups.

RELIGIOUS RECORDS: The dominant historical religion of Poland is Roman Catholicism. There were significant Jewish communities in Russian and Austrian Poland, and Mennonites in the Vistula Delta area. Lemkos, who inhabited the Lower Beskid range of the Carpathian Mountains, followed eastern Catholic traditions (learn more at **<lemko. org>**).

Catholic parish records can include parishioner lists, marriage banns, announcements, religious education rolls, and registers of lay

ecclesiastical movements and religious orders. Priests consistently recorded parishioners' individual sacraments as early as 1547; in 1782, they also began keeping registers of Jews and other non-Christians. Rabbis and ministers of other Christian faiths also recorded births, marriages and deaths.

Four key Catholic church records with rich genealogical details on the person and family members are baptismal records, marriage records, death certificates and burial records (these may reference the churchyard, but not specific plots). Term graves, the tradition of reusing graves, is a common practice in Poland even today; the family pays a leasing fee.

Determine the parish your ancestors likely attended based on their village in Stanisław Litak's *The Latin Church in the Polish Commonwealth in 1772* or, more currently, *Roman Catholic Parishes in the Polish People's Republic in 1984* by Lidia Mullerowa (both from the PGSA). For southern Poland, turn to Gerald A. Ortell's *Polish Parish Records of the Roman Catholic Church: Their Use and Understanding in Genealogical Research* (PGSA). You can order microfilmed copies of most extant parish records through your FHL branch Family History Center, or mail a request to local parish offices. Images of church books from parishes in the Częstochowa, Gliwice, Lublin and Radom dioceses are online at **<familysearch.org>**.

CIVIL RECORDS: Civil registrations of births, marriages and deaths before about 1800 exist most frequently for noble and middle-class families. Beginning in 1804, universal civil registrations were recorded in the Russian partition of Poland under the Napoleonic code; similar records began in the Prussian sector in 1874. You'll find excellent genealogical information in these records: Birth registrations may name birth date, time and place; parents' names, ages and father's occupation; and grandfathers' first names.

Most civil registrations older than 100 years are at Polish regional archives. The Polish national archives website **<www.archiwa.gov.pl/en>** directs you to regional archives. Click on State Archives, then List of Archives. If you request records, be prepared to pay an hourly rate.

Microfilm of most pre-1880 records are available through Family History Centers. An index of Jewish Poles listed in civil records is at **<jri-poland.org>**.

Vital registrations less than 100 years old are in civil records offices at town halls across Poland. Address a request for a typed abstract (photocopies aren't permitted of these records) to the Urząd Stanu Cywilnego, [town], Poland. Or hire a local researcher to visit the office for you.

COMMUNITY HISTORIES: These are incredibly important in Polish research. The 15-volume *Słownik Geograficzny Królestwa Polskiego* (Geographical Dictionary of the Kingdom of Poland) was published between 1880 and 1902. This amazing resource describes every Polish village's geography, history, government, churches, demographics, history, schools, names of landowners and inhabitants, and more. Sources for further reading are suggested for each village, too. Find it online at **<dir.icm.edu.pl/pl/Slownik_geograficzny>**.

Yizkor books published by former residents of European Jewish communities pay tribute to their hometowns and Holocaust victims. The JewishGen Yikzor Book Project maintains a database listing all known books. Search under your ancestor's town and region at **<www.jewishgen.org/yizkor>**, then check other areas of the website for available print and web versions, translations, mentions of your ancestors in the necrology index, etc. You also can read digitized versions of 650 yizkor books at the New York Public Library at **<legacy.www.nypl.org/research/chss/jws/yizkorbookonline.cfm>**.

SHIP DEPARTURES: Poles most frequently departed from Bremen, Hamburg and Stettin, Germany (Stettin is now in Poland); and to a lesser degree, Antwerp and Rotterdam, Netherlands. Some traveled by land and ferry to England and departed from a British port.

Seven million emigrants sailed from Bremerhaven between 1832 and 1974. Unfortunately, lists from 1875 to 1908 have been destroyed, and all but about 3,000 lists for 1920 to 1939 were lost in World War II. Surviving lists are indexed at **<www.passengerlists.de>**.

Hamburg Direct and Indirect Passenger Lists and Indexes (1850–1934) are on microfilm through Family History Centers and on Ancestry.com. The database is indexed for 1885 to 1914; browse handwritten indexes for the 1855 to 1934.

Manifests for Stettin (now Szczecin, Poland) also are fragmentary. Surviving departure lists for 1871, 1876 to 1891 and 1896 to 1898 are in the *Vorpommersches Landesarchiv* **<www.landesarchiv-greifswald.de>** in Greifswald, Germany.

The search for these records may be a long, winding road. But chances are good you'll discover the ghosts of traveling companions along the way—like that freedom-fighting uncle—who will introduce you to long-gone relatives in Poland. That's the best thing about travel: the people you meet.

RESOURCES

ORGANIZATIONS AND ARCHIVES

ARCHDIOCESE OF POZNAN
Kuria Metropolitalna w Poznaniu, ul. Ostrów Tumski 2, 61-109 Poznań, Poland
Phone: +48 61 851 28 00
Fax: +48 61 851 28 14
E-mail: kuria@archpoznan.pl
<www.archpoznan.pl>

CONNECTICUT POLISH AMERICAN ARCHIVES
Central Connecticut State University, 1615 Stanley St., New Britain, CT 06053
Phone: (860) 832-2060
<library.ccsu.edu/help/spcoll/cpaa>

FEDERATION OF EASTERN EUROPEAN FAMILY HISTORY SOCIETIES
Box 321, Springville UT 84663
E-mail: conference@feefhs.org
<www.feefhs.org>

INDIANA UNIVERSITY POLISH STUDIES CENTER
1217 E. Atwater Ave., Bloomington, IN 47401
Phone: (813) 855-1507
Fax: (812) 855-0207
<www.indiana.edu/~polishst>

THE KOSCIUSZKO FOUNDATION
2025 O St. NW, Washington, DC 20036
Phone: (202) 785-2320
Fax: (202) 785-2159
<www.thekf.org>

POLISH AMERICAN ASSOCIATION
3834 N. Cicero Ave., Chicago, IL 60641
Phone: (773) 282-8206
<www.polish.org>

POLISH EMBASSY
2640 16th St. NW, Washington, DC 20009
Phone: (202) 499-1700
Fax: (202) 328-6271
E-mail: washington.amb@msz.gov.pl
<washington.mfa.gov.pl/en>

POLISH GENEALOGICAL SOCIETY OF AMERICA
984 N. Milwaukee Ave., Chicago, IL 60622
E-mail: pgsamerica@pgsa.org
<www.pgsa.org>

POLISH NATIONAL TOURIST OFFICE
5 Marine View Plaza, Suite 303 b, Hoboken, NJ 07030
Phone: (201) 420-9910
<www.poland.travel>

POPE JOHN PAUL II POLISH CENTER
3999 Rose Drive, Yorba Linda, CA 92886
Phone: (714) 966-8161
E-mail: polishcenter@sbcglobal.net
<www.polishcenter.org>

STATE ARCHIVES OF POLAND
ul. Rakowiecka 2D, 02-517 Warszawa, Poland
Phone: +48 22 565 46 00
Fax: +48 22 565 46 14
E-mail: ndap@archiwa.gov.pl
<www.archiwa.gov.pl>

U.S. CONSULAR AGENCY
Ulica Paderewskiego 8, 61-770 Poznan, Poland
Phone: +61 851 8516
Fax: +61 851 8966
E-mail: capoz@post.pl
<poland.usembassy.gov/service/poznan-consular-agency.html>

U.S. CONSULATE GENERAL
Ulica Stolarska 9, 31-043 Krakow, Poland
Phone: +61 12 424 51 38
Fax: +61 12 424 51 45
E-mail: krakowairc@state.gov

US EMBASSY

Aleje Ujazdowskie 29/31, 00-540 Warsaw, Poland
Phone: +61 48 22 504-2000
E-mail: airc_warsaw@state.gov
<poland.usembassy.gov>

BOOKS

Essentials in Polish Genealogical Research by Daniel M. Schlyter (Polish Genealogical Society of America)

First Names of the Polish Commonwealth: Origins and Meanings by William F. Hoffman, and George W. Helon (Polish Genealogical Society of America)

Going Home : A Guide to Polish-American Family History Research by Jonathan D. Shea (Language & Lineage Press)

A Guide to Chicago and Midwestern Polish-American Genealogy by Jason Kruski (Clearfield)

Index to the Newsletters, Journals, and Bulletins of the Polish Genealogical Society of America, 1979–1996 by Rosemary A. Chorzempa, George W. Helon and William F. Hoffman (Polish Genealogical Society of America)

Poland, 1799 Map (Jonathan Sheppard Books)

Polish and Proud: Tracing Your Polish Ancestry by Janneyne L. Gnacinski and Leonard T. Gnacinski (Janlen Enterprises)

Polish Customs, Traditions and Folklore by Sophie Hodorowicz Knab (Hippocrene Books)

Polish Family Research, revised edition, by J. Konrad (Summit Publications)

Polish Genealogy and Heraldry: An Introduction to Research by Janina W. Hoskins (Hippocrene Books)

Polish Parish Records of the Roman Catholic Church: Their Use and Understanding in Genealogical Research, 3rd revised edition, by Gerald A. Ortell (Genun Publishers)

Polish Roots (Korzenie Polskie) by Rosemary A. Chorzempa (Genealogical Publishing Co.)

Polish Surnames: Origins and Meanings by William F. Hoffman (Polish Genealogical Society of America)

The Polish Way: A Thousand-Year History of the Poles and Their Culture by Adam Zamoyski (Hippocrene Books)

Roman Catholic Parishes in the Polish People's Republic in 1984 by Lidia Mullerowa (Polish Genealogical Society of America)

Russian Language Documents from Russian Poland: A Translation Manual for Genealogists by Jonathan D. Shea (Genealogy Unlimited)

Sto Lat: A Modern Guide to Polish Genealogy by Cecile Wendt Jensen (Michigan Polonia)

Tracing Your Polish Roots by Maralyn A. Wellauer (Maralyn A. Wellauer)

Translation Guide to 19th-Century Polish-Language Civil-Registration Documents (Birth, Marriage and Death Records) by Judith R. Frazin (Jewish Genealogical Society of Illinois)

PERIODICALS

Bulletin of the Polish Genealogical Society of America (1994-)

Dziennik Zwiazkowy, 1908-1917 (still published in Chicago as *Polish Daily News* <ecollections.crl.edu/cdm4/index_dz.php?CISOROOT=/dz>)

Polish Eaglet (Polish Genealogical Society of Michigan, 1981–)

Polish Genealogical Society Newsletter (Polish Genealogical Society, 1979–1992)

Rodziny (Polish Genealogical Society, 1993-)

WEBSITES

Bremen Passenger Lists
<www.passengerlists.de>

Cyndi's List: Poland
<www.cyndislist.com/poland>

East European Genealogical Society
<www.eegsociety.org>

Galizien German Descendants
<www.galiziengermandescendants.org>

Geographical dictionary of Polish Kingdom and other Slavic countries
<dir.icm.edu.pl/pl/Slownik_geograficzny>

Gesher Galicia
<www.geshergalicia.org>

HalGal
<www.halgal.com>

Index of Polish Parish Records
<brightonlibrary.info/php/polishindex>

JewishGen
<jewishgen.org>

Kashubian Association of North America
<www.ka-na.org>

Michigan Polonia
<www.mipolonia.net>

PolandGenWeb
<rootsweb.ancestry.com/~polwgw>

Poland.net
<www.poland.net>

Polish American Congress
<www.pac1944.org>
The Polish Genealogy Project
<www.polishgeno.com>

Polish Genealogy Society of America
<www.pgsa.org>

Polish Genealogy Society of New York State
<www.pgsnys.org>

Polish government online
<poland.pl>

PolishMigration.org
<www.polishmigration.org>

The Polish Mission
<www.polishmission.com>

PolishOrigins
<polishorigins.com>

PolishRoots
<www.polishroots.com>

Polish World
<www.polishworld.com>

PolTran
<www.poltran.com>

Poznań Marriage Indexing Project
<poznan-project.psnc.pl/project.php>

Type Polish Characters

CHAPTER NINE

EASTERN EUROPE

By Lisa A. Alzo and James M. Beidler

astern Europe may seem like a disparate cluster of countries, each with
an indecipherable language, complex history and individual record
customs. But many genealogical techniques translate to every country:
Learning the history and starting at home are essential no matter your ancestral homeland. Passenger and emigration records are invaluable, along with
church records both here and abroad. Eventually you'll need to write abroad
for records and perhaps enlist the help of a local expert. Our country-specific
guides get you started.

CZECH REPUBLIC AND SLOVAKIA

Nearly 3.5 million Americans claim Czech or Slovak ancestry—and if you
count yourself among them, you're undoubtedly eager to celebrate the polka
and *pirohi* in your past. But with your homeland's well-known historical and
political complexities, how do you start finding your family tree? Make our tips
a central part of your research strategy.

The modern Czech and Slovak republics formed only recently: Before their
amicable "Velvet Divorce" in 1993, these neighboring states existed as a single
country, Czechoslovakia. But don't let that 75-year union fool you into lumping
Czechs and Slovaks into one all-encompassing nationality: Though both groups
have Slavic origins and similar languages, historical circumstances led them to

develop distinct cultural identities. Today's Slovak Republic corresponds to the centuries-old region of Slovakia, while the Czech Republic has its roots in the ancient kingdoms of Bohemia and Moravia. Those three areas were united as Great Moravia in the ninth century, but they evolved into separate regions after that empire collapsed. (Bohemia and Moravia were known collectively as the Czech lands.)

The republics' location in the geographical center of Europe—bordered by present-day Germany to the west, Poland to the north, Ukraine and Romania to the east, and Austria and Hungary to the south—put them at the crossroads of expanding empires.

It would take volumes to detail these nations' long, complicated pasts. But every family historian should know some key events in the region's history. The Hapsburg Empire (later renamed the Austrian empire) began ruling the Czech lands in 1526. Following a long period of unrest, Austria formed a dual monarchy with Hungary in 1867; Bohemia and Moravia became Austrian provinces, and Slovakia remained under Hungarian control.

The treaties ending World War I dissolved the Austro-Hungarian Empire and joined Bohemia, Moravia and Slovakia (along with parts of the Polish province Silesia) into Czechoslovakia in 1918. Independence was short-lived: Just two decades later, Nazi Germany annexed much of Bohemia and Moravia, and Slovakia—though officially "independent"—became a German puppet state. After World War II, a restored Czechoslovakia (minus the eastern region called Subcarpathian Rus') fell within the Soviet sphere of influence until the "Velvet Revolution" ended communist rule in 1989.

Tracing Immigrants

Your quest to trace your roots to the old country begins with identifying and documenting the immigrant generation. The majority of Czech and Slovak immigrants arrived before the 20th-century political upheavals. That includes approximately 400,000 Czechs and some 620,000 Slovaks who flocked to America's shores between 1850 and 1914—some sought better economic and social conditions; others wanted to avoid political persecution or conscription into the Austrian army.

Pre-Civil War Czech immigrants were farmers who settled in Iowa, Illinois, Texas, Wisconsin, Nebraska and the Dakotas; those who arrived after the Civil War opted for larger industrial or mining areas. Slovak immigrants began arriving en masse in the 1880s and sought employment in American factories, mines and mills in cities such as Chicago, Cleveland and Pittsburgh.

Not all Czech and Slovak immigrants intended to settle in the United States permanently—some planned to stay only until they could earn enough money to purchase land back home. These "birds of passage" sometimes returned several times before settling in America for good. So be sure to look for immigrant ancestors on multiple passenger arrival and departure lists.

You'll find passenger lists online, too. Some US-bound Czechs and Slovaks came through Canada, so if you can't find evidence of your ancestors arriving through a US port, check border-crossing records. The United States began keeping them in 1895; you can view them on microfilm at NARA, its regional facilities, the FHL and FHCs. You'll find background on Canadian census, immigration and vital records on the Library and Archives of Canada website **<www.collectionscanada.ca/index-e.html>**.

Czechs and Slovaks embarked primarily from three European ports: Bremen and Hamburg, Germany, and Antwerp, Belgium. The Hamburg State Archives has preserved that port's passenger lists, which include the "direct" records of those sailing straight to America and the "indirect" lists of people who changed ships en route. Search both so you don't overlook your ancestor. Hamburg's archives has posted lists from 1890 to 1905 on Ancestry.de **<search.ancestry.de>**. The FHL has the complete set of records on microfilm.

Unfortunately, few of Bremen's and Antwerp's passenger lists have survived. Thanks to an ongoing reconstruction effort, you can view Bremen's 1920 to 1939 records online at **<www.passengerlists.de>**. For Antwerp, only the 1855 lists are fully intact; incomplete, unindexed lists also exist for 1920 to 1940. See the Belgium Roots Project **<belgium.rootsweb.ancestry.com/migr/emig/antwerp>** for more information.

Researching Names and Places

To successfully trace your Czech or Slovak ancestors in Europe, you'll need two key clues: the immigrant's original name and hometown. Prepare yourself for a challenge—the changing town and county names, confusing

TIME LINE

1350	Prague is capital of Holy Roman Empire.
1389	Turks defeat Serbs at Kosovo.
1402	Czech Protestant reformer Jan Hus begins preaching in Prague.
1456	Hungary defeats Ottomans at Belgrade.
1526	Hungary is defeated at Battle of Mohács; lands divided between Turks and Hapsburg Empire.
1563	Council of Trent orders churches to keep vital records.
1584	Hapsburg Empire adopts Gregorian calendar.
1671	Hungary becomes province of Austria.
1701	Europe's first philharmonic society established in Ljubljana, Slovenia.
1754	First census of Hapsburg territories.
1848	Serfdom abolished in Austria-Hungary following Hungarian rebellion.
1867	Dual monarchy of Austria-Hungary begins.
1878	Romania achieves independence.
1880–1920	Eastern Europe immigration to the United States peaks.
1908	Bulgaria gains independence.
1918	Czechoslovakia forms.
1931	Hungarian-American Bela Lugosi stars in Dracula.
1955	Warsaw Pact forms.
1989	Communist governments collapse.
1991	Yugoslavia breaks up.
1993	Czech and Slovak republics split.

geographical borders, exotic-sounding surnames and unfamiliar languages can frustrate even the most experienced researcher.

ANCESTORS' NAMES: The surrounding countries of Germany, Hungary and Poland strongly influenced Czech and Slovak names. Surname spellings often vary in grammatical context—for example, male Czech surnames may end in *-úv*, or *-ovec*. You may encounter patronymic surnames (ones derived from the father's name, such as *Janaček*, meaning "little John," or *Štepanek*, meaning "little Stephen"), as well as surnames that reflect social status or personal features, trade or occupation. Female surnames typically have the suffix *-ova* at the end.

Note first-name practices, too. Orthodox and Catholic families frequently named their children for saints. You'll need to recognize regional and cultural translations: Great-great-grandma might appear as Elizabeth on her naturalization application, *Alžbeta* in Slovak parish registers and *Erzsébet* in Hungarian census returns. For help sorting out your family's monikers, download William F. Hoffman's article "Mutilation: The Fate of Eastern European Names in America" from **<www.pgsa.org/PDFs/Mutilation.pdf>**.

TOWN NAMES: Identifying ancestral cities or villages isn't as easy as looking up a place name on a modern map—it's often a complicated process. So take it one step at a time, starting with some US sources that might name your family's village.

Once you've found the name of your ancestral town or village, you'll need to determine both its pre- and post-WWI locations using maps, atlases and gazetteers—because of the postwar political changes, some towns and villages were renamed or referred to in different languages. The FHL has an extensive collection of maps and gazetteers. Note that the library catalogs its Czech and Slovak materials based on spellings in the 1929 gazetteer *Místopisný Slovník Československé Republiky*.

You'll find helpful maps online, as well: In particular, see the Federation of Eastern European Family History Societies' Map Room **<www.feefhs.org/maplibrary.html>** and Osztrák-Magyar Monarchia (1910) **<lazarus.elte.hu/hun/maps/1910/1910ind.htm>**. JewishGen's Communities Databases and Gazetteer **<www.jewishgen.org/Communities>** can help you locate Eastern European towns, too, whether or not you have Jewish roots.

Finding and Using Records

If you're sleuthing for Slovak ancestors, you'll discover the FHL has microfilmed church registers, censuses and other records for hundreds of Slovak localities. That means you can tap many sources stateside. Czech roots seekers aren't so lucky: The library has far fewer Czech records, primarily because the FHL hasn't reached microfilming agreements with the Czech government. Of course, historical records of Czechs and Slovaks extend well beyond the FHL's holdings, and we'll outline other ways to get them in the next section. But first, let's take a look at those countries' record-keeping practices, so you know what's available.

VITAL RECORDS: Called *matriky* in Czech and Slovak, vital records—especially churches' parish registers—are the most complete and reliable source for family tree details. Most parishes didn't keep records until the 1600s (although some Bohemian and Moravian records date back to the late 1500s). After 1624, Austria prohibited Protestantism throughout its empire, including the Czech lands, so all vital events until 1849 were recorded in Catholic registers. Protestants who refused the Catholic authority weren't recorded. But a compromise in Hungary allowed certain Protestants to practice their religions. The Hungarian government (which ruled Slovakia) recognized four denominations in 1645: Calvinism, Catholicism, Lutheranism and Unitarianism. Greek Catholic parishes started keeping records in the mid-18th century. Until 1868, records of Jews may also be found in Catholic books. In general, check your ancestors' parish—but be aware that some villages' church records were kept in different parishes or larger, nearby towns.

Civil registration in Czech lands began in 1869; in Slovakia, it initiated in 1895. After World War I, the new Czechoslovak state adopted its own vital-record-keeping policies. In 1952, the government began gathering all registers more than 100 years old into state regional archives (*statni oblastni archivy*). More recent records (and a few older ones) remain in local records offices.

CENSUS: The Austrian government first enumerated Czechs by name in 1651, then again in 1754 and 1770. Earlier censuses (*sčitánílidu*) were merely head counts taken for taxation. The most genealogically useful enumerations for Slovak researchers are Hungary's 1869 census and 1848 census of Jews. You can get the Hungarian records on microfilm from the FHL.

MILITARY RECORDS: In 1868, Austria instituted universal conscription, requiring every male citizen to serve three years of active duty in the military (modified to a two-year term in 1912). The system remained until the empire's dissolution. Muster rolls and qualification lists, taken from the 1700s through 1915 (mostly by Austria), often contain the names of the enlistee's hometown and parents, as well as his religion. The FHL has them on microfilm. The catch: You have to know which regiment your ancestor belonged to in order to use them.

Besides these key record groups, the FHL has a few volumes of unindexed Austrian tax lists (*berní ruly*) written in Czech, and some nobility documents for the kingdom of Hungary. Your ancestors' names also might appear in town histories or "chronicles"—check with the town historian and county or regional archives.

Although the Czech and Slovak archival systems rank among the world's best, genealogists have to cope with access limitations. You can write to the Slovak Administration of Archives of the Ministry of Interior to request pre-1900 records; for later vital records, contact the Slovak embassy. To the dismay of Czech roots seekers—who have relied heavily on letter-writing in the absence of microfilms—recent developments suggest that the Czech government no longer accepts records requests by mail. Consult the Czech embassy in Washington, DC (listed in the Resources), to gain an understanding of the policy changes.

HUNGARY

By the time Eastern European immigrants were flocking to America (1880s to 1920s), Austria-Hungary had swallowed up the center of the Continent—including areas of present-day Croatia, Romania, Serbia, Slovakia and Ukraine in Hungary's domain.

As a result, the 1.4 million Americans who claim Magyar ancestry share their Hungarian roots with people whose ancestors came from all over Eastern Europe. They also share a number of genealogical challenges: confusing geography, unfamiliar languages, and surname and place name changes. If you're hoping to trace your family tree in Hungary, this might sound like a recipe for disaster. But don't let the challenges discourage you.

Getting Started

The Magyars originated in Asia and settled in what's now Hungary—along the Danube River in the Carpathian Basin—in 896. For the next 100 years, the Magyars raided the kingdoms of Europe until they eventually met their match in the Germans. Over the next few centuries, Hungary found itself on the other end of invasions—by the Mongols in 1241 and later the Turks, whose victory at the 1526 Battle of Mohács paved the way for Hungary's royal union with the Hapsburgs of Austria.

In 1867, Austria and Hungary established a dual monarchy, giving birth to Austria-Hungary. Austria controlled Bohemia and Moravia (the modern Czech Republic), Silesia (in what's now Poland) and Galicia (divided between Poland and Ukraine), Bukovina (Romania), Carniola (Slovenia), Dalmatia (Croatia), Lower and Upper Austria, Salzburg, Tyrol, Carinthia, Austrian Littoral and Styria.

In addition to its modern-day territory, Hungary ruled Slovakia, Transylvania and Banat (in what's now in Romania), Subcarpathian Rus´ (now in Ukraine) and the rest of Croatia, including Slavonia. Bosnia was jointly administered from 1878 to 1908. The end of World War I spelled the end for Austria-Hungary—the peace treaties created Czechoslovakia and Yugoslavia; Hungary also lost territory to Romania, Poland and Ukraine.

GET GEOGRAPHICAL AIDS. Modern maps might not show Great-grandpa's village. To get an accurate picture of the region during his time, turn to historical atlases such as *The Palgrave Concise Historical Atlas of Eastern Europe* by Dennis P. Hupchick and Harold E. Cox (Palgrave Macmillan) and *Historical Atlas of Central Europe* by Paul Robert Magocsi (University of Washington Press). Be sure to bookmark the Eötvös University cartography department's online maps **<lazarus.elte.hu/hun/maps/1910>**. You can buy historical maps from Genealogy-Unlimited **<www.genealogyunlimited.com>**.

You'll also need gazetteers to research your ancestral village. We recommend the 1877 *Magyarország Helységnévtára Tekintettel a Közigazgatási Népességi és Hitfelekezeti Viszonyokra* by Janos Dvorzsák. Volume 1 indexes all Hungarian communities, with cross-references for variant names. Volume 2 gives each town's county and district, along with religious statistics (number of residents who practiced each faith and churches they attended). You can rent microfilm of this gazetteer from the Family History Library (FHL) **<familysearch.org>**.

Check libraries for two helpful resources from Talma Publishers: *Atlas and Gazetteer of Historic Hungary 1914* and *Dictionary of Hungarian Place-Names* by György Lelkes. The Hungarian Village Finder, Atlas, and Gazetteer for the Kingdom of Hungary CD (available from **<www.hungarianvillagefinder.com>**), JewishGen's Gazetteer **<www.jewishgen.org/communities/loctown.asp>** and Radix's Hungarian place locator **<www.bogardi.com/gen/g056.htm>** also can help you pinpoint your family's origins.

TRY TRANSLATION TOOLS. Once you take your research back to the old country, you'll encounter records in Hungarian, which differs from other European languages because of the Magyars' Asian origins. With Hungary's dominion once spanning so many ethnic groups, expect to run into other languages, too—including Latin, Slovak and German, among others. You don't have to be fluent to decipher most genealogical records, but a working knowledge of key terms and phrases will help. Start with the FHL's genealogical word lists (download Hungarian, German and Latin from **<www.familysearch.org/learn/wiki/en/Category:Word_List>**); use the free online Hungarian-English dictionary at **<www.freedict.com/onldict/hun.html>** for quick lookups.

Seeking Sources

The more genealogical clues you have to go on, the better off you'll be when you venture into unfamiliar Hungarian sources. Focus your initial research on gleaning every scrap of ancestral information from American records, including censuses, passenger lists, naturalizations and vital records. Obituaries often reveal immigration details, too—especially those in ethnic newspapers. The University of Minnesota's Immigration History Research Center (IHRC) **<www.ihrc.umn.edu>** houses a large Hungarian-American newspaper collection.

Tracing your family in Hungary relies on two key ingredients—the immigrant's name and the ancestral town or village. Some tips for researching them follow.

NAMES: An immigrant's name is often your first stumbling block when you begin searching for records, especially online. Surnames that seem unusual to you—Balog, Horváth, Kovács, Nagy—find more at **<www.bogardi.com/gen/g023.htm>**—might be as common in Hungary as Smiths and Johnsons are here, making surname searches of databases and indexes impractical.

To use Hungarian records, you need to know your ancestors' original name in the old country—which might have changed multiple times after their arrival in America. Ask your living relatives for all possible spellings. Two more naming traditions you should be aware of: Hungarians commonly put their family names before their given names, the reverse of most Western cultures. And women often won't appear by their own name, but by adding the suffix *-né* to their husbands'—for example, Great-grandma might show up as Kovács Mátyásné (equivalent to Mrs. Mátyás Kovács, or Matthew's wife) instead of Erzébet.

PLACES: If you don't know your ancestral town or village, building your family tree will be next to impossible. That's because Hungarian records are stored and organized geographically—by county (*megye*), district (*járás*) and locality (*község*). Over time, county and district borders moved, and names changed. Of course, you'll also encounter misspellings and transcription errors in US sources, so it's important to determine the correct names. Before 1918, many Hungarian records listed both a village and county name—for instance, Pósa, Zemplén. Try not to confuse the two: Pósa is the village; Zemplén is the former county. Use your gazetteers to sort out those jurisdictional distinctions.

Using Church Records

Now you're ready to move on to the main course: Hungarian church records (*egyházi anyakönyv*). Although Roman Catholicism predominated throughout Hungarian history, Orthodoxy, Greek Catholicism, Protestantism (Lutheran, Reformed, Mennonite and Baptist), Judaism and even Islam also were practiced there. Prior to the October 1895 start of civil registration, religious authorities recorded all vital events. From 1781 on, each denomination maintained its own set of records.

Before 1781, however, the Roman Catholic Church kept official tabs on everyone—meaning your 18th-century ancestors will show up in Catholic records regardless of their faith. Record-keeping began when the Council of Trent (1545 to 1563) required parishes to maintain baptism and marriage registers; a directive to record burials followed in 1614. Unfortunately, most of the earliest registers haven't survived, but coverage typically goes back at least through the 1700s.

The national archives in Budapest houses all ecclesiastical registers for modern Hungary (see **<www.natarch.hu/english/menu_31.htm>**). But you don't necessarily have to travel there or hire a local researcher: The FHL has microfilmed many Hungarian church records up to 1895—including ones for places now in other countries.

You can use gazetteers to identify the assigned religious jurisdiction for your ancestors' town in the period you're researching. If you can't find your family in that parish's records, try broadening your search. Perhaps your ancestors' town didn't have a church or synagogue for their faith, so they went to a neighboring parish. Also be aware that religious affiliation may not be static from generation to generation. If your family disappears from the church records, check other denominations.

What will the records tell you? Baptisms (*keresztelő*) include the child's name, date (cluing you in to an approximate birth date), parents' and witnesses' names, and town of residence. Some Greek Catholic registers list the grandparents. Marriages (*házasság*) typically give the date; the bride's and groom's names, residence, prior marital status and sometimes their ages; and the names of witnesses and possibly the parents. Burials (*temetés*) aren't as detailed, but they'll provide the decedents' names, ages, last residences and perhaps marital status. For children who died, the records usually list the fathers. In general, records became more thorough—and easier to read and interpret—over time.

Tapping Government Records

Of course, you won't want to limit your research to parish registers—you'll need other sources to fill in gaps, expand your search and create a fuller picture of your family. Sample these next:

CENSUSES: The Austro-Hungarian Empire periodically enumerated its residents for taxation, conscription and statistical purposes. The four most genealogically useful censuses (*népszámlálások*) are from the 19th century: The 1828 land and property census, recorded in Latin, provides conscription information and property owners' names. An 1848 census of Hungary's Jews gives all household members' names, ages and birthplaces. The 1857 census—in German and Hungarian or German only, depending on which form the enumerator used—gives all household members' names and their relationships to the head of household, plus birth dates, religion, house numbers and sometimes place of origin. Likewise, the 1869 enumeration (in Hungarian) names all villagers, with details on their residences, ages, religions and relationships to the head of household.

The FHL has microfilmed many of these censuses. For others, try writing to the Hungarian national archives. Get guidance at **<www.progenealogists.com/hungary/census-fhl.htm>**.

MILITARY RECORDS: Because Hungary required service, your male ancestors will likely show up in military records. Muster rolls (*katonai nyilvántartási jegyzék*) list each soldier's name, birth date, residence at the time of enlistment and parents' names. The FHL has microfilm of unindexed muster rolls for about 150 current Hungarian military districts—they're listed along with years covered at **<www.progenealogists.com/hungary/military.htm>**. Unless you know what unit your ancestor belonged to, be prepared to search the records unit by unit.

During the dual monarchy, Austria and Hungary had one unified army. You're most likely to find pre-1867 records for conscripts and officers at the Austrian State Archives' war records division **<www.oesta.gv.at>**. After 1867, Hungary began storing military records for its own districts. These documents are organized by regiment. To learn more, download "An Introduction to Austrian Military Records" from **<feefhs.org/journal/10/austrian.pdf>**.

CIVIL REGISTRATIONS: Hungary's privacy laws restrict access to birth registers for 90 years, marriage registers for 60 years and death registers for 30 years. So you'll have just a few decades of civil vital records to work with after their 1895 start. The FHL has microfilmed many of the publicly available civil registrations (*állami anyakönyv*); they're cataloged at the town level.

When it comes to your Hungarian research, you can never have too many cooks in the kitchen. After you've exhausted these sources—or if you get stuck along the way—consider hiring a professional genealogist who knows the language and is familiar with the archive system.

CROATIA

The Croats were first identified as a distinct Slavic group in the 7th century, when they moved following the shape of a crescent—first to the area between the Danube, Drava and Sava rivers (called Slavonia); then westward to the Gulf of Venice (Istria); and finally southward along the Adriatic coast (known as Dalmatia since Roman times). After rule by Frankish kings including Charlemagne, the Kingdom of Croatia was created in 925 when Duke Tomislav united the dukedoms. The Venetian Republic and its successor states, though, for many years held some areas ethnic Croats inhabited along the Adriatic coastline.

Croatia—*Hrvatska* in the local tongue—was called a kingdom until the end of World War I in 1918, but it was independent only until 1102. For the next 400 years, Croatia was in personal union with Hungary—though some scholars claim Hungary occupied Croatia. Then, after the Ottoman Turks surged into to the area, resulting in the death of the Croatian and Hungarian King Louis II in the 1526 Battle of Mohács, Hungarian and Croatian nobles elected a member of the Austrian Hapsburg family as their king.

The Croats became part of the multiethnic Hapsburg Empire, and even after the European powers began to drive back the Ottoman Turks in the 1600s, Croatia remained an area of border fortresses under Austrian military control. After the 1848 Hungarian revolution, Croatia spent 17 years subject to "Germanization" while under Austrian supervision, before moving to the Hungarian half of the Austro-Hungarian dual monarchy.

In the 20th century, the Croats became part of the Slav-dominated Yugoslavian conglomeration that resulted from the World Wars. In 1991, Croatia declared independence from Yugoslavia, standing alone as a nation for the first time in nearly 900 years. Wars with Serbia—primarily regarding the status of Bosnia, which lies between the two countries—followed in the 1990s.

Getting Started

Although the attic's still the first place to explore for Croatian ancestors, you may be confused over ethnic identities. Genealogy expert Adam S. Eterovich notes that records of a Croatian family in America might not yield useful information, especially regarding the crucial spelling of surnames. "In many cases, individuals tracing their Croatian roots do not know the correct spelling of the name and location of village, town or city in Croatia," Eterovich says, let alone the name and address of the church, city hall or archive. "I recommend researching Croatian benevolent societies, clubs, churches and cemeteries in America."

Not only will such organizations likely afford you the opportunity to break through Croatian brick walls, they also will give you windows to your ancestors' traditional culture and social life. The Croatian Immigrant History Project **<www.croatia-in-english.com/cihp>** is collecting old photos and short biographies of Croatians who emigrated before 1920, though its database has mostly southern Croatians from the Dubrovnik area who ended up in California.

Language can be a barrier—and not only the native Croatian tongue. Some areas, such as northern Dalmatia, might have parish records in Italian, Latin, Croatian and Hungarian during various eras, in addition to a Croatian dialect script called Glagolitic (see an article on Glagolitic script at **<www.feefhs.org/journal/12/mcdaniel.pdf>**). Because Croatia is home to a Serbian minority, its version of Serbo-Croatian written with a Cyrillic alphabet also can come into play.

For language help, use FamilySearch resources including a letter-writing guide and glossary of key words in Serbo-Croatian **<wiki.familysearch.org/en/croatia>**. They're essential if you plan to write to Croatia—the number of English speakers is few, so record requests are unlikely to be answered unless you write in Croatian. Croatia GenWeb **<rootsweb.ancestry.com/~hrvwgw>** can assist new researchers with language dilemmas.

The online Croatian Genealogy Newsletter, archived at **<www.durham.net/facts/crogen/newsltr-archival.html>**, is a terrific spot for finding new resources. Quite a number of these are in Croatian, which means you'll probably need language assistance from folks on the GenWeb site, the Croatian-English dictionary **<www.rjecnik.com>** and Google translation tools **<google.com/language_tools>**.

Finding and Using Records

Today, almost 4 million Croatians live in Croatia, but an estimated 4.5 million have spread throughout the rest of the world. Some left their homeland as early as the Ottoman conquests in the 1500s, but most of the emigrants are more recent. Ethnic Croats dug into the 1849 California Gold Rush, but it wasn't until the late 1800s and early 1900s that larger numbers of Croats migrated overseas, primarily for economic reasons. Their destinations included the United States (particularly industrial areas stretching from Pittsburgh to the Midwest) and Canada, as well as South America, Australia and New Zealand. Once you're ready to trace your ancestors in Croatia, look for the following records.

CHURCH RECORDS: For many villages in Croatia, the best records will be those of the churches. In most cases, Croatians historically have been Roman Catholic, Orthodox and Greek Catholic. The Family History Library (FHL) **<familysearch.org>** has microfilms of the parish registers from all these faiths. Search the library's online catalog for the village name; you can rent film through your local Family History Center **<library.familysearch.org>.**

In general, church registers include baptisms, marriages and deaths. Some begin as early as the 1460s and usually run through World War II. Most begin before the late 1600s, offering the opportunity to document quite a few generations. In addition to vital records, you can sometimes find confirmations and communion records, as well as a book called *Knjiga Duša* (A Book of Souls), a genealogical record of any one generation that lists the man and woman upon marriage and each child as he or she was born, with comments about death and emigration. The FHL collection includes only church records deposited with the Croatian State Archives. If a village church's records hadn't made their way to the archives, you'll need to write to the parish priest of that particular church to request the documents you are seeking. Look for directories of churches through the FHL. You can also write to regional archives for help. JewishGen has a primer online at **<www.jewishgen.org/infofiles/croatia.htm>**.

CIVIL REGISTRATION: Government tracking of births, marriages and deaths began only in 1946, after World War II heralded the reformation of Yugoslavia, of which Croatia was a republic. Local civil registry offices in city halls hold these records (look for small towns' registries in the next larger town). Write to request these records. For contact info, try the directory of Catholic parishes at **<www.croatian-genealogy.com/cro-parishes>**.

MILITARY RECORDS: Many Croatians, including those in Slavonia, are listed in the many rolls of military records from the Military Archives (known by its German name *Kriegsarchiv*) in Vienna, Austria. Since Croatia spent much of the 1600s and early 1700s as part of the border, the military had a large role in its affairs in this era. The records are on FHL microfilm and end in 1869. Originals of the records relating to Croatia are in the Croatian State Archive. These records are in German, the language of the Austrian Empire.

CENSUSES: Some censuses, compiled beginning in 1785 for taxation purposes and others to facilitate conscription, exist in municipal and district archives (find addresses online at **<wiki.familysearch.org/en/Croatia_Archives_and_Libraries>**).

The FHL has two rolls of census microfilms. A civil census was conducted during 1804-1805, and regular censuses were conducted in 1857, 1869 and every ten years between 1880 and 1910.

ROMANIA AND BULGARIA

Tracing ancestors back to Bulgaria or Romania is similar to researching kin from other East European countries. Your first objective is to identify the immigrant's original name and—even more important—the name of the family's home village. These two details will serve as the foundation for all further research.

Dig for clues to names and the village in old family documents (look for letters and envelopes, naturalization certificates, photographs, obituaries and so forth). Then search every possible record you can find of your family on this side of the ocean—including but not limited to vital and census records, church documents, burial and cemetery records, naturalization petitions, school records and fraternal organization records.

Once you've determined a place or origin, you'll also need to know what jurisdiction the village is in now, as well as historically. For this task, maps, atlases and gazetteers—geographical dictionaries that list all localities and often key identifiers such as churches)—will be your key excavation tools. Start with the Federation of East European Family History Societies' online Map Library **<www.feefhs.org/maplibrary.html>** and the *A Monarchia III. Katonai Felmérése* (3rd Military Mapping Survey of Austria-Hungary) **<lazarus.elte.hu/hun/digkonyv/topo/3felmeres.htm>**.

Romanian Research Tips

Romania has long been a land of ethnic diversity. Romanians are the primary ethnic group, but the area also has been home to Hungarians, Ukrainians, Germans, Serbs, Roma (Gypsies), Jews and others over a history stretching back to the year 106, when the Roman Empire under Trajan expanded into what's now Romania. In fact, the name Romania (Latin: *Romanus*) means "citizen of the Roman Empire."

IMMIGRATION: A small group of Romanians immigrated to California during the 1849 gold rush, but lack of success drove them to Mexico. The first major influx of Romanians to the United States took place between 1895 and 1920, when 145,000 émigrés from Wallachia, Moldavia and other areas arrived. The threat of Nazi occupation of Romania during World War II spurred another surge of immigrants to the United States.

KEY HISTORY: The map of Romania has changed considerably over its long history. The original Romanian principalities of Moldavia and Wallachia make up most of the eastern half of modern Romania. To the west, Transylvania and part of the Banat were formerly in the old kingdom of Hungary. The eastern coastal area of Dobruja belonged to Bulgaria under Turkish rule until 1878.

Romania became a kingdom in 1881. Following the breakup of the Austro-Hungarian Empire in 1918, Romania expanded to include Transylvania, Bukovina, part of Banat and the Russian province of Bessarabia. In 1945, it ceded the Bessarabian portion of Moldavia and part of Bukovina to the Soviet Union. (See the resources section to learn more about Romanian history and culture).

GEOGRAPHICAL AIDS: What does this patchwork of peoples and political changes mean for your research? Pinpointing the correct spelling of your ancestral village name and its jurisdiction becomes more challenging. You may have multiple languages to deal with: For example, the Transylvanian city of Braşov is known as Brassó in Hungarian and Kronstadt in German.

Maps can be helpful, but gazetteers are better because of the further identifying detail they provide. A useful gazetteer of modern Romania is the 1974 *Index of Localities of Romania*, or *Indicatorul Localitatilor din Romania* (*Editura Academiei Republicii Socialiste Romania*), on FamilySearch microfilm 1181561 (item 1). For places in Transylvania formerly under Hungarian rule, try the 1877 *Gazetteer of Hungary*, or *Magyar Helsegnevtara*, by Janos Dvorzak (Havi Fuzetek), on FamilySearch microfilms 599564 (volume 1) and 973041 (volume 2). This gazetteer will help you determine the former Hungarian spelling, and the nearest parish or synagogue; learn how to use it at **<www.iabsi.com/gen/public/dvorzsak_gazetteer.htm>**.

Gazetteers exist for Transylvania, Banat and Bukovina, as well, so check the FamilySearch catalog **<familysearch.org/catalog-search>** for films you can rent for viewing at your local Family History Center (find one at **<familysearch.org/locations/centerlocator>**) or those you can get via interlibrary loan.

ADMINISTRATIVE DIVISIONS: Knowing the jurisdiction of the village is critical for anticipating the type of records available. Romanian, Hungarian and Austrian record-keeping traditions varied. For instance, civil registration began in the Kingdom of Romania in 1865, the Hungarian Empire in 1895 and in Austria only after World War II. But religious vital records and transcripts created for civil authorities exist for all places back to earlier periods.

Romania has 43 archive branches, one for each *judetul* (district), plus a central archive and municipal archive in Bucharest. For areas previously in Hungary, note that current boundaries of these districts often don't correspond to the historical boundaries.

CHURCH RECORDS: Because civil registration began relatively late, religious vital records—Roman Catholic, Calvinist/Reform, Lutheran and Jewish—will figure prominently into your research. Each denomination maintained its own set of records. In most cases, the religious authorities kept their own records after 1895 but were no longer required to do so by the civil authorities. Hungarian church records from the 1700s and 1800s—available on FamilySearch microfilm—cover parts of present-day Romania.

CIVIL REGISTRATION: By law, government vital records are kept in local civil records offices and parish offices for seventy-five years, then transferred to the state archives in Bucharest or the district capital. Romanian civil registrations are restricted because they're considered identity documents, so your best chance is to acquire the religious copy if you can.

CENSUSES: The Austro-Hungarian Empire conducted censuses in Transylvania, Banat and Bukovina in 1785, 1805, 1828, 1857, 1869, 1880, 1890, 1900 and 1910. Romania took censuses in 1912, 1930, 1941, 1956 and 1966. Except for FamilySearch microfilm of a few early Austro-Hungarian census returns for parts of Transylvania, these records are accessible only at the national archives of Romania and Hungary. A 1942 Jewish census covering Moldova and Ukraine is available on JewishGen **<www.jewishgen.org>** and Ancestry.com.

FamilySearch hasn't microfilmed records from the Romanian national archives, except for records of the ethnic German minority in Banat and Transylvania Saxon villages (which were filmed in Germany).

Although you might have luck doing research by correspondence in Romanian (use FamilySearch's letter-writing guide **<www.familysearch.org/learn/wiki/en/Romania_Letter_ Writing_Guide>** to compose your letters), you'll likely find that hiring a professional researcher is the most effective route for tapping into Romanian records. Find a list of on-site researchers at **<www.jewishgen.org/infofiles/researchers.htm>**.

Sometimes you may find records in unexpected places. For example, Ancestry.com has a limited number of databases unique to Romania **<search.ancestry.com/places/europe/romania>**. These are mostly resources from Bessarabia (now Moldova), some of which you can search for free. If your research expedition leads you into the neighboring countries of Macedonia and Turkey, get tips from the FamilySearch Wiki at **<www.familysearch.org/learn/wiki/en/Macedonia>** and **<www.familysearch.org/learn/wiki/en/Turkey>**.

Bulgarian Research Tips

Bulgaria ranks as the third-largest country in southeastern Europe, bordering Romania, Serbia, Macedonia, Greece, Turkey and the Black Sea. It's situated in the geographical territory today referred to as the Balkans, along with Greece, Albania, Macedonia, Romania, Yugoslavia (Serbia and Montenegro) and Bosnia Herzegovina.

The history of this entire area is complex, due to successive waves of invasions, partitions, sporadic anarchy and internal turmoil. Despite its turbulent history, Bulgaria is the oldest surviving European state to have kept its original name—since 681, when the Bulgars invaded the south Danube region. Bulgarians were the first people to use the Cyrillic alphabet after its inception in the ninth century. The recognition of the Bulgarian Patriarchate by the Patriarchate of Constantinople in 927 makes the Bulgarian Orthodox Church the oldest Slavic Orthodox Church in the world.

IMMIGRATION: Bulgarians first started immigrating to the United States in significant numbers between 1903 and 1910. Approximately 50,000 ethnic Bulgarians arrived from Turkish-occupied Macedonia and from Bulgaria proper. The 1924 National Origins Act limited the number of Bulgarians who could enter the United States to a mere 100 a year (the quota was lifted in 1965). During restricted years, some Bulgarians are believed to have entered with non-Bulgarian passports or found other routes in via Canada or Mexico. Bulgarians may have been recorded as Turks, Greeks, Serbs, Romanians, Russians or Yugoslavs in American records.

The Bulgarian and Macedonian Cultural Center in West Homestead, Pa. **<www.bmnecc. org>**, houses correspondence, legal documents, manuscripts, files and oral histories of immigrants who lived and worked in America since the late 1800s, as well as other Bulgarian and Macedonian ethnography (see **<www.librarything.com/profile.php?view=bmnecc>**).

KEY HISTORY: Keep in mind that Bulgaria was under the former Ottoman Empire from 1396 to 1878—it was the first state to join the Ottoman Empire and the last to be liberated (by the Russian army). Bulgaria became an autonomous principality under Ottoman control. Eastern Rumelia, the southeastern portion of Bulgaria, was added in 1885. Prince Ferdinand proclaimed Bulgaria's full independence in 1908 and assumed the title of czar. Bulgaria added more territory by 1913 during the Balkan wars. It aligned with Germany in both World Wars. Following decades under Soviet influence, Bulgaria became an independent country in 1990.

ADMINISTRATIVE DIVISIONS: Bulgaria is divided into 28 districts (provinces), each taking its name from its respective capital city. The provinces subdivide into 264 municipalities. See **<www.familysearch.org/learn/wiki/en/File:Bulgariadistricts.jpg>**.

In addition to the geographic aids mentioned earlier, the 1989 *Dictionary of Villages and Village names in Bulgaria, 1878–1987* (in Bulgarian, *Rechnik na Selishchata i Selishchnite Imena v Bulgariia, 1878–1987*) by N. Michev and P. Koledarov (*Nauka i Izkustvo*) is a helpful tool for identifying Bulgarian jurisdictions. This book is available at the Family History Library (FHL) in Salt Lake City, or you can possibly get it via interlibrary loan.

An official archive system formed during the communist era. Each district has an archive (find addresses at **<www.archives.government.bg/436-ARD>**; be sure to click English in the upper right corner), and the Central State Archives in Sofia serves as a national archive. Some Bulgarian records for the Ottoman era are in Turkey and Greece.

CIVIL REGISTRATIONS: Bulgaria instituted civil registration in 1893. The records are housed in district archives. FamilySearch has microfilmed civil registrations for the districts of Sofia and Plovdiv—these usually cover 1893 to 1912. To find them, do a place-names search of the FamilySearch catalog (type Bulgaria into the box and select a district and locality from the list) and look under the Civil Registration heading. You can then rent microfilm to view at your local Family History Center.

CHURCH RECORDS: Churches recorded vital events prior to the government. You'll find church vital registers mainly from the Bulgarian Orthodox and Roman Catholic religions; these typically date back to 1850 and as early as 1797 for some Catholic books.

Most church records are still located in the churches that created them. To get them, you must either write to the church, conduct research on-site or—usually most effective—hire a local professional to do the research for you. Find contacts at **<rootsweb.ancestry.com/~bgrwgw/ researchguide/contact.html>**.

CENSUSES: Bulgaria conducted its first national census in 1880, but the name lists for 19th-century censuses haven't all survived. Ottoman censuses of males—taken for taxation and military conscription—covering 1831 to 1872 are believed to be in the Ottoman Archives in Istanbul (see **<www.familysearch.org/learn/wiki/en/Macedonia_Beginning_Research>**).

Scarce information is available on other Bulgarian sources, including land, probate and military records. Because of Bulgaria's alliance with Germany in both World Wars, records for certain ethnic groups, such as Sephardic Jews, were hidden. You'll need to go to synagogues and Sephardic organizations to learn where to find those records.

Overcoming Language Barriers

The prospect of reading your ancestors' records can seem daunting. Bulgarian records were kept in Bulgarian—whose Cyrillic alphabet poses an added challenge—Turkish, Greek and Old Church Slavonic. Find help with some common Bulgarian genealogy words at **<rootsweb. ancestry.com/~bgrwgw/researchguide/quickresearchguide.html>**. Records from western Romania and Transylvania are usually in Hungarian and sometimes in German. Elsewhere, they might be in Romanian or even written in Cyrillic. Download a list of Romanian terms from **<net.lib.byu.edu/fslab/researchoutlines/Europe/Romania.pdf>**.

EASTERN EUROPE RESOURCES

ORGANIZATIONS AND ARCHIVES

EAST EUROPEAN GENEALOGICAL SOCIETY
Box 2536, Winnipeg, Manitoba, R3C 4A7
Canada
Phone: (204) 989-3292
E-mail: info@eegsociety.org
<www.eegsociety.org>

FEDERATION OF EAST EUROPEAN FAMILY HISTORY SOCIETIES
Box 321, Springville UT 84663
<feefhs.org>

IMMIGRATION HISTORY RESEARCH CENTER
University of Minnesota, College of Liberal Arts, 311 Andersen Library, 222 21st Ave. S, Minneapolis, MN 55455
Phone: (612) 625-4800
Fax: (612) 626-0018
E-mail: ihrc@umn.edu
<www.ihrc.umn.edu>

BOOKS

Following the Paper Trail: A Multilingual Translation Guide by Jonathan D. Shea and William F. Hoffman (Avotaynu)

Historical Atlas of East Central Europe by Paul Robert Magocsi with Geoffrey J. Matthews (University of Washington Press)

In Search of Your European Roots: A Complete Guide to Tracing Your Ancestors in Every Country in Europe by Angus Baxter (Genealogical Publishing Co.)

Overcoming Obstacles to Eastern European Research by Serah Fleury Allen (Closson Press)

Where Once We Walked: A Guide to the Jewish Communities Destroyed in the Holocaust by Gary Mokotoff and Sally Amdur Sack (Avotaynu)

Where Once We Walked Companion by Gary Mokotoff (Avotaynu)

WEBSITES
Cyndi's List: Eastern Europe
<www.cyndislist.com/eastern-europe>

EastEuropeGenWeb
<rootsweb.ancestry.com/~easeurgw>

E-Transcriptum
<www.e-transcriptum.net/eng>

JewishGen Shtetl Seeker
<www.jewishgen.org/ShtetlSeeker>

Repositories of Primary Sources: Europe
<www.uidaho.edu/special-collections/euro1.html>

BULGARIA RESOURCES

ORGANIZATIONS AND ARCHIVES

BULGARIAN CENTRAL STATE ARCHIVES (CENTRALEN DARZAVEN ARHIV)
5 Moskovska Str., 1000 Sofia, Bulgaria
Phone: +359 (2) 9400153
<www.archives.government.bg/6-CSA>

BULGARIAN MACEDONIAN EDUCATIONAL AND CULTURAL CENTER
449 W. Eighth Ave., Homestead, PA 15120
Phone: (412) 461-6188
<www.bmnecc.org>

EMBASSY OF THE REPUBLIC OF BULGARIA
1621 22nd St. NW, Washington, DC 20008,
Phone: (202) 387-0174
<www.bulgaria-embassy.org>

BOOKS

The Bulgarian Americans by Claudia Carlson (Chelsea House)

Peter Menikoff: The Story of a Bulgarian Boy in the Great American Melting Pot by Peter Dimitrov Yankoff (Cokesbury Press)

Under the Yoke by Ivan Vazov (Twayne Publishers)

WEBSITES

Bulgarian Alphabet
<rootsweb.ancestry.com/~bgrwgw/researchguide/tips.html>

Bulgarian Genealogy Forum
<genforum.genealogy.com/bulgaria>

Bulgarian Genealogy Links
<www.genealogylinks.net/europe/bulgaria>

Bulgarian Phone Directories
<world.192.com/europe/bulgaria>

Family Search Wiki: Bulgaria
<familysearch.org/learn/wiki/en/Bulgaria>

History of Bulgaria
<www.bulgaria.com/history/bulgaria>

International Jewish Cemetery Project: Bulgaria
<www.iajgsjewishcemeteryproject.org/bulgaria>

Looking 4 Kin: Bulgaria Genealogy
<www.looking4kin.com/group/bulgariagenealogy>

CROATIA RESOURCES

ORGANIZATIONS AND ARCHIVES

CROATIAN FRATERNAL UNION OF AMERICA
100 Delaney Drive, Pittsburgh, PA 15235
Phone: (412) 843-0380

Fax: 412.823.1594
E-mail: info@croatianfraternalunion.org
<www.croatianfraternalunion.org>

CROATIAN GENEALOGICAL AND HERALDIC SOCIETY
2527 San Carlos Ave., San Carlos, CA 94070
Phone: (650) 592-1190
E-mail: croatians@aol.com
<www.croatians.com>

CROATIAN STATE ARCHIVES
Marulić Square 21, 10 000 Zagreb, Croatia
Phone: +385 1 4801 999
Fax: +385 1 4829 000
E-mail: hda@arhiv.hr
<www.kultura.hr/eng/Institutions/CSA>

EMBASSY OF THE REPUBLIC OF CROATIA
2343 Massachusetts Ave. NW, Washington, DC 20008
Phone: (202) 588-5899
Fax: (202) 588-8936
<www.croatiaemb.org>

BOOKS

Cassell's New English-Croatian and Croatian-English Dictionary (MacMillian Publishing Co.)

Croatia: Land, People, Culture edited by Frances H. Eterovich (University of Toronto Press)

Croatian Pioneers in America, 1685–1900 by Adam S. Eterovich (Ragusan Press)

Finding Your Ethnic-American Roots: Croatian by Robert D. Reed and Danek S. Kaus (Ultramarine Publishing Co.)

A Guide to Croatian Genealogy by Adam S. Eterovich (Ragusan Press)

Jugoslavija Auto Atlas (Yugoslavia Road Atlas) (*Jugoslavenski Leksikografski Zavod*)

Searching for Your Croatian Roots by Robert Jerin (self-published)

WEBSITES

Croatia GenWeb
<rootsweb.ancestry.com/~hrvwgw>

Croatia in English
<www.croatia-in-english.com>

Croatian Genealogy
<www.appleby.net/genealogy.html>

Croatian Genealogy and Family History
<www.croatian-genealogy.com>

Croatian Heritage
<www.croatians.com>

Croatian Regional State Archives
<zagreb.arhiv.hr/en/hr/drugi-arhivi/fs-ovi/
arhivi-hrvatska.htm>

Croatian Roots
<www.croatianroots.com>

Early Croatian Given Names
<www.s-gabriel.org/names/walraven/croat>

How To Do Croatian Genealogy
<www.durham.net/facts/crogen>

Online Croatian Genealogy Newsletter
<www.durham.net/facts/crogen>

Zagreb cemetery burials
<www.gradskagroblja.hr/trazilica>

CZECH REPUBLIC & SLOVAKIA RESOURCES

ORGANIZATIONS AND ARCHIVES

ARCHIVES OF THE CZECHS AND SLOVAKS ABROAD
University of Chicago Library, 1100 E. 57th St.,
Chicago, IL 60637
Phone: (773) 702-8456
<www.lib.uchicago.edu/e/su/slavic/acasa.
html>

CZECH REPUBLIC STATE ARCHIVES
Archivní 4/2257, 149 00 Prague 4, Chodovec,
Czech Republic
Phone: +420 (3) 974 811 111
<www.nacr.cz/eindex.htm>

CZECHOSLOVAK GENEALOGICAL SOCIETY INTERNATIONAL
Box 16225, St. Paul, MN 55116
Phone: (651) 964-2322
E-mail: info@cgsi.org
<www.cgsi.org>

NATIONAL CZECH AND SLOVAK MUSEUM AND LIBRARY
1400 Inspiration Place SW, Cedar Rapids, IA
52404
Phone: (319) 362-8500
<www.ncsml.org>

SLOVAK NATIONAL ARCHIVES
Ministerstvo Vnútra SR, Odbor Archivníctva a
Spisovej Služby, Križkova 7, 811 04 Bratislava
Phone: +421 (2) 52 49 60 51

BOOKS

The Czech Americans by Stephanie Saxon-Ford
(Chelsea House)

*Genealogical Research for Czech and Slovak
Americans* by Olga K. Miller (Gale Research Co.)

*Handbook of Czechoslovak Genealogical
Research* by Daniel Schlyter (Genun)

The Slovak Americans by M. Mark Stolarik
(Chelsea House)

WEBSITES

The Carpathian Connection
<www.tccweb.org>

Carpatho-Rusyn Genealogy Web Site
<www.rusyn.com>

Carpatho-Rusyn Knowledge Base
<www.carpatho-rusyn.org>

Czech GenWeb
<rootsweb.ancestry.com/~czewgw>

It's All Relative Genealogy
<www.iarelative.com>

Online Czech-English Dictionary
<www.wordbook.cz>

Slovak GenWeb
<rootsweb.ancestry.com/~svkwgw>

Slovakia.org
<www.slovakia.org>

HUNGARY RESOURCES

ORGANIZATIONS AND ARCHIVES

AMERICAN HUNGARIAN FOUNDATION
300 Somerset St., Box 1084, New Brunswick, NJ 08903
Phone: (732) 846-5777
Fax: 732-249-7033
E-mail: info@ahfoundation.org
<www.ahfoundation.org>

BUDAPEST FŐVÁROS LEVÉLTÁRA (BUDAPEST CITY ARCHIVES)
1139 Budapest, Teve Utca 3-5, Hungary
Phone: +36 (1) 298-7500
E-mail: bfl@bparchiv.hu
<bfl.archivportal.hu/?lang=en>

HUNGARIAN GENEALOGICAL SOCIETY OF GREATER CLEVELAND
c/o Betty Bower, 1197 Parkview Drive, Seven Hills, OH 44131
<hungariangensocietycleveland.org>

MAGYAR ORSZÁGOS LEVÉLTÁR (NATIONAL ARCHIVES OF HUNGARY)
1250 Budapest, Postafiók 3, Hungary,
Phone: +36 (1) 225-2800
Fax: +36 (1) 225-2817
E-mail: info@mnl.gov.hu
<www.mol.gov.hu>

BOOKS
A Concise History of Hungary by Miklós Molndár and Anna Magyar (Cambridge University Press)

Contents and Addresses of Hungarian Archives, 2nd edition, by Edward Reimer Brandt (Genealogical Publishing Co.)

Finding Your Ancestral Village in the Former Austro-Hungarian Empire by John A. Hudick (self-published)

Handy Guide to Hungarian Genealogical Records by Jared H. Seuss (Everton Publishers)

A History of the Habsburg Empire, 1526–1918 by Robert A. Kann (University of California Press)

How and Where to Research Your Ethnic-American Cultural Heritage: Hungarian Americans by Robert D. Reed and Danek S. Kaus (R&E Publishers)

WEBSITES
Austro-Hungarian Genealogy
<www.felix-game.ca>

Church Record Translations
<vader.bmi.net/jjaso>

Eastern Slovakia Genealogy Research Strategies
<www.iabsi.com/gen/public>

Eötvös University Department of Cartography
<lazarus.elte.hu>

GenForum: Hungary Genealogy Forum
<genforum.genealogy.com/hungary>

Hungarian Heraldry
<www.heraldica.org/topics/national/hungary.htm>

Hungarian Online Resources: *Genealógia*
<hungaria.org/hal/genealogia>

Hungarian Village Finder and Gazetteer
<www.hungarianvillagefinder.com>

Hungarotips
<www.hungarotips.com>

Hungary Genealogy Links
<www.genealogylinks.net/europe/hungary>

Hungary GenWeb
<rootsweb.ancestry.com/~wghungar>

JewishGen: Hungarian Special Interest Group
<www.jewishgen.org/hungary>

Radix: Genealogy Research in Hungary
<www.bogardi.com/gen>

Wideweb: Genealogy
<www.wideweb.hu/hungary/
hungarians-abroad/genealogy>

Your Guide to Researching Hungarian Ancestors
<www.barbsnow.net/Hungary.htm>

ROMANIA RESOURCES

ORGANIZATIONS AND ARCHIVES

BUKOVINA SOCIETY OF THE AMERICAS
Box 81, Ellis, KS 67637
<www.bukovinasociety.org>

EMBASSY OF ROMANIA
1607 23rd St. NW, Washington, DC 20008
Phone: (202) 332-4848
<washington.mae.ro/en>

NATIONAL ARCHIVES OF ROMANIA
Bulevardul M. Kogalniceanu 29, 70602
Bucuresti, Romania

ROMANIAN-AMERICAN HERITAGE CENTER
2540 Grey Tower Road, Jackson, MI 49201
Phone: (517) 522-8260

BOOKS
The Romanian Americans by Arthur Diamond
(Chelsea House)

The Romanians in the United States and Canada by
Vladimir Wertsman (ProQuest)

Historical Dictionary of the Republic of Moldova by
Andrei Brezianu (Scarecrow Press)

*Jewish Roots in Ukraine and Moldova: Pages From
the Past and Archival Inventories* by Miriam Weiner
(Routes to Roots Foundation/YIVO Institute)

WEBSITES
Emigration/Romania Ancestry
<marinel.net/romania/ancestry.html>

FamilySearch Wiki: Romania
<familysearch.org/learn/wiki/en/Romania>

JewishGen: Romania-Moldova Special Interest
Group
<www.jewishgen.org/RomSIG>

Romanian-English Dictionary
<en.bab.la/dictionary/romanian-english>

The Romanian Gap
<www.genealogy.ro/gap.htm>

Romanian Research Outline
<net.lib.byu.edu/fslab/researchoutlines/
Europe/Romania.pdf>

Romanian Voice
<www.romanianvoice.com/directory>

Romanian Tribune Newspaper
<ro-am.net/roam/romanian-tribune-
newspaper.html>

Unitarian Transylvanian Archives Project
<archives.unitarian.ro>

CHAPTER TEN

RUSSIA AND THE BALTIC REGION

By Lisa A. Alzo

T he five countries that make up the Russian and Baltic region have a few things in common: complex border changes and multilingual records. Knowing the region's history and geography will be essential to tracking down your Russian, Ukrainian and Baltic forebears.

RUSSIA

"The astonishing thing about Russian genealogy is the fact that it is possible at all," says Russian research expert Mikhail Kroutikhin. Wars, revolutions and even ignorance have led to significant record losses. Although genealogy flourished in czarist Russia at the beginning of the 20th century, Kroutikhin notes, it was quickly quashed following the revolution in 1917.

"Persecution—and even massacres—of people belonging to 'wrong' classes discouraged the transition of family memories to young generations," he says. "Only a decade ago [did] Russian genealogists start to come out in the open."

Certainly, researching roots in Mother Russia is fraught with challenges: record destruction, recent political instability, language barriers and the historical persecution that led past generations to keep details mum. For family history researchers used to fairly complete and easily accessible American records, the challenges of Russian genealogy might seem especially difficult to surmount. But the seven strategies described here will help you get past the hurdles that otherwise could potentially thwart answers about your Russian ancestors.

Getting Started

As you begin your search for Russian ancestors, you'll apply the basic principles of genealogy: Start with home and family sources to identify the immigrant's name and his/her town or village of origin. Ask them plenty of questions, and be sure to always ask where key events took place. Get tips at **<www.family treemagazine.com/article/20-questions>**.

In addition to any available family resources, you'll need to check all accessible North American records you can find before moving on to research across the ocean. Some key US and Canadian resources to investigate for clues to the name of the ancestral town or village: censuses immigration and naturalization records; birth, marriage and death records; military draft and service records; cemetery burial cards; tombstone inscriptions; and obituaries.

Understanding Names

In order to successfully research across the pond, you'll need to know your immigrant ancestor's original name. Many immigrants "Americanized" their names once they arrived in the United States. Some adopted the English equivalent, while others chose a similar-sounding name or made the spelling more American. (Despite popular lore, Ellis Island immigration officials didn't change people's names—learn more in an article by immigration historian Marian Smith **<www.ilw.com/articles/2005,0808-smith.shtm>**.)

Many changes were inevitable: If your ancestors hailed from the former Soviet Union or Russian Empire (Russians, Belarusians and Ukrainians), their names would be

TIME LINE

859	The Rus', Viking traders, establish first Russian state at Novgorod.
860	Cyrillic alphabet invented.
1147	Moscow founded.
1237	Tatars defeat Kievan Rus'.
1400	Vodka introduced to Russia.
1560	St. Basil's Cathedral completed.
1582	Russia occupies Siberia.
1598	Time of Troubles.
1698	Peter the Great westernizes Russia.
1784	First permanent Russian settlement in North America, on Kodiak Island.
1849	Moscow Kremlin completed.
1861	Emancipation of Russian serfs.
1864	Leo Tolstoy begins *War and Peace*.
1866	Fyodor Dostoyevsky publishes *Crime and Punishment*.
1867	Russia sells Alaska to US for $7.2 million.
1912	First issue of *Pravda*, the official Communist Party newspaper.
1917	Bolshevik Revolution.
1918	Russia pulls out of WWI; Ukraine and Baltic states gain independence.
1920	Science-fiction writer Isaac Asimov born in Russia.
1939	Igor Sikorsky builds first helicopter.
1948	George Gamow presents his big-bang theory.
1957	Sputnik I satellite launched.
1987	Gorbachev launches glasnost ("openness") policy.
1991	USSR dissolves.
2001	Mir space station retired.

transliterated from the Cyrillic to the Roman alphabet. Russian female surnames end in *-a*. You'll need to pare down names to their "root" forms to track your ancestors. Russian names spelled in Cyrillic letters have various—and sometimes peculiar—versions when spelled in French, German or English. For example, the letter *V* easily becomes *W*, or *FF*. One resource to check is *A Dictionary of Period Russian Names* **<heraldry.sca.org/paul>**.

Consider Russian naming customs, too, as Jonathan D. Shea and William F. Hoffman advise in their book *Following the Paper Trail: A Multilingual Translation Guide*: "Generally, Moscow has forced even non-Russians under its control to comply with Russian customs regarding names." The system works like this: Each person has a given name, patronymic and surname. The patronymic usually ends in *-ovich* for men or *-ovna* for women.

Orthodox and Catholic families frequently named children for saints, selecting one whose feast day was close to the child's birthday. Jewish families named children after close deceased relatives. Jews in the Russian Empire didn't adopt surnames until the government began requiring their use in the early 19th century.

Studying Geography and History

Russia is the world's largest country, covering almost twice the territory of the next-largest nation, Canada. It boasts the world's eighth-largest population, with 149 million people. Historically, Russia's population consisted of Slavic tribes: East Slavs were Russians, Ukrainians and Belarusians; West Slavs were Poles, Czechs and Slovaks; and South Slavs included Bulgarians, Croats, Macedonians Serbs and Slovenians. Russia was an independent country for many centuries, then following the Bolshevik Revolution of 1917 and the subsequent Russian Civil War of 1918–1930, it became the Russian Soviet Federative Socialist Republic (RSFSR), a republic of the Union of Soviet Socialist Republics (USSR). Since the dissolution of the Soviet Union in December 1991, Russia has been known as the Russian Federation. To gain a deeper understanding of Russia's rich and complex history, consult the books and online resources listed in this chapter's resources.

Russia today shares land borders with 14 countries (including Norway, Finland, Poland, Ukraine, China and North Korea), and the United States and Japan are not far away—with small stretches of water (the Bering Strait and La Pérouse Strait, respectively) in between. The Russian Federation spans nine time zones, so you can appreciate the need to get a handle on the geography—otherwise pinpointing records for your ancestors will be next to impossible.

You'll want to familiarize yourself with terms for administrative divisions. Imperial Russia (aka the Russian Empire) was divided into *gubernias* (provinces), which were divided into *uyezds* (districts). Soviet Russia and Ukraine and other former Soviet republics were, and are still, divided into *oblasts* (provinces), which were and are divided into *raions* (districts). The Caucasus—a geopolitical region at the border of Europe and Asia, situated between the Black and the Caspian sea—sometimes use the term *krai* instead of *raion* for district. Archives from all over the former Soviet Union concentrate their holdings according to *oblast* borders. You'll need to know both the old and the new jurisdictions—in particular for smaller places. For example, the FamilySearch catalog **<familysearch.org/catalog-search>**, which lists the vast microfilm holdings of the Family History Library (FHL) in Salt Lake City, uses the new jurisdictions for Ukraine, but the old ones for Russia. Most of FamilySearch's Russian and Ukrainian microfilms are from the Imperial time, and of course documents refer to the old jurisdictions.

Maps, atlases and gazetteers (geographical dictionaries) will be your friends as you sift through old and new borders. Start with the *Palgrave Historical Atlas of Eastern Europe* (Palgrave Macmillan, $13), and view a map of 1912 Russian Empire jurisdictions at **<familysearch.org/learn/wiki/en/File:Russian_Empire_Jurisdictions.jpg>**. You can browse maps of the Russian empire online via the Federation of East European Family History Societies (FEEFHS) map room **<www.feefhs.org/maplibrary.html>** and read up on the FHL's collection of gazetteers **<familysearch.org/learn/wiki/en/Russia_Gazetteers>**.

Surveying Records

When you're ready to cross the pond, avoid the temptation to dive right in without some preparation. You should first create a research plan that outlines the "Who, What, When, Where and Why" of what specifically you wish to accomplish. For help putting together your plan, consult the article "Road Map to Your Roots" in the January 2011 *Family Tree Magazine* and view a sample research plan at **<www.familytreemagazine.com/article/sample-research-plan>**.

Keep in mind that most records you seek will still have to be accessed by direct research in Russian archives—though that doesn't necessarily mean travel to Russia, as we'll explain later. Among the helpful resources online and on microfilm: the Russians to America Passenger Data File, 1834–1897, available via the National Archives and Records Administration's (NARA) Access to Archival Databases **<aad.archives.gov/aad/fielded-search.jsp?dt=2126&cat=GP44 &tf=F&bc=,sl>**, and Records of Former Russian Agencies (otherwise known as Russian Consular Records) held by NARA. See record group M-1485 for the U.S. and M-1742 for Canada. An index to the records was compiled as *The Russian Consular Records Index and Catalog* by Sallyann Amdur Sack and Suzan F. Wynne, available on microfilm from NARA **<www.archives. gov/research/guide-fed-records/groups/261.html>**. Check the FamilySearch catalog, too, for microfilm you can order for a modest fee to view at your local Family History Center or participating library (search the catalog for *Russian Consular Records*).

For documents created between 1898 and 1922 by the consular offices of the Russian Empire in Canada, see Library Archives Canada's Likacheff-Ragosine-Mathers (LI-RA-MA) collection (MG 30 E406). The index and digitized images of the files of the Passport/Identity Papers series are available online **<www.collectionscanada.gc.ca/databases/li-ra-ma/index-e.html>**.

You must also understand what types of Russian records you'll find. Record-keeping in the Russian Empire mostly resembled the practices elsewhere in Europe. Vital records were the purview of the church before the government stepped in. Older parish registers are usually held by an archive, while more recent ones (within the past 75 years) are in civil registration offices, explains Kahlile Mehr, former Slavic Collection Manager for the FHL and FamilySearch. The government took ten poll-tax censuses, referred to as revision lists (*revizskie skazki*), between 1719 and 1859. They're organized by place, then by social class, such as nobility (*dvorianstvo*), peasants (*krest'iane*), Cossacks (*kazaki*) and Jews (*yevreyski*). Surviving revision lists are in regional and historical archives, as are remaining copies of the 1897 census of the entire empire. FamilySearch has some digitized records (indexes, images, or both) online. See **<familysearch. org/search/collection/list#page=1&countryId=1927021>**.

For more help, consult the FamilySearch Wiki **<familysearch.org/learn/wiki/en/Russia_ Genealogy>**. While FamilySearch has made great strides in bringing data collections online, its Russian collections barely scratch the surface of what may be hidden. Remember to keep checking back (or sign up for a free FamilySearch account to be notified when new data sets are added or current collections are updated).

Researching Russian Immigrants

If the trail back to Great-grandpa grows cold, try cluster genealogy—the process of studying your ancestor as part of a group, or "cluster," of relatives, friends, and neighbors and associates. The cluster approach can help you find (or confirm) details you might miss by looking only at an individual ancestor. Study up on Russian immigration, too.

Early Russian immigrants to America settled in Alaska and along the West Coast. Larger numbers came after 1880. The largest influx came during the "great migration" of the late 19th and early 20th centuries, with 2.3 million immigrants from czarist Russia arriving in the US between 1871 and 1910. When the Soviets loosened immigration restrictions in 1969, thousands left, including many Jews. Other "clusters" of Russian immigrants can be found in various localities in New York, New Jersey, Pennsylvania and other states. Scour US census records for relatives or others from the same town, look at traveling companions on passenger lists and note names of witnesses on baptismal and marriage certificates, and naturalization petitions.

Accessing the Archives

When records aren't available via FamilySearch, you must determine which Russian archive houses them. The Russian Federal Archive Service **<www.rusarchives.ru>** has contact information for all archives and links to an archive's website when one exists. You can use Google **<translate.google.com>** to translate the basic information on the site; a more in-depth knowledge of Russian may help you use it more effectively.

Also check Repositories of Primary Sources **<www.uidaho.edu/special-collections/Other. Repositories.html>**, a key portal the University of Idaho created. Organized by country, it lists a variety of public and private archives and libraries that maintain websites.

Be prepared for your research to take you to archives for the countries bordering Russia if your ancestor came from border areas (see the resources section for links). If you're searching early historical time periods, be aware that regional archives keep records dating back only to about 1790. You might find earlier information in federal archives in Moscow or St. Petersburg.

You have three options for getting records from archives: You can send a written request, which usually requires advance payment, long wait times, varied response and no guarantee of positive results. You can travel to Russia and do the research yourself—a costly and often difficult route. Or you can hire a researcher who can research on your behalf.

The latter option is often your best bet because a Russia-based researcher can speak the language, knows the archives and can research in libraries. Fees will vary depending on the volume of the records to be translated and explained, says Kroutikhin. To avoid surprises, always ask the researcher for an initial estimate up front. To find a reliable researcher, check with the Association of Professional Genealogists **<www.apgen.org>**, ProGenealogists **<www.progenealogists. com>**, or Routes to Roots **<www.routestoroots.com>** (specialists in Jewish research), or ask for recommendations from fellow genealogists using social media.

Learning the Language

Once you get to the records you need to view, you'll need to figure out how to read them or find someone who can. Although Russian is among the most difficult languages for English speakers to learn (see **<www.foreigntranslations.com/languages/russian-translation/russian-language>**, you can dabble with short and basic DIY translations using free tools such as BabelFish **<www.babelfish.com>**, Google Translate **<translate.google.com>**, and the Russian Dictionary iPhone/iPad app **<itunes.apple.com/us/app/russian-dictionary-free/ id401396814?mt=8>**.

To be sure you don't miss any important information, you'll need to learn more about the Russian language. Begin with the series of free tutorials on familysearch.org **<familysearch.org/ learningcenter/results.html?q=*&fq=place%3A%22Russia%2>**, which will acquaint you with the Russian alphabet (a variation of the Cyrillic alphabet); explain Russian names, dates, and key words; and teach you the basics of reading Russian genealogical records including birth, marriage, and death records.

When you're ready to really dive in, FamilySearch also has a PDF Russian Word List you can download for free from **<familysearch.org/learn/wiki/en/images/8/86/Russian_Word_List. pdf>**. Find more language helps in the resources section.

If you decide to take a chance on sending a written request to a Russian archive, you'll need to prepare your correspondence in Russian—don't expect that the archive officials will speak or read English. Typically, all correspondence is done in Russian.

Jonathan Shea has excellent sample letters in his book *Going Home: A Guide to Polish American Family History Research* (Langline, available from **<www.langline.com>**). Don't let the title fool you: While the book focuses on Polish research, it has several pages of Russian Vocabulary in addition to the sample letters. For more accurate results, look for a human translator (rates will vary). See if your local college or university can make any recommendations, or check out Cucumis **<www.cucumis.org/translation_1_w>**, Freelang **<www.freelang.net/translation>** and Linguanaut **<www.linguanaut.com>**. With these tools and research strategies, your Russian roots discoveries soon will speak for themselves.

UKRAINE

Just two decades ago, if you were trying to trace your Ukrainian roots, you probably got used to having a lot of doors slammed in your face. After all, the long-ruling Soviet regime wasn't particularly cooperative: The government had a monopoly over information and restricted who was allowed access to it. Even the most innocent query about your great-great-grandfather would likely be met with suspicion. Add to the mix a complex history and a limited availability of resources in North America, and genealogy research could feel like an exercise in futility.

But Ukraine eventually gained its independence. Many of those officially closed doors started to open. And in recent years, microfilmed records and online resources have begun to offer alternatives to expensive and obstacle-ridden long-distance research for the almost 1 million Americans of Ukrainian descent. Follow our guide to help you sort through the ups and downs unique to Ukrainian genealogy.

Getting Started

"Anyone just starting out needs to be patient," advises Matthew Bielawa, who lectures on Ukrainian and Polish genealogy and runs the website Genealogy of Halychyna/Eastern Galicia (Hal-Gal) **<www.halgal.com>**.

He recommends reading up on Ukrainian history and geography before you begin. First lesson: "Many folks mistakenly say 'the Ukraine.' You wouldn't say 'the France' or 'the Italy,'" Bielawa notes.

Located in Eastern Europe, Ukraine is bordered on the north by Belarus, on the north and east by Russia, on the south by the Sea of Azov and the Black Sea, on the southwest by Romania and Moldova, and on the west by Hungary, Slovakia and Poland.

Ukraine was the center of the first eastern Slavic state, Kyivan Rus', which during the 10th and 11th centuries was the largest and most powerful state in Europe. But it was weakened by internal quarrels and Mongol invasions. Various parts of what's now Ukraine have at times been claimed by Russia, Poland, the Austrian Empire, Hungary, Romania and Czechoslovakia. Present boundaries were set in 1954; Ukraine finally became independent in 1991.

Becoming comfortable with history and geographical terminology also will help you learn where genealogical records might be located and what language they could be in. "It's not haphazard disorganization," Bielawa notes. "If you know that your family is from Lviv in Western Ukraine,

which was in Poland before World War II and in the Austrian Empire before World War I, you can understand why your ancestors' records could be housed in either a Ukrainian or Polish archive. Vital records are usually in Latin with some Polish, Ukrainian and Church Slavic—a church language of the Eastern rite Catholics and Orthodox Christian. And if your family was from Uzhhorod in southwest Ukraine, you can expect to find some Hungarian records."

"With a little background in history, you won't be shocked to find an ancestor who was born in the Austrian Empire, attended school in Poland, married in the Soviet Union and died in independent Ukraine—all without ever leaving home," Bielawa adds.

"The overwhelming majority of Ukrainians in North America have roots in western Ukraine or southeastern Poland," writes John D. Pihach in his book *Ukrainian Genealogy*, considered by many as the authoritative guide to Ukrainian research.

Novice researchers also can look to online resources as jumping-off points, including HAL-GAL, the Ukrainian research outlines at **<net.lib.byu.edu/fslab/researchoutlines/Europe/Ukraine.pdf>**, InfoUkes **<www.infoukes.com/genealogy>** and the FamilySearch Wiki pages for Ukraine **<www.familysearch.org/learn/wiki/en/Ukraine>**.

Understanding Ukrainian Immigration

Ukrainian immigration to North America occurred in waves, Pihach says. We'll focus on helping you find family in three waves.

Ukrainians began arriving in large numbers in the United States by 1870 to escape czarist rule. Some went to Alaska before the United States purchased it in 1867, with many continuing south to California. Others flocked to work in Pennsylvania mines and the factories and mills of industrial cities in New York, Ohio, Illinois and Michigan. Some 250,000 Ukrainians arrived in the United States by 1914, when World War I and immigration quotas halted the influx.

In Canada, whose Ukrainian-descended population exceeds that of the United States, more than 171,000 Ukrainians arrived between 1891 and 1914. Most emigrants were peasants from Galicia and Bukovina. In contrast to their US counterparts, many headed for farms in the prairie provinces of Manitoba, Saskatchewan and Alberta, in response to Canada's settlement campaign. Winnipeg and Edmonton had bloc settlements **<esask.uregina.ca/entry/ukrainian_settlements.html>**, but other Ukrainians sought work in Quebec or Ontario.

A smaller wave of Ukrainian immigrants, numbering about 15,000, arrived in North America between the world wars. Another major immigration wave followed World War II. It consisted mainly of well-educated students, scholars and other professionals who had spent time in refugee camps in Austria and Germany.

Learn more about Ukranian immigrants and culture at **<www.everyculture.com/multi/Sr-Z/Ukrainian-Americans.html>** and **<ist.uwaterloo.ca/~marj/genealogy/thevoyage.html>**. For a more complete picture of how Ukraine's political history influenced your family history and emigration decisions, consult *A History of Ukraine* by Paul Robert Magocsi.

Finding Your Ancestral Village

The first thing you should do is to locate the village or town in Ukraine (or a neighboring country) where your Ukrainian ancestor lived. Keep in mind that Ukraine is a large country—the second largest in Europe, a little smaller than Texas. With 24 provinces and an autonomous republic, this might not be an easy task.

Start with records created during your immigrant ancestor's life in North America. Besides records that you'd use for any North American ancestor—census, immigration, naturalization and vital records—look for records from the church or synagogue your ancestors attended. Unlike other records in which Eastern European names could get mangled, religious records from an ethnically Ukrainian church or synagogue often include proper spellings of names because the clerk was usually able to understand and correctly record them. These records also often contain specific geographic information, such as a county or province your family was from, as well as the correct spelling of the town or village name. Contact the church or synagogue directly with records requests, or if it no longer exists, a regional office.

No matter which database you're searching, try alternate spellings of names. For example, if a surname ends in *-wicz*, try searching on a spelling ending in *-wycz, -wich, -vich* or *-vych*. You'll find more search tips at **<www.halgal.com/passengerlists.html>**.

Once you determine the name of the town or village, you need to pinpoint its location. Note that village names might be repeated all over the country, even in the same province and district. Knowing the right village in the right province (*oblast* in Ukrainian) or district (*raion*) is key. Pinpoint the right place by consulting online tools, maps, atlases and gazetteers. Ukraine Gen-Web has a Guide to Finding Your Town tool, which coaches you through the process of locating a town based on what you know **<rootsweb.ancestry.com/~ukrwgw/ukrainetown.html>**. The Federation of East European Family History Societies Map Library **<feefhs.org/links/ukraine. html>** has a good collection of online maps, as does Harvard University **<hcl.harvard.edu/ news/articles/2010/ukraine_maps.cfm>** and InfoUkes **<www.infoukes.com/ua-maps>**.

Gazetteers may be most helpful to you. Search the Family History Library (FHL) online catalog **<familysearch.org>** for Ukraine to find gazetteers in print and on microfilm. A must-have resource for any Western Ukrainian genealogist is the *Genealogical Gazetteer of Galicia* by Brian J. Lenius **<www.lenius.ca/Gazetteer/Gazetteer.htm>**. It contains information critical to locating an ancestral village in the former province of Galicia, now located in southeastern Poland and western Ukraine. The book includes village names in Ukrainian and Polish, and can help you identify the correct village for repeated place names.

Overcoming Language Barriers

When you're ready to delve into foreign records, you'll have a number of challenges to consider. "Language is the most critical roadblock to Ukrainian genealogy," Bielawa advises. "A Ukrainian researcher might discover vital records in Russian, Church Slavonic, Latin, Polish or Hungarian depending on the time frame and location of the record."

At first glance, this looks overwhelming. But knowing the historical background will go a long way in sorting out language issues. Learning Cyrillic, even if only to understand names and places, will greatly assist you: It'll come in handy whether you're trying to read names on a headstone (immigrants' headstones may be inscribed in their native Ukrainian), a road map or a Ukrainian website. See a table showing Cyrillic characters and English transliterations for each one at **<en.wikipedia.org/wiki/Romanization_of_Ukrainian>**. You can find transliterations for common genealogy words in Ukrainian, Latin, Polish and Russian at **<freepages.genealogy.rootsweb.ancestry.com/~atpc/genealogy/articles/records-common-fgn-words.html>**. You'll find advice for reading Cyrillic records at **<www.sggee.org/research/translation_aids#sampleRus>**.

Your ancestors' names could have been transliterated into English or another language, such as Polish (for a Polish passport), or German or Dutch (for a passenger list). Transliteration isn't an exact science, so it can result in a range of name variations. Furthermore, you might find Ukrainian names written in the national language of the ruling country. A Ukrainian named Ivan Kovalchuk (Іван Ковальчук) could have his name written as Jan Kowalczuk in Polish, Janos Kovalcsuk in Hungarian or Johann Kowaltchuk in German. Your Uncle Nick could have been called Mykola by his Ukrainian parents, but known as Mikolaj in a Polish document and Nikolai in a Russian document. You'll find a list of common Ukrainian given names and their transliterations at **<www.behindthename.com/names/usage/Ukrainian>**. Common Ukrainian surname suffixes are *-enko, -ko, -yuk, -yuk, -yak, -ak, -yshyn* or *-ishyn*. The suffixes *-ets* or *-iets* and *-iv* are common to the Galician region.

Knowing how a name and its nicknames are spelled in different languages is important when searching not only foreign documents, but also North American immigration, naturalization and census records. For language help, try *Teach Yourself Ukrainian Complete Course* by Olena Bekh (McGraw-Hill) and *In Their Words: A Genealogist's Translation Guide to Polish, German, Latin, and Russian Documents: Volume I: Polish and Volume II: Russian* by Jonathan D. Shea and William F. Hoffman (Langline).

Using Genealogical Records

The best records for tracing Ukrainian ancestors in Europe are birth or baptismal, marriage and death records kept by churches. Ukrainians have traditionally been Eastern Christians, divided since 1596 into an Orthodox majority and a minority of Eastern Rite (Uniate) Catholics, who predominate in the west. Latin Rite Catholicism, which includes Roman Catholicism, is generally limited to ethnic Poles and Hungarians. Protestant, Jewish and Muslim (mostly a Turkic ethnic group called Crimean Tatar) communities also exist in Ukraine.

Several large collections of Ukrainian records have been microfilmed and are available to rent through the FHL and your local Family History Center. This includes the huge collection—more than 7,000 Ukrainian Catholic church registers—of the Ukrainian Catholic Consistory housed in the Central State Historical Archives of Ukraine in the city of Lviv in western Ukraine, and a large collection from the Kyiv (Kiev in Russian) Orthodox Consistory **<rootsweb.ancestry. com/~ukrwgw/fhc.html>**.

Also look for digitized records from Ukraine at **<https://familysearch.org/search/collection/ list#page=1&countryId=1927132>**. You'll get context for the records in the FHL collection if you check out the UkraineGenWeb information at **<rootsweb.ancestry.com/~ukrwgw/fhc.html>**.

For help deciphering records in church books, see the Guide to Reading Old Church Slavonic, used in some Eastern Orthodox and Eastern Catholic churches as a liturgical language, at **<www.familysearch.org/learn/wiki/en/images/6/66/Old_Church_Slavonic_Numbers,_ Dates,_and_Months_by_Matthew_Bialawa.pdf>**.

Certainly, most of the records in Ukraine have yet to be filmed or digitized, but the numbers are growing. If the documents you need aren't on microfilm, you can mail requests for these records to the Ukrainian archives **<www.archives.gov.ua/Eng>** or hire a local researcher. In addition to civil registration (birth, marriage and death records), archives may have land records, school records and nobility documents. Not all archives have all these types of records for all towns and villages, however, and staff typically charge fees for filling requests.

Branching Out

Reaching out to others with Ukrainian roots can bring research advice, translation help and more. Groups I've consulted include the Ukrainian Genealogical Society **<rootsweb.ancestry. com/~ukrgs>**, East European Genealogical Society in Winnipeg, Canada **<www.eegsociety. org>**, and Toronto Ukrainian Genealogy Group **<www.torugg.org>**.

You can also post to bulletin boards and listservs where knowledgeable researchers are willing to answer questions, including GenForum **<genforum.genealogy.com/ukraine>**, Ancestry. com **<boards.ancestry.com/localities.eeurope.ukraine/mb.ashx>** and Yahoo! Groups **<groups.yahoo.com/group/GaliciaPoland-Ukraine>**.

The path to Ukraine's independence was long, and your quest to build your Ukrainian family tree may seem the same. But once you discover your ancestral town, you can start looking for long-lost cousins and records, and perhaps even plan that dream trip to Ukraine.

THE BALTIC REGION

Each of the Baltic states—Estonia, Latvia and Lithuania—has its own cultural identity. But all three countries, bordered by the brackish Baltic Sea to the west and largely overshadowed by Russia to the east, have in common a tumultuous history, characterized by centuries of foreign occupation and domination interspersed with brief interludes of independence.

Despite the occupations and other turmoil, many records in the Baltic nations have been well-preserved—you just need to look in the right places. Start discovering your Baltic roots by following these fundamental steps.

Getting Started

You may be tempted to go right for the "good stuff"—the records housed in archives, churches and town offices in the old country. But your chances of success over there depend on how well you do your homework here. Start by talking to your relatives to learn your immigrant ancestor's correct name and hometown. Be careful not to buy into family lore too much, though. For instance, you may find that an ancestor immigrated through Baltimore or even arrived in Canada—not New York, as your aunt told you.

Take what you learn from relatives, and check all available US records—that includes census, vital, immigration and naturalization records. You can find many of these documents on subscription websites such as Ancestry.com **<ancestry.com>** and Fold3 **<fold3.com>**, as well as on free websites such as FamilySearch **<familysearch.org>**. Be sure to research your kin in deeds, court records, ethnic newspapers and other offline sources, too.

In the early stages of your research, it helps to seek out other people who share your interest. "One thing you have to realize is that genealogy is a team sport," says genealogist Thomas Sadauskas, an expert in Lithuanian research. Organizations such as the Lithuanian Global Genealogical Society **<www.lithuaniangenealogy.org>**, the Estonian Genealogical Society **<www.genealoogia.ee>** and the American Latvian Association **<http://www.alausa.org/en/>** are excellent resources for genealogical and cultural information.

Understanding Baltic History

You may be wondering why certain records say your Lithuanian ancestor was born in Poland or your Estonian ancestor emigrated from Russia. It helps to understand the region's complex past—in particular, each country's relations with neighboring states.

In the 13th century, crusading German knights subjugated the territory of modern-day Estonia and Latvia. Later, Sweden dominated the northern Baltic lands and the Polish-Lithuanian Commonwealth the southern. Russia gained control during the 18th century.

After World War I, Estonia and Latvia enjoyed a brief period of independence before the Red Army imposed Soviet control in 1940. The Soviets brought in masses of Russians to industrialize the area; subsequently, the Estonian and Latvian shares of the population significantly decreased. When the Soviet Union collapsed in 1991, both states regained their independence.

As for Lithuania, it allied with Poland in 1385, when Grand Duke Jogaila (later Wladyslaw II) of Lithuania married Queen Jadwiga of Poland. Jogaila's cousin Vytautas assumed power in 1392 and extended Lithuania's borders from the Baltic to the Black Sea. Lithuania stayed connected to Poland in some form for about 400 years.

In 1569, the two kingdoms formally united as the Polish-Lithuanian Commonwealth, which was partitioned in 1772, 1792 and 1795 by Russia, Prussia and Austria. Russia occupied Lithuania and much of present-day Poland. Both countries re-emerged as independent states in 1918, but then Lithuania was annexed by the Soviets in 1940. Like its two neighbors, Lithuania regained independence in 1991.

After 1918, Finland was considered a Baltic state, but today Finland is more often grouped with the Nordic countries. To study each of the Baltic nations' histories in more detail, look to online sources such as Wikipedia **<en.wikipedia.org>**, Cyndi's List **<cyndislist.com/baltic>** and WorldGenWeb **<www.worldgenweb.org>**.

Learning Immigration Patterns

Aside from a few early settlers in the 1600s, Estonian immigration to the United States was limited until the late 1800s, with the first significant wave coming after the failure of the 1905 revolution. About 15,000 Estonian immigrants arrived in the United States after World War II; many settled in Chicago.

If you're searching immigration records predating 1922, when Estonia's independence was officially recognized, you'll most likely find your Estonian ancestors listed as Russian. Or you might find them listed as Germans or Swedes, depending on the language they spoke.

The first four Latvian immigrants arrived in 1638 from the Swedish-controlled northern region of Livonia, in what's now Latvia and Estonia. Emigration from Latvia to the United States began in earnest between 1880 and 1920.

Latvian immigrants fall into two distinct groups: the Old Latvians (or *veclatvieši*), who settled in the United States before WWII, and the Latvians who arrived after the war. Most of the early immigrants were young, single men who journeyed to America in search of their fortunes—or to escape being drafted into the Russian czar's army—although some single women and families also came to the States at the end of the 19th century. These immigrants settled primarily on the East Coast, in Boston, New York and Philadelphia, and in Midwestern cities such as Cleveland and Chicago. Some went to the West Coast, putting down roots in Seattle, Portland and San Francisco. Political views further divided the early immigrants into two groups: those who supported the creation of an independent Latvia and those who supported socialism. Until the 1930 census, the US government lumped Latvians in with Lithuanians and Russians.

Lithuanians were by far the largest of the three Baltic immigrant groups. A number of Lithuanians immigrated to the New World before the American Revolution, but the first significant wave of Lithuanian immigration began in the late 1860s. During the late 19th and early 20th centuries, an estimated 300,000 Lithuanians journeyed to America. Then the immigration tide slowed considerably because of World War I and US-imposed quotas.

Exact immigration numbers are hard to pinpoint because US census records didn't officially recognize Lithuanian as a separate nationality until the 20th century. The 1920 census was the first to allow "Lithuania" to be listed as a place of birth. Prior to the 1920 census, "Lithuanian" was an acceptable entry only for the language category. Your ancestors' ethnicity may have been recorded as Russian, Polish or Jewish.

Lithuanians settled predominantly in the large cities and industrial towns of the Northeast and Midwest, and the coal fields of Pennsylvania and southern Illinois. Many of the first immigrants were mobile, searching for work all over the United States. Some were so-called "birds of passage," who intended to work hard for a few years and then return to Lithuania with enough money to purchase land.

Lithuanian-American communities also sprouted in small industrial towns in Massachusetts, Connecticut, New Jersey and Pennsylvania. But by 1930, nearly half of all Lithuanian-Americans lived in just 10 metropolitan areas, including Chicago, Cleveland, Detroit, Pittsburgh, New York and Boston. After 1945, WWII refugees flocked to many of the same areas as their predecessors.

For a more complete picture of Baltic immigration, read this article from the journal *Lituanus*: **<www.lituanus.org/1983_1/83_1_02.htm>**.

Studying Names

In US records, you won't necessarily find your ancestor's first name or surname spelled the same way it was in the old country. "One family surname I was researching started out in Lithuania as Derliunas, which went through several variations (Derlunas, Derlun, Darlunas) in the United States, finally ending up as Darlun," Sadauskas says. You may find changes in both given names and surnames. For instance, men with the given name of Kazimieras (Casimir) might've gone by Charles; men named Vincas/Vincentas may have changed their name to William (rather than to the more expected Vincent).

Sadauskas says that prior to the formalization of the Lithuanian language in 1918, the letters *sz* (pronounced sh, as in should) and *cz* (ch, as in chain) were used in lieu of the current *š* and *č* used to represent those sounds. So if you're using spellings from pre-1918 documents, remember that you might need to translate them to the modern Lithuanian spellings.

Furthermore, married women had surnames ending in *-iene* (for example, Sadauskas became Sadauskiene), while unmarried women had names ending in *-aite, -ute* or *-yte*, depending on the family surname (Sadauskas became Sadauskaite). Typically, Lithuanian male given names ended in a consonant (Vytautas and Jonas, for instance), while female given names ended in a vowel (Birute, Ona, Egle). For more help, read the Polish Genealogical Society of America's article on name changes **<www.pgsa.org/PDFs/Mutilation.pdf>**.

Common Estonian surnames include Tamm, Pärn, Sokk and Kask. Estonian men tend to have first names ending with the letter *o* (as in Arno, Eino, Ivo and Ülo). Other common given names include Jaak, Jaan, Peeter and Rein. Common female names include Aime, Ester, Krista,

Leida and Mari. Learn more by visiting Pronunciation and Meaning of Estonian Names **<www.fredonia.edu/faculty/emeritus/EdwinLawson/estoniannames>**.

In the 1830s, all Estonians received surnames, says Kahlile Mehr, Slavic collection manager at FamilySearch. Before that, they'd followed the naming customs of their ethnic heritage. Germans used surnames, Swedes followed the Nordic patronymic system and Estonians used nicknames and parents' names plus their given names. An Estonian may have gone by Murrista Jaco Madde, where Murrista was a nickname, Jaco was the father's name and Madde was the given name.

Surnames such as Irbe, Sniedze, Viesturs, Dzintars and Auseklis are unique to Latvians. The most popular man's name in Latvia is Jānis; you'll also see Andris, Juris, Edgars, Māris and Aivars. For women, the most common names are Anna, Kristīne, Marija, Inese, Inga and Ilze.

Grasping Geography

To trace your Baltic heritage successfully, you need to pinpoint the location of the ancestral town or village. Two obstacles may stand in your way: spelling differences and border changes. "Most likely you will not find the exact place of birth in Lithuania on the first document you find," Sadauskas says. "If you do, it might use the German or Polish spelling of the place name." To keep track of place names, he maintains a spreadsheet listing place names in Lithuanian, Polish, Russian, German and Yiddish.

The same principle applies to Estonia and Latvia—don't expect clear-cut geographic or political boundaries. You'll need to consult both historical and modern-day maps, atlases and gazetteers and learn the administrative makeup of the area. A good place to begin is with *The Palgrave Concise Historical Atlas of Eastern Europe* by Dennis P. Hupchick and Harold E. Cox (Palgrave).

FEEFHS has an excellent collection of 19th- and 20th-century maps online **<www.feefhs.org/maplibrary.html>**, including one of the Baltic states circa 1882. For maps of Estonian territorial division, see **<www.genealoogia.ee/English/maps.html>**.

Under imperial Russia, the administrative structure of the Baltics consisted of the town or village, the *uezd* (county) and the *guberniya* (province or state). Modern Estonia comprises the Estonia guberniya and the northern half of Livonia guberniya. Modern Latvia includes the Kurland guberniya, the southern half of Livonia and a small piece of the Vitebsk guberniya. Modern Lithuania consists of the Kovno guberniya, and half of Vilno and half of Suwalki (Polish) gubernii.

There were six Lutheran consistories: Kurland (which included Kurland, Vitebsk, Mogilev, Minsk, Vilna, Grodno and Kovno), Estonia, Livonia and the cities of Oesel, Reval (Tallinn) and Riga. There were two Catholic dioceses: Samogitia (comprising Kovno, Estonia and Livonia) and Vilnius (Vilna south to Brest). Orthodox dioceses shared boundaries with civil jurisdictions.

Finding Foreign Records

When you're ready to cross the pond in search of your Baltic ancestors, seek record groups similar to those on this side of the Atlantic. Look for the following resources in particular.

- **Metrical books:** These church registers of births, marriages and deaths were first recorded in the 1700s.
- **Census records:** The 1897 census was the only universal one in czarist Russia. Estonian censuses exist for 1860 to 1917. Estonian and Latvian personal registers for 1926 to 1940 also exist.
- **Military records:** As of 1874, all 21-year-old males were eligible for military service. Look for conscription lists of those entering or drafted into the military.
- **Revision lists:** Called *Seelenlisten* and kept from 1795 to 1858 to support a national Russian poll tax, these lists are comparable to a census and contain each individual's name, age and relationship to the head of household.

Other records such as resident books (compiled in Estonia and Latvia), nobility and genealogy collections and passport applications (available for Latvia only) may provide additional personal or genealogical information.

You can access some of these records in online databases or on microfilm through the Family History Library's (FHL) branch Family History Centers (find locations at **<familysearch.org>**). For records not on microfilm or online, you'll need to write to the archives where they're stored. Of course, most of these foreign records won't be in English. Consult online or print dictionaries, translation aids or the aforementioned FHL word lists. The German Gothic handwriting guide **<www.familysearch.org/learn/wiki/en/Germany_Handwriting>** and examples at **<www.genealoogia.ee/English/gothic.html>** also may help.

Tapping Online Resources

Although you won't find a ton of Eastern European records online, the Estonian Historical Archives website **<www.eha.ee/english/english.htm>** offers inventories of records and images for free. For general research assistance, visit the Estonian Genealogical Society website **<www.genealoogia.ee/English/english.html>**. You'll find a database of Estonian WWII casualties at **<www.okupatsioon.ee/en/lists/327-hukkunute-nimekiri-6666-nime>**.

Following the Estonian Historical Archives' lead, the Latvian State Historical Archives also provides a database of digitized records called Raduraksti **<www.lvva-raduraksti.lv/en.html>**. Currently, the database contains more than 5.7 million images of genealogical records, including church records and the 1897 Russian imperial census. Raduraksti is just one of the resources offered by Latvia's state archival system. To access other databases, go to **<www.arhivi.gov.lv/index.php?&3>**. The Lithuanian Archives Department website **<www.archyvai.lt/archyvai>** lets you search for descriptions of record groups housed in the State Historical Archive.

To access foreign records that aren't accessible online or on microfilm here in the United States, your best bet may be to hire a professional researcher based in your ancestral homeland and knowledgeable about the area's geography, history and languages. For research in Estonia, check with the Estonian Biographical Center **<www.isik.ee/english>**. If your ancestors were victims of Nazi persecutions, contact the International Tracing Service **<www.its-arolsen.org>**.

Just two decades ago, the opportunities for researching in Estonia, Latvia and Lithuania were limited. Thankfully, the tides have turned, and today, getting back to your Baltic roots is easier than ever.

REGIONAL RESOURCES

ORGANIZATIONS AND ARCHIVES

EAST EUROPEAN GENEALOGICAL SOCIETY
Box 2536, Winnipeg, Manitoba, R3C 4A7
Canada
Phone: (204) 989-3292
<www.eegsociety.org>

FEDERATION OF EAST EUROPEAN FAMILY HISTORY SOCIETIES
Box 321, Springville UT 84663
<feefhs.org>

GENEALOGY UNLIMITED INTERLINK BOOKSHOP
4687 Falaise Drive, Victoria, British Columbia, V8Y 1B4 Canada
E-mail: orders@genealogyunlimited.com
<www.genealogyunlimited.com>

IMMIGRATION HISTORY RESEARCH CENTER
University of Minnesota, College of Liberal Arts, 311 Andersen Library, 222 21st Ave. S, Minneapolis, MN 55455
Phone: (612) 625-4800
Fax: (612) 626-0018
E-mail: ihrc@umn.edu
<www.ihrc.umn.edu>

ROUTES TO ROOTS FOUNDATION
136 Sandpiper Key, Secaucus, NJ 07094
Phone: (201) 866-4075
Fax: (201) 864-9222
<www.rtrfoundation.org>

BOOKS

A Dictionary of Jewish Surnames from the Russian Empire by Alexander Beider (Avotaynu)

Following the Paper Trail: A Multilingual Translation Guide by Jonathan D. Shea and William F. Hoffman (Avotaynu)

In Search of Your European Roots: A Complete Guide to Tracing Your Ancestors in Every County in Europe by Angus Baxter (Genealogical Publishing Co.)

The Penguin Historical Atlas of Russia by John Channon with Robert Hudson (Viking)

Where Once We Walked: A Guide to the Jewish Communities Destroyed in the Holocaust by Gary Mokotoff and Sallyann Amdur Sack with Alexander Sharon (Avotaynu)

WOWW Companion: A Guide to the Communities Surrounding Central and Eastern European Towns by Gary Mokotoff (Avotaynu)

WEBSITES

Family History Library Catalog
<www.familysearch.org>

FEEFHS Map Room: Russian Empire
<www.feefhs.org/maplibrary.html>

GenForum
<genforum.genealogy.com/regional/countries>

JewishGen
<www.jewishgen.org>

Mailing Lists
<rootsweb.ancestry.com/~jfuller/gen_mail.
html>

Petro Jacyk Resource Centre
<pjrc.library.utoronto.ca>

BELARUS RESOURCES

ORGANIZATIONS AND ARCHIVES

NATIONAL HISTORICAL ARCHIVES OF BELARUS
55, Kropotkina St., Minsk, 220002, Republic of Belarus
Phone: +375 (17) 268-65-22
E-mail: niab@niab.by
<archives.gov.by/eng/index.php?id=503226>

NATIONAL HISTORICAL ARCHIVES OF BELARUS IN GRODNO
2, Tizengauza Square, Grodno, 230023, Republic of Belarus
Phone: +375 (152) 77 28 56
Fax: +375 (152) 74 31 04
E-mail: niab_grodno@tut.by, niabgrodno@rambler.ru
<archives.gov.by/eng/index.php?id=377130>

BOOKS
Belarusans in the United States by Vitaut Kipel
(University Press of America)

Historical Dictionary of Belarus by Jan Zaprudnik (Scarecrow Press)

WEBSITES
Belarus GenWeb
<rootsweb.ancestry.com/~blrwgw>

Belarusian Genealogy
<www.belarusguide.com/genealogy1>
Belarus Message Boards
<boards.ancestry.com/mbexec/board/an/
localities.eeurope.belarus>

Belarus SIG
<www.jewishgen.org/belarus>

Genealogy/Family History
<archives.gov.by/eng/index.php?id=12>

ESTONIA RESOURCES

ORGANIZATIONS AND ARCHIVES

ESTONIAN AMERICAN NATIONAL COUNCIL
243 E. 34th St., New York, NY 10016
Phone: (212) 685-0776
<www.estosite.org>

ESTONIAN BIOGRAPHICAL CENTER
Tiigi 10-51, 51003 Tartu, Estonia
Phone/fax: +372 742 0882
E-mail: info@isik.ee
<www.isik.ee/english>

ESTONIAN GENEALOGICAL SOCIETY
Pk 4419, 10511 Tallinn, Estonia
<www.genealoogia.ee/English/english.html>

ESTONIAN HISTORICAL ARCHIVES (*AJALOOARHIIV*)
J. Liivi 4, 50409 Tartu, Estonia
Phone: +372 (7) 387 500
Fax: +372 7/387 510
E-mail: ajalooarhiiv@ra.ee
<www.eha.ee/english/english.htm>

NATIONAL ARCHIVES OF ESTONIA (*RAHVUSARHIIV*)
J. Liivi 4, Tartu 50409, Estonia
Phone: +372 738 7500
Fax: +372 738 7510
E-mail: rahvusarhiiv@ra.ee
<rahvusarhiiv.ra.ee/en/national-archives>

NATIONAL LIBRARY OF ESTONIA
Tõnismägi 2, 15189 Tallinn, Estonia,
Phone: +372 630 7611
E-mail: nlib@nlib.ee
<www.nlib.ee/en>

STATE ARCHIVES OF ESTONIA (*RIIGIARHIIV*)
Maneézi 4, 15019 Tallinn, Estonia
Phone: +372 693 8036
Fax: +372 661 6230
E-mail: archive@ra.ee
<www.riigi.arhiiv.ee>

BOOKS
Estonia and the Estonians by Toivo U. Raun (Hoover Institution Press)

Estonian Experience and Roots by Sigrid Renate Maldonado (As Was Publishing)

The Estonians in America, 1627–1975: A Chronology and Fact Book by Jaan Pennar (Oceana Publications)

Following the Paper Trail: A Multilingual Translation Guide by Jonathan D. Shea and William F. Hoffman (Avotaynu)

A Guide to Jewish Genealogy in Latvia and Estonia by Arlene Beare (Jewish Genealogical Society of Great Britain)

WEBSITES
English-Estonian Dictionary
<dict.ibs.ee>

Estonia Genealogy Resources
<feefhs.org/links/estonia.html>

Estonia Message Boards
<boards.ancestry.com/mbexec/board/an/localities.scan-balt.estonia>

Estonica
<www.estonica.org>

How to Find Relatives in Estonia
<www.aai.ee/~urmas/urm/vast.html>

LATVIA RESOURCES

ORGANIZATIONS AND ARCHIVES

AMERICAN LATVIAN ASSOCIATION
400 Hurley Ave., Rockville, MD 20850
Phone: (301) 340-1914
Fax: (301) 341 8732
E-mail: alainfo@alausa.org
<www.alausa.org>

LATVIAN STATE HISTORICAL ARCHIVES
Slokas iela 16, Riga 1050, Latvia,
Phone: +371 67613118
Fax: +371 67612406
E-mail: vestures.arhivs@arhivi.gov.lv
<www.arhivi.lv/index.php?&3>

STATE ARCHIVES OF LATVIA
Bezdeligu 1, Riga 1048, Latvia
Phone: +371 67462317
Fax: +371 67460462
E-mail: lva@arhivi.gov.lv
<www.archiv.org.lv/indexe.php?id=11>

BOOKS
A Guide to Jewish Genealogy in Latvia and Estonia by Arlene Beare (Jewish Genealogical Society of Great Britain)

The Jews of Lithuania: A History of a Remarkable Community 1316–1945 by Masha Greenbaum (Gefen Books)

The Latvians: A Short History by Andrejs Plakans (Hoover Institution Press)

The Latvians in America, 1640–1973: A Chronology and Fact Book edited by Maruta Karklis, Liga Streips and Laimonis Streips (Oceana Publications)

The Latvians: A Short History by Andrejs Plakans (Hoover Institution Press)

The Latvians in America, 1640–1973: A Chronology and Fact Book by Maruta Karklis (Oceana Publications)

WEBSITES

Latvia Message Boards
<boards.ancestry.com/mbexec/board/an/localities.scan-balt.latvia>

Latvian-English Dictionary
<dictionary.site.lv/dictionary>

Latvian GenWeb
<rootsweb.ancestry.com/~lvawgw>

The Latvian Language
<www.codefusion.com/latvian>

Latvians.com
<www.latvians.com>

LITHUANIA RESOURCES

ORGANIZATIONS AND ARCHIVES

BALZEKAS MUSEUM OF LITHUANIAN CULTURE
6500 S. Pulaski Road, Chicago, IL 60629
Phone: (773) 582-6500
E-mail: info@balzekasmuseum.org
<www.lithaz.org/museums/balzekas>

LITHUANIAN CENTRAL STATE ARCHIVES
O. Milašiaus 21, LT-10102, Vilnius, Lithuania
Phone: +370 5 247 7811
Fax: +370 5 276 5318
E-mail: lcva@archyvai.lt
<www.archyvai.lt/en/archives/centralarchives.html>

LITHUANIAN GLOBAL GENEALOGICAL SOCIETY
Box 109, Redondo Beach, CA 90277
<www.lithuaniangenealogy.org>

LITHUANIAN SPECIAL ARCHIVES
Gedimino 40/1, LT-01110, Vilnius, Lithuania
Phone: +370 5 251 4210
Fax: +370 5 251 4211
E-mail: lya@archyvai.lt
<www.archyvai.lt/en/archives/specialarchives.html>

LITHUANIAN STATE HISTORICAL ARCHIVES
Gerosios Vilties 10, LT-03134 Vilnius, Lithuania
Phone: +370 5 213 7482
Fax: +370 5 278 43 69
E-mail: istorijos.archyvas@lvia.lt
<www.archyvai.lt/en/archives/historicalarchives.html>

BOOKS

Address List of Roman Catholic Churches in Lithuania by Jonathan D. Shea (Language and Lineage Press)

Gazetteer of Lithuania: Names Approved by the United States Board on Geographic Names (Defense Mapping Agency)

The Jews of Lithuania: A History of a Remarkable Community 1316–1945 by Masha Greenbaum (Gefen Books)

Lithuania: Past, Culture, Present edited by Saulius Zukas (Baltos Lankos)

Lithuanian Customs and Traditions by Danuté Brazyté Bindokiené (*Pasaulio lietuviu bendruomene*)

The Lithuanian Pioneers: A Study of Lithuanian Immigration to the United States Before World War I by Jessie Ecker Daraska (J.R. Daraska)

Spisok Naselennykh Mest Estliandskoi Gubernii (Revel)

WEBSITES

Lithuania Message Boards
**<boards.ancestry.com/mbexec/board/an/
localities.scan-balt.lithuania>**

Lithuanian Genealogical Research
**<www.rootsweb.com/~ilwinneb/lithuani.
htm>**

Lithuanian Genealogical Resources
<www.feefhs.org/links/lithuania.html>

Lithuanian Heritage Magazine
<www.lithuanianheritage.com>

Lithuanian Place Name Changes
**<www.rootsweb.com/~ilwinneb/placelit.
htm>**

MOLDOVA RESOURCES

ORGANIZATIONS AND ARCHIVES

CENTRAL STATE ARCHIVES (*SERVICIUL DE STAT DE ARHIVA*)
67b Gheorghe Asachi St., Kishinev 277028,
Republic of Moldova
Phone: +373 22 73 58 27
Fax: +373 22 72 10 57
E-mail: arhiva.national@gmail.com
<www.arhiva.gov.md>

BOOKS

*Historical Dictionary of the Republic of
Moldova* by Andrei Brezianu (Scarecrow Press)

*Jewish Roots in Ukraine and Moldova: Pages
from the Past and Archival Inventories* by
Miriam Weiner (Routes to Roots Foundation/
YIVO Institute)

WEBSITES

Moldova GenWeb
<rootsweb.ancestry.com/~mdawgw>

Moldova Message Boards
**<boards.ancestry.com/mbexec/board/an/
localities.eeurope.moldova>**

RUSSIA RESOURCES

ORGANIZATIONS AND ARCHIVES

**AMERICAN HISTORICAL SOCIETY OF
GERMANS FROM RUSSIA**
631 D St. , Lincoln, NE 68502
Phone: (402) 474-3363
<www.ahsgr.org>

**AMERICAN SOCIETY OF RUSSIAN NAVAL
HISTORY**
c/o Richard A. Russell, 12201 Jonathons Glen
Way, Herndon, Virginia 20170
**<www.feefhs.org/links/Russia/ASRNH/
FRGASRNH.HTML>**

**CENTRAL HISTORICAL ARCHIVE OF
MOSCOW (TSIAM)**
117393, Moscow, ul. Union, 80, Russia
Phone.: +8 (499) 128-68-06,
E-mail: mosarch@mos.ru
<www.rusarchives.ru/state/ciam>

**CENTRAL STATE MOSCOW HISTORICAL
ARCHIVES (*CENTRALNYJ ISTORICHESKIJ
MOSKOVSKIJ ARCHIV, CIMA*)**
ul Profsoyuznaya 80, 117393
Moskva (Moscow), Russia

**CENTRAL STATE HISTORICAL ARCHIVE OF
ST. PETERSBURG**
ul. Pskovskaia, 18, 190121, St. Petersburg, Russia
Phone: (812) 495-29-61
E-mail: cgia@mail.wplus.net
<www.rusarchives.ru/state/cgiaspb>

EAST EUROPEAN GENEALOGICAL SOCIETY
Box 2536, Winnipeg, MB
Canada R3C 4A7
Phone: (204) 989-3292
E-mail: info@eegsociety.org
<www.eegsociety.org/Home.aspx>

EMBASSY OF THE RUSSIAN FEDERATION

2650 Wisconsin Ave. NW, Washington, DC 20007
Phone: (202) 298-5700
<www.russianembassy.org>

FEDERAL ARCHIVAL SERVICE OF RUSSIA (*ROSARKHIV*)

103132, Moscow, ul. Il're inka, 12, Russia
Phone: + (8) 495 (606) 35-31
E-mail: rosarchiv@gov.ru
<archives.ru/rosarhiv/contact.shtml>

FEDERATION OF EAST EUROPEAN FAMILY HISTORY SOCIETIES (FEEFHS)

Box 321, Springville UT 84663
<www.feefhs.org>

STATE ARCHIVE OF THE RUSSIAN FEDERATION (GARF)

119992, Moscow, ul., Most Pirogovskaya 17, Russia
Phone: + 8 (495) 580-88-41
E-mail: garf@statearchive.ru
<www.rusarchives.ru/federal/garf>

BOOKS

Archives of Russia: A Directory and Bibliographic Guide to Holdings in Moscow and St. Petersburg edited by Patricia Kennedy Grimsted (M.E. Sharpe)

Dictionary of Russian Personal Names by Morton Benson (Cambridge University Press)

Following the Paper Trail: A Multilingual Translation Guide Jonathan D. Shea and William F. Hoffman (Avotaynu)

In their Words: A Genealogist's Translation Guide to Polish, German, Latin and Russian Documents, Volume II: Russian by Jonathan D. Shea and William F. Hoffman (Available through The Polish Genealogical Society of America)

Migration from the Russian Empire series edited by Ira A. Glazier (Genealogical Publishing Co.)

The Palgrave Historical Atlas of Eastern Europe by Dennis P. Hupchick (Palgrave Macmillan)

The Russian Americans by Paul Robert Magocsi (Chelsea Hous)

Where Once We Walked: A Guide to the Jewish Communities Destroyed in the Holocaust, Revised Edition by Gary Mokotoff and Sallyann Sack with Alexander Sharon (Avotaynu)

WEBSITES

All Russia Family Tree
<www.vgd.ru/about_en.htm>

ArcheoBiblioBase International Institute of Social History
<www.iisg.nl/abb/>

BLITZ Glossary of Russian Genealogy Terms
<feefhs.org/members/blitz/bz-gloss.html>

Doukhobor genealogy
<www.doukhobor.org/index.html>

FamilySearch Wiki Russia
<www.familysearch.org/learn/wiki/en/Russia>

Genealogia.ru
<www.genealogia.ru/gene/bpg/default.asp>

Geographical Atlas of the Russian Empire
<www.familytree.ru/en/maps/state-ru3.htm>

Germans From Russia Heritage Collection
<library.ndsu.edu/grhc>

HalGal
<www.halgal.com>

History of Russia (in Russian)
<www.ostu.ru/personal/nikolaev/russia.html>

Information on the area of Murom, Russia
<www.feefhs.org/links/Russia/MUROM/
murom.html>

Index of Russian Genealogy Terms
<www.doukhobor.org/Terms-General.htm>

JewishGen
<www.jewishgen.org>

Looking 4 Kin Genealogy & Family History
Network (Russia)
<www.looking4kin.com/group/
russiagenealogy>

Maps: Russian Empire
<www.feefhs.org/maplibrary.html>

Online English-Russian-English Dictionary
<www.freedict.com/onldict/rus.html>

Routes to Roots
<www.routestoroots.com>

Russian Message Boards
<boards.ancestry.com/localities.asia.russia/
mb.ashx>

Russian Ancestry Research Services
<www.feefhs.org/members/blitz/frgblitz.
html>

Russian Empire Genealogical Primer
<familysearch.org/learn/wiki/en/
images/3/30/Russian_Empire_Genealogical_
Primer.pdf>

Russia Genealogy Research Group on Facebook
<www.facebook.com/RussiaGenealogy>

Russian GenWeb
<www.rootsweb.ancestry.com/~ruswgw>

Russia Mailing Lists
<www.rootsweb.ancestry.com/~jfuller/gen_
mail_country-rus.html>

Russian Life Magazine
<www.rispubs.com>
Russian Central State Military Historical Archive
<www.feefhs.org/links/Russia/MUROM/
csmha.html>

Russian Word List (FamilySearch)
<familysearch.org/learn/wiki/en/
images/8/86/Russian_Word_List.pdf>

Russian Word List
<net.lib.byu.edu/fslab/researchoutlines/
Europe/Russia.pdf>

Sher's Russian Index
<www.websher.net/inx/icdefault1.htm>

St. Petersburg Genealogy Portal
<petergen.com/indexe.htm>

UKRAINE RESOURCES

ORGANIZATIONS AND ARCHIVES

CENTRAL STATE HISTORICAL ARCHIVE OF UKRAINE IN KYIV
Solomianska St., 24, 03110 Kyiv-110 Ukraine
Phone: +380(44) 275-30-02
Fax: +380(44) 275-30-02
E-mail: mail@cdiak.archives.gov.ua
<www.archives.gov.ua/Eng/Archives/ca03.
php>

CENTRAL STATE HISTORICAL ARCHIVE OF UKRAINE IN LVIV
Soborna Sq., 3A, 79008 Lviv-8 Ukraine
Phone: +380 (32) 235-45-08
Fax: +380 (32) 235-45-08
E-mail: office@cdial.org.ua
<www.archives.gov.ua/Eng/Archives/ca04.
php>

UKRAINIAN MUSEUM-ARCHIVES
<www.umacleveland.org>
1202 Kenilworth Ave., Cleveland, OH 44113
Phone: (216) 781-4329
E-mail: staff@umacleveland.org

BOOKS

Sources for Researching Ukrainian Family History by Paul J. Himka (Canadian Institute of Ukrainian Studies)

The Ukrainian Americans by Myron B. Kuropas (University of Toronto Press)

Ukrainians in North America edited by Dmytro M. Shtohryn (Association for the Advancement of Ukrainian Studies)

WEBSITES

Genealogical Research
<www.archives.gov.ua/Eng/genealogia.php>

Genealogy of Halychyna/Eastern Galicia
<www.halgal.com>

InfoUkes
<www.infoukes.com>

Ukraine Genealogy Resources
<feefhs.org/links/ukraine.html>

Ukraine Message Boards
<boards.ancestry.com/mbexec/board/an/localities.eeurope.ukraine>

Ukraine WorldGenWeb
<rootsweb.ancestry.com/~ukrwgw>

Ukrainian Genealogy Group: National Capitol Region
<ukrainiangenealogygroup-ncr.org>

Volhynia
<www.volhynia.com>

CHAPTER ELEVEN

ITALY

By Sharon DeBartolo Carmack

REGIONAL GUIDE

Ask a researcher tracing Italians "What's new?" and you're likely to get a shoulder shrug, a toe kicking the dirt and a mumbled "Not much."

It seems Italian genealogy is moving into the electronic age at a sloth's pace. A minuscule number of Italian records are popping up on sites such as Ancestry.com **<ancestry.com>** and FamilySearch **<familysearch.org>**, but I bet they aren't the ones you need.

The reason for this sluggish progress? In Italy, records—births, marriages, deaths, recent censuses and church records—are kept at the local level, in town halls and churches. Given that, in its Italian research outline **<familysearch. org/learn/wiki/en/Italy>**, the Family History Library (FHL) boasts "about 60,000 microfilms and microfiche containing information about people who've lived in Italy," that's a lot of records to digitize. And remember, the FHL doesn't have every record on microfilm for every town and every time period. So you can see the magnitude of the problem for going to all those local repositories and getting their records digitized and online.

The news isn't all gloom and doom, though, and the sidebar on page 214 outlines the process for digging into your Italian roots. But first, let's focus on ten steps that will enhance your research and get you going—without requiring you to go to Italy.

STEP 1 ✦ Comuni Italiani

This website <en.comuni-italiani.it> is *molto bene*! By clicking on one of the regions in Italy, Apulia (Puglia in Italian), say, you'll learn the names of all the provinces. Then click on a province—I chose my ancestors' province of Bari—to get a list of all its towns and cities. Then click on the town, in my case Terlizzi, and you'll discover helpful genealogy links.

One link gives you a Google map of the area. You can zoom in for a detailed street map. Another link delivers you to a phone directory so you can track down potential relatives with your surname. I tried *DeBartolo* but didn't get any hits—which I thought odd, as I've visited DeBartolo cousins in the town. When I entered just *Bartolo*, however, it brought up all the DeBartolos in Terlizzi.

By clicking on the town's official site, I could take a virtual tour of the area or look at photos of local landmarks. And if you're wondering who the town's patron saint is—or the mayor—you can find that information along with the number of families who live there.

The town page on Comuni Italiani gives you the address and the phone and fax numbers for the town hall, as well as an e-mail link. Of course, you'll need to write your letter or e-mail in Italian. See page 211 for translation sites.

STEP 2 ✦ Social Histories

Genealogical research gives you only half the story—the who (names), where (places) and when (dates). But social history research gives you the other half: the how, what and why. How did your ancestors live their lives? Why did they leave Italy? What was it like to be an Italian immigrant in America?

Unless you're fortunate enough to have surviving letters and diaries—or even better, the immigrant generation still alive to tell you—reading social history books can give you details that fill out the bare bones on your ancestor charts.

Italian-American life and immigration is well explored in classic books such as *La Storia: Five Centuries of the Italian American Experience* by Jerre Mangione and Ben Morreale (Harper Perennial), *Italian-American Folklore*, by Frances M. Malpezzi and William M. Clements (August House Publishers) and *Blood of My Blood: The Dilemma of the Italian-Americans* by Richard Gambino (Guernica Editions).

More recent publications include oral histories, autobiographies and memoirs of Italian-American life and culture. For example, *The Italian American Reader* by Bill Tonelli (Harper Paperbacks) is an anthology bearing the description "part manifesto, part Sunday dinner." It's a collection of excerpts from Italian-American–authored novels, memoirs, short stories, essays and poems, covering a broad spectrum of lives from little Italian grandmas to gangsters.

STEP 3 ✦ Italian Newspapers

The country's largest collection of Italian language and Italian-American newspapers and periodicals is archived at the Immigration History Research Center (IHRC) at University of Minnesota in Minneapolis **<www.ihrc. umn.edu/research/periodicals/italian.php>**. The IHRC is open to researchers weekdays; see the website for hours. You can purchase copies of most IHRC microfilm or borrow it through interlibrary loan (ask your librarian to make the request for you). In extraordinary circumstances, the staff can conduct research for you at a charge of $40 per hour.

Not many Italian papers have been digitized, but continue to check newspaper websites such as GenealogyBank **<www. genealogybank.com>**. If your Italian ancestors settled in major cities such as Boston, New York or Chicago, you're more likely to find obituaries or other news items about them in mainstream newspapers that are digitized online.

STEP 4 ✦ Order Sons of Italy in America

According to its website **<www.osia.org/ about/history.php>**, the Order Sons of Italy in America (OSIA) was originally called *Figli d'Italia*. A group of Italian immigrants who came to the United States during the great Italian migration from 1880 to 1923, including Dr. Vincenzo Sellaro, established the organization in New York City's Little Italy on June 22, 1905. They wanted to create a support system that would help Italian immigrants become US citizens, assimilate to American life, and obtain health and death

TIME LINE

753 B.C. ✦	Rome founded.
509 B.C. ✦	Rome becomes a republic.
44 B.C. ✦	Julius Caesar assassinated
30 B.C. ✦	Virgil writes *The Aeneid*.
27 B.C. ✦	Roman Empire established; Augustus crowned first emperor.
476 A.D. ✦	Visigoths conquer Rome, ending the Empire.
1054 ✦	Roman Catholic and Orthodox churches split.
1096 ✦	World's first university founded at Salerno.
1202 ✦	Leonardo Fibonacci's Liber Abaci introduces Arabic numerals.
1321 ✦	Dante Alighieri completes *The Divine Comedy*.
1340 ✦	Italian Renaissance begins (–c. 1550).
1492 ✦	Christopher Columbus lands in West Indies.
1512 ✦	Michelangelo finishes the Sistine Chapel ceiling.
1524 ✦	Giovanni da Verrazzano is first person to sight New York.
1532 ✦	Niccolo Machiavelli's *The Prince* published posthumously.
1582 ✦	Gregorian calendar introduced.
1659 ✦	Sicilian Francisco Procopio perfects ice-cream making.
1861 ✦	Kingdom of Italy declared.
1865 ✦	The capital moves from Turin to Florence.
1870 ✦	Rome becomes the capital of Italy.
1895 ✦	Guglielmo Marconi invents the telegraph.

1900 ◆	Puccini's *Tosca* first performed.
1905 ◆	First pizzeria in New York City.
1908 ◆	A 7.1-magnitude earthquake kills as many as 200,000 people in Sicily and southern Italy.
1915 ◆	Italy enters World War I aligned with the French and British.
1922 ◆	Benito Mussolini becomes prime minister.
1940 ◆	Italy invades Greece, entering World War II.
1943 ◆	Nazi troops occupy Northern Italy.
1946 ◆	Italy becomes a republic.
1955 ◆	Italy joins the United Nations.
1960 ◆	Rome hosts the Summer Olympics.
1968 ◆	Luciano Pavarotti debuts in the United States.
1972 ◆	Francis Ford Coppola films *The Godfather*.
1998 ◆	Italy's Oscar-winning *Life Is Beautiful* earns a record $57 million.
1999 ◆	Restoration of Leonardo da Vinci's *Last Supper* completed.
2006 ◆	Turin hosts the Winter Olympics.

benefits and educational opportunities. More than 600,000 members of this still-active group belong to 650 chapters (or lodges) across the country, and membership is open to men and women of Italian heritage.

The IHRC in Minneapolis is the depository for the organization's historical membership and other records. If you think a relative was a member, visit **<www.ihrc.umn.edu/research/vitrage>** and type *Order Sons of Italy* into the Search field to learn what records the IHRC holds. But as mentioned above, if you find a promising entry, you'll need to visit the center or hire someone to check the records for you.

STEP 5 ◆ Naming Traditions

Learning the traditional naming pattern many Italians followed might help you identify more relatives in Italian records. Most couples stuck to the custom of naming the first son after the father's father; the second son after the mother's father; the third son after the father; the first daughter after the father's mother; the second daughter after the mother's mother; and the third daughter after the mother. If you haven't identified your immigrant ancestor's parents, you can make an educated guess about their given names based on this pattern.

For example, Salvatore and Angelina (Vallarelli) Ebetino named their children—listed in birth order—as follows:

1. Francesco
2. Fortunato
3. Fortunato
4. Stella
5. Isabella

6. Felice
7. Michele
8. Michele
9. Salvatore

From this, we can reasonably guess that Salvatore's parents' names were Francesco and Stella, the names of his first son and daughter, and that Angelina's parents were Fortunato and Isabella, the names of her second son and daughter. My further research confirmed this was exactly the case.

Notice, also, that they named two children Fortunato and two Michele. This is because the first Fortunato and the first Michele died in infancy. To preserve the naming pattern, Salvatore and Angelina used the names again for the next child born of the same sex. This type of name is known as a necronym and was common in Italian families. To find out more about Italian names, visit Behind the Name **<www.behindthename.com/names/usage/italian>**, which gives you Italian name details such as pronunciation, origin and masculine or feminine usage. For more sites on Italian first and last names, visit **<www.angelfire.com/ok3/pearlsofwisdom/ italynames.html>**.

STEP 6 ✦ Translation Tools

Translating words from Italian genealogy records is as easy as typing them into a translation website. For just a word or two, you can use an online translation dictionary, such as Reverso **<dictionary.reverso.net/english-italian>**. For longer phrases and sentences, try Babylon.com **<translation.babylon.com/Italian/to-English>** or Google **<translate.google.com>**.

If you're writing a short records request to an Italian town hall, you can paste your letter in English and then have it translated into Italian. Remember, though, that you'll get a literal translation. For best results, compose your English version in formal language, avoiding contractions, slang and colloquialisms (otherwise, your letter might sound like one of those foreign spam e-mails asking to deposit millions of dollars into your bank account). You also can use FamilySearch's Italian letter-writing guide to compose your request **<familysearch.org/learn/ wiki/en/Italy_Letter_Writing_Guide>**. It also tells you how much money to send and in what currency, and where to mail your request.

Historical records can be more tricky to translate because of the dialects and archaic language. To help you translate civil registration birth, marriage and death records that you've found on microfilm from the Family History Library, there are full translations of those records in Lynn Nelson's *A Genealogist's Guide to Discovering Your Italian Ancestors* (Betterway Books). The book is out of print, but you might be able to find used copies online or at a library. Some websites also offer, for a fee, a human to translate your letter or document, or you can find a translator using the Association of Professional Genealogists directory **<apgen.org/directory>**.

ITALIAN RECORDS AT A GLANCE

CIVIL REGISTERS OF BIRTH, MARRIAGE AND DEATH
- begin in 1809 for most of Italy
- begin about 1820 for Sicily
- begin in 1866 for other areas

The Family History Library (FHL) has microfilmed civil registers up to 1866 for much of central and southern Italy and some of northern Italy. In some cases, FHL film goes up to 1910. The original records are kept at local registrars' offices in each town or city.

CHURCH RECORDS
- baptism records begin about 1500
- marriage and death records begin about 1520

The FHL has records from some parishes up to 1900 and some up to 1925. Surviving records are kept at the local parish church.

MILITARY RECORDS
- begin in 1792 for enlisted men
- conscription of all males began in 1865

The FHL has microfilmed records from the 1800s through the early 1900s for the provinces of Parma, Cosenza, Catania and Torino. Copies of original records are kept in local military archives and, after 75 years, transferred to the provincial archives and made public.

STEP 7 ✦ Research Guides

FamilySearch also offers free Italian research helps at **<familysearch.org/learn/wiki/en/Italy>**. Listed along with the letter-writing guide mentioned in step 6, you'll find links to maps of Italy, a Historical Background of Italy, the PDF pamphlet "Finding Records of Your Ancestors" with details on how to find and read Italian civil records, and several step-by-step guides for finding and using different types of Italian records.

STEP 8 ✦ Italian Genealogical Group

Though it's based in New York City, the Italian Genealogical Group **<www.italiangen.org>** has membership worldwide. The group's website includes a database of surnames and Italian localities members are researching. If you find a name and place that match your interests, click the e-mail link and ask for the name of the submitter.

The IGG site also has several databases of records, but they're mostly for New York. You'll find naturalization and vital records indexes, including New York City Deaths, 1898 to 1948, and New York City Births (this currently indexes records from 1880 to 1909). Links let you print forms to request the records from the city's vital records office **<http://www.nyc.gov/html/records/html/archives/geneology.shtml>**.

ORGANIZATIONS AND ARCHIVES

AMERICAN ITALIAN HERITAGE ASSOCIATION
Box 3136, Albany, NY 12203
Phone: 518 435 1979
E-mail: aiha.albany@gmail.com
<www.aiha-albany.org>

ITALIAN GENEALOGICAL GROUP
Box 626, Bethpage, NY 11714
<www.italiangen.org>

ITALIAN GENEALOGICAL SOCIETY OF AMERICA
Box 3572, Peabody, MA 01961
<www.italianroots.org>

ISTITUTO GENEALOGICO ITALIANO
E-mail: iagifaig@gmail.com
<www.iagi.info>

NATIONAL ITALIAN AMERICAN FOUNDATION
1860 19th St. NW, Washington, DC 20009
Phone: (202) 387-0600
Fax: (202) 387-0800
E-mail: information@niaf.org
<www.niaf.org>

PURSUING OUR ITALIAN NAMES TOGETHER
Box 82309, Dept. PHP, Las Vegas, NV 89180
<www.point-pointers.net>

BOOKS

Annuario delle Diocesi d'Italia, 1951 (Yearbook of the dioceses of Italy) (Marietta)

Archivio biografico italiano (Italian biographical archive) (K.G. Saur)

Archivio biografico italiano: Nuova serie (Italian biographical archive: New Series) (K.G. Saur)

Archivio genealogico (Genealogical studies) (Società Italiana di Studi Araldici e Genealogici)

Cataloghi a stampa di periodici delle biblioteche italiane (1859–1967): bibliografia descrittiva (Descriptive bibliography of periodicals in Italian libraries) by Gertrude Nobile Stolp (Leo S. Olschki)

Enciclopedia storico-nobiliare italiana (Historical encyclopedia of Italian nobility) (Enciclopedia storico-nobiliare italiana)

Finding Italian Roots: The Complete Guide for Americans, 2nd edition, by John P. Colletta (Genealogical Publishing Co.)

A Genealogist's Guide to Discovering Your Italian Ancestors: How to Find and Record Your Unique Heritage by Lynn Nelson (Betterway Books)

Genealogy in Italy by Guelfo Guelfi Camajani (Istituto genealogico italiano)

Indice biografico italiano (Italian biographical index) 4 volumes (K.G. Saur)

Indirizzi e numeri di telefono di tutta Italia (Addresses and telephone numbers of all of Italy) (Topware CD Service)

Internationaler biographischer Index (World biographical index) 3rd CD-ROM edition (K.G. Saur)

The Italian American Experience: An Encyclopedia, edited by Salvatore J. LaGumina, Frank J. Cavaioli, Salvatore Primeggia and Joseph A. Varacalli (Garland Publishing Co.)

A word of caution, though: When you initially click on an Italian Genealogy Group database link, you'll get a page that says "No More Databases! Unless … " This is a plea for indexing help from this volunteer organization. You can still get to the databases by scrolling down and clicking on the "To continue on to the databases" link.

While you're on the site, also look at the organization's newsletter articles on Italian genealogy. Not all the newsletters are posted online, so you may want to consider joining the group to get future issues.

STEP 9 ✦ Point

Pursuing Our Italian Names Together <www.point-pointers.net> is another membership organization. Its quarterly journal, *POINTers: The American Journal of Italian Genealogy*, is filled with articles on tracing Italian ancestry. The organization also sponsors a national conference every other year—it's one of the best conference bargains around.

Check out the link on POINT's home page to local chapters across the United States. If there is a POINT near you, it's a great way to network with other Italian researchers. And you can subscribe to the free POINT e-mail list by following another link on the site.

STEP 10 ✦ Mangia, Mangia!

What would an article on Italian resources be without bringing up food? Being Italian and loving food go hand in hand. But how, you may ask, will that help with my genealogy?

The answer is that food preferences are regional and local in Italy. Just as learning social history helps you better understand your ancestors, researching their dietary habits might shed light on why the family always ate fish on Christmas Eve (a Southern Italian tradition) or preferred polenta (historically, a staple in Northern Italy) to pasta. Details like these not only give more depth to your family's story, but they also provide ways to carry on the traditions of your heritage.

At the website LifeInItaly.com <www.lifeinitaly.com/food-wines>, you'll find several helpful articles on Italian food and wine for the different regions. In the link for Nonna's Food,

> ## CENSUS
> The first Italian census was taken in 1871; successive censuses were once each decade.
>
> The censuses taken from 1871 to 1901 are of limited use and are inconsistent in content. In most regions, the census named only the head of household, his occupation and the number of persons in the house. However, after 1911, the censuses list the names, ages, occupations, birthplaces and relationships to the head of the household for each resident.
>
> Census records up to 1991 are held in the state archive of each province. Census records from 1911 or 1921 to 1991 are also usually found in each *comune's anagrafe* (register's office). The availability to the public differs from *comune* to *comune*.

FOUR STEPS TO FINDING ITALIAN ANCESTORS

Those of us who have been tracing our Italian roots since the Dark Ages, long before the word *online* existed, have managed just fine. In fact, I traced my DeBartolo and Vallarelli lines back to the mid-1700s without leaving US shores and without the aid of a computer. If I can do it, you can, too—following these four key steps.

NUMERO UNO

If you know the town where your ancestors originated, you're one step further toward connecting your immigrant ancestor to his forebears in Italy. But sound genealogical research means starting with the present and working back one generation at a time. So first, gather all the identifying information you can in US sources. After all, you don't want to be tracing the wrong Antonio DeLeo in Italian records. Plus, your ancestor's name may be different in America from what it was in Italy: An immigrant I've helped research named Frank Miller was born Francesco Mollo. Ask family members if they know your immigrant ancestor's Italian name. In US census records (on microfilm in large libraries and online at subscription sites such as Ancestry.com **<ancestry.com>**) search first for the American name. If you get no results, try the Italian name.

NUMERO DUE

Next, move on to other US genealogical records such as births, marriages and deaths, again checking under both the American and Italian names.

Once you have a good idea of your ancestor's original name, you're ready to search passenger lists. These lists, created at the port of departure, are online at Ancestry.com, as well as on microfilm at many large libraries. New York arrival lists are free at CastleGarden.org **<castlegarden.org>** (1820 until the 1890s) and EllisIsland.org **<ellisisland.org>** (1892 to 1924). Even married Italian women usually used their maiden names when they traveled. My great-grandmother Angelina Ebetino, who was married when she immigrated in 1910 with her small children, was on the arrival list of the Verona as Angelina Vallarelli, her maiden name. But her children were listed with the surname Ebetino.

Francesco Mollo, age 30, sailed on the *Nord America*, arriving in New York Oct. 1, 1903. The list shows him as a married male whose occupation was "peasant." His last residence was "Rogiano." If you don't know where in Italy your ancestor came from, the passenger list might be your ticket back to the old country. If your ancestor became a US citizen after 1906, the town of origin should be recorded on his naturalization record.

Especially important to note on the passenger list is the column "Whether ever before in the United States; and if so, when and where?" Many Italians were "birds of passage," sailing back and forth between Italy and America one or more times before finally bringing their families to the United States. Frank, for example, had lived in Philadelphia from 1896 to 1901. That means there's another passenger list to look for and the 1900 census to check.

NUMERO TRE

Once you've exhausted the potential records America has to offer on your ancestor and you've learned his Italian hometown, it's time to cross the Atlantic. The Mollo family knew that "Rogiano" was actually Roggiano Gravina in the province of Cosenza and the region of Calabria. But if you're not sure of the spelling or full name of the town, run a Google search to find alternate spellings. Or try an online gazetteer, such as the Directory of Cities, Towns, and Regions in Italy **<www.fallingrain.com/world/IT>**. Next, check **<comuni-italiani.it>** for details such as the town's province and region.

NUMERO QUATTRO

Armed with the name of the town, province and region, check the online catalog of the Family History Library (FHL) in Salt Lake City to see what records are on microfilm. Run a place search on the town name and Italy. Most FHL Italian holdings are civil registrations of births, marriages and deaths, originally kept in town halls across Italy. Records from Roggiano Gravina include *registri dello stato civile* (civil registers) from 1809 to 1910.

The family believed Frank was born Aug. 18, 1873, so the microfilm reel with the 1873 volume was a logical place to start. Sure enough, Francesco Mollo was born that date. He was the son of Vincenzo Mollo and Maria Raffaella Aita, and the grandson of Francesco Saverino Mollo (after whom Francesco was named) and Giovanni Aita. The beauty of Italian records is that they typically name three generations.

These records are in Italian, but they're not all that difficult to use once you get the hang of it. Use the FamilySearch research guides and word lists **<https://familysearch.org/learn/wiki/en/Italian_Genealogical_Word_List>**. Typically, each year had its own volume for births, marriages and deaths, and the volumes are usually indexed. Be aware, however, that the index may be at the beginning or end of the volume. Occasionally, if a supplementary volume was used for that year, the index will be in the middle.

discover bits of wisdom on food and spices in the Italian diet, as well as herbal remedies. You'll also find recipes and tips for cooking pasta and making Italian bread and pizza. If you've ever wondered how good olive oil is produced, you'll learn about that here, too. And while you're on the site, check out the links for Heritage and History under the Culture tab at the top.

Maybe much hasn't changed in the way you'll research Italian ancestors, but there are more resources than ever before to help you fill in the gaps in your tree. *Buona fortuna* in your search!

Italian Genealogical Records: How to Use Italian Civil, Ecclesiastical, and Other Records in Family History Research by Trafford R. Cole (Ancestry)

Italian Repatriation from the United States, 1900–1914 by Betty Boyd Caroli (Center for Migration Studies)

Italians to America, Lists of Passengers Arriving at U.S. Ports, 1880–1899 (Scholarly Resources)

Italy and Associated Areas: Official Standard Names Approved by the U.S. Board on Geographic Names (US Government Printing Office)

La Storia: Five Centuries of the Italian American Experience by Jerre Mangione and Ben Morreale (HarperCollins)

Libro d'Oro della Nobiltà italiana (Golden book of the Italian nobility) (Collegio Araldico)

Our Italian Surnames by Joseph G. Fucilla (Genealogical Publishing Co.)

South Italian Folkways in Europe and America: A Handbook for Social Workers, Visiting Nurses, School Teachers and Physicians by Phyllis H. Williams (Russell & Russell)

The Unknown Internment: An Oral History of the Relocation of Italian Americans during World War II by Stephen Fox (Twayne Publishers)

PERIODICALS

Bollettino della Società di studi Valdese (Bulletin of the Society of Waldensian studies, Società di Studi Valdesi, 1935–)

POINTers: The American Journal of Italian Genealogy (POINT: Pursuing Our Italian Names Together, 1987–)

WEBSITES

Cyndi's List
<cyndislist.com/italy>

D'addezio: Italian Genealogy Search Tools and Articles
<www.daddezio.com/italgen.html>

Genealogia Italiana
<www.genealogiaitaliana.it/en>

ItalianAncestry.com
<www.italianancestry.com>

Italian Genealogical Group
<www.italiangen.org>

Italian Genealogy Homepage
<www.italgen.com>

Italian Genealogy Mailing Lists
<rootsweb.ancestry.com/~jfuller/ gen_mail_country-ita.html>

Italian Genealogy Online and All Things Italian
<www.angelfire.com/ok3/pearlsofwisdom>

Italy Genealogy Forum
<genforum.genealogy.com/italy>

Italy Maps
<www.lib.utexas.edu/Libs/PCL/Map_collection/italy.html>

Italy WorldGenWeb
<www.italywgw.org>

ItalyGen
<www.italygen.com>

Joe's Italian Genealogy Page
<www.caropepe.com/italy>

My Italian Family
<www.myitalianfamily.com>

Professional Italian Genealogy Research
<www.italianfamilytree.com>

CHAPTER TWELVE

GREECE

By Thomas MacEntee

REGIONAL GUIDE

What does it mean to have Greek heritage? Whether your family hails from the northern areas of Macedonia and Thrace, or the Peloponnese in the South, or one of the 200-plus inhabited islands, Greece is your homeland—your ancestry. A way of life. For a Greek-American, culture permeates every aspect of life: religion, food, music, language.

More than 1.3 million people in the United States claim Greek ancestry, including the likes of Jennifer Aniston, George Stephanopoulos, Tina Fey, Pete Sampras and Olympia Dukakis. Pursuing Greek roots isn't without challenges; you'll need an understanding of the country's sometimes-turbulent history, geopolitical changes, migration patterns, language, culture, naming traditions and available records. The journey, though, is immensely rewarding—and it begins with these records and resources.

History in the making

At its geographical peak during the Hellenic period, Greek civilization reached from Greece to Egypt and to the Hindu Kush mountains in Afghanistan. After the Romans arrived in the second century, Greece became part of Byzantium. Christianity took hold late in the third century. The Great Schism in 1054 split the Catholic church into its Western and Eastern Orthodox components, still in existence today.

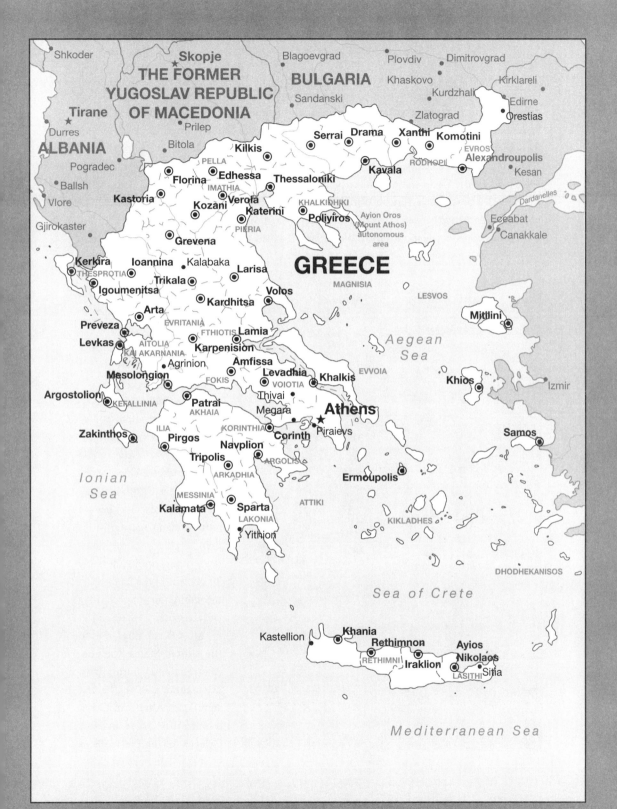

The Ottoman Turks invaded Greece in the mid-15th century and began a long period of domination, finally ending with Greek independence in the 1830s. Greece sought to enlarge its boundaries to include ethnic Greeks who'd settled outside the country proper. Britain returned the Ionian Islands in 1863. The Ottomans ceded Thessaly. After the Balkan Wars with Turkey (1912–1913), Greece claimed Epirus, southern Macedonia, Crete and the Aegean Islands. In 1947, it added the Dodecanese Islands from Italy.

In 1923, a post-Greco-Turkish War treaty made homeless about 1.5 million Greeks: A mass population exchange between Greece and Turkey kicked them out of Anatolia, Eastern Thrace and Pontus. Nazi occupation during World War II killed thousands of Greeks and deported Greek Jews. A postwar power vacuum helped cause the Greek Civil War, which lasted from 1946 to 1949. A military coup in 1967 led to the end of the monarchy in 1973. Democracy was eventually restored in 1975.

These political and economic forces converged to launch a massive immigration of Greeks to the United States and elsewhere starting in the late 18th century. Geography also has been a contributing factor: More than 75 percent of the country is mountainous, and only 30 percent of the land is fertile enough to support crops and livestock.

Most Greek migration to the United States, Canada, Australia and South Africa began around 1880. The first significant American Greek community arose in New Orleans during the 1850s; it built the country's first Greek

Temple of Zeus ruins, Athens

Orthodox church in 1866. By 1890, almost 15,000 Greeks lived in the United States. Most of these immigrants had come from Asia Minor and Aegean Islands still under Ottoman rule. Many passed through New York's Castle Garden immigration depot (the forerunner of Ellis Island), which they pronounced "Kastigari."

The influx picked up, with more than 450,000 Greeks arriving between 1890 and 1920. Almost 90 percent were men, who generally had every intention of returning home once they made enough money. In fact, you might discover passenger records showing several trips back and forth to Greece over a period of 10, 20 or 30 years.

Most Greek immigrants worked in major Northeastern cities, with some working railroads and mines in the West. An enterprising spirit often led them to establish businesses. Owning a restaurant attracted Greeks for a simple reason: The business was a family affair and relatives would become waiters, waitresses, dishwashers and cooks. In 1919, one in three Chicago restaurants was Greek-owned.

Today, the Windy City, New York City, Detroit, Boston, Baltimore, Dallas and Cleveland have high concentrations of Greek Americans. But the population prize goes to Tarpon Springs, Fla., where about 11 percent of residents have Greek roots.

In the 1920s, with US immigration restrictions and continued war in Greece, other countries saw an influx of immigrants from Greece and Cyprus. Almost 700,000 Australians claim Greek heritage, as do more than 250,000 Canadians.

Time Line

776 B.C.	First Olympic Games are held.
c.750– 700 B.C.	Homer writes *The Iliad* and *The Odyssey*.
c.750– 500 B.C.	City-states are formed throughout the Mediterranean that function as political units or *polis*, each ruled by a king and council.
490– 479 B.C.	Greek Persian Wars.
461– 446 B.C.	First of the Peloponnesian Wars begins between Sparta and Athens.
399 B.C.	Socrates is tried and executed for his opposition to the Thirty Tyrants.
356 B.C.	Alexander the Great is born.
267 A.D.	Goths ruin Athens, Sparta and Korinth.
286	Emperor Diocletian divides the Roman Empire in two, forming modern Greece (the Byzantine Empire).
641	Slavs overrun Greece.
1147	Roger II of Sicily takes Corfu from the Byzantines and pillages Corinth, Athens and Thebes.
1205	The duchy of Athens is founded by the crusader Othon de la Roche.
1303	Mercenaries employed by Byzantine Emperor Andronicus II defeat the Ottomans but turn against the empire.
1430	Sultan Murat II captures the Thessalonica, held by Venice since 1423.
1458	The Turks occupy Athens.

1770	At the instigation of Russian agents, the inhabitants of the Peloponnese rise up against Ottoman rule. The revolt is put down by the Turks with Albanian support.
1821	Archbishop Germanos of Patras calls for a Greek uprising against the Ottomans. The Ottomans begin a campaign of repression following a Greek massacre of Turks in the Peloponnese.
1823	Turks withdraw.
1830	Independence guaranteed by London Conference.
1863	Prince William of Denmark becomes King George of Greece.
1893	Corinth Canal opens.
1897	War with Ottoman Empire.
1913	King George is assassinated. His son Constantine, the duke of Sparta, becomes king.
1917	Pro-German King Constantine is forced by the Allies to abdicate.
1941	Greece attacked by Germany.
1946	Prolonged civil unrest threatens to start a civil war.
1949	The civil war ends with the defeat of the Communists
1952	Women are granted the right to vote.
1973	President George Papadopoulos ousted in a military coup.
1976	Pollution threatens to destroy the Acropolis.
1981	Greece joins the European Community (now Union)
1987	A heat wave kills 700.
2004	Athens hosts the Summer Olympics
2010	Greece faces a major debt crisis

Wars, a coup and the switch from a monarchy to republic mean that location names may have changed since your ancestors departed their homeland. Search by place in online with "Name Changes of Settlements in Greece" <**pandektis.ekt.gr/pandektis/handle/10442/4968**>, which draws from a database of name changes resulting from official administrative acts in Greece between 1913 and 1996. In addition to your ancestors' town name, you'll want to learn the municipality (*dímos*) to which the town belongs, as well as the district (*eparchia*) and county (*nomos*).

It's All Greek

Understanding the basics of the Greek alphabet and genealogy words will be invaluable when it's time to decipher resources. Invest in a Greek-English dictionary and use these learning aids:

- Lica Catsakis' Greek Genealogy Transliteration Chart <**greekgenealogy.org/index_files/Page679.htm**>
- Kefalonian Roots' Small Greek Grammar for Family History Researchers <**www.keffyroots.com/grammar.htm**>
- online translation tools such as Google Translate <**translate.google.com**>

Translating Greek names requires additional tools and knowledge. What might seem like complicated conventions to the non-Greek are part of Greek customs. Some of the following traditions are changing in the modern world, but they can offer clues to family historians.

GIVEN NAMES: The Greek tradition of naming a newborn after a grandparent can be traced back to antiquity. Usually, the first-

Santorini village

born son is named after the paternal grandfather, the first daughter after the paternal grandmother, the second son after the maternal grandfather, and the second daughter after the maternal grandmother. A baby also may be named after an older child who died. This continuous use of a name can help you theorize about grandparents' names. Another tradition: A child is never named after a living parent.

Because most Greek children are named after saints, a child celebrates his "name day" on that saint's feast day. Typically, a Name Day celebration was more important than a birthday. See **<www.namedays.gr>,** Greek Name Days, to find a specific Name Day based on a given name.

Watch out for alternate forms for a given name. For example, Aikaterini (which translates to Katherine) may appear as Katina; Dimitrios (James) could appear as Dimos. It was common for Greeks to Americanize their names to the closest English equivalent, or occasionally, an unrelated name. A helpful resource is the First Name Translator at **<www.daddezio.com/genealogy/greek/names.html>,** which lets you to translate to and from Greek and English.

For middle initials, children of both sexes took the first letter of their father's given name. Upon marriage, a Greek woman would usually change her middle initial to the first letter of her husband's name. When requesting records or asking for information from Greek repositories, it's best to leave a middle initial as is: Georgios I. Metropoulos, not Georgios Iannis Metropoulos.

SURNAMES: Most Greek surnames are patronymic: They derive from the first name of the original father of the family, often with the addition of the suffix *-opoulos*, meaning "descendant of," or *-akis* (associated primarily with Crete and the Aegean Islands). If you can learn the suffix or prefix, you may find clues to your family's origin (see the sidebar on page 225). A girl's surname was the possessive form of her father's given name.

Official records will use a formal style with names. For example, Metropoulos Georgios tou Iannis translates as "George of John Metropoulos" or George Metropoulos, son of John Metropoulos.

Greek immigrants often shortened their surnames after arriving in America. The name Papadopoulos might have become Pappas, or Mastoropoulos became Poulos. You'll find more specifics on naming traditions at **<en.wikipedia.org/wiki/Greek_name>**.

For the Record

The best method for tracing your Greek ancestors is to start with their lives in America. Verify where they settled, determine when and where they arrived and gather records from as many US sources as possible. Then if needed, start working with resources in Greece. The following US records will be particularly helpful.

CENSUS RECORDS: Trace your family in every census record available during their lifetime. The easiest way is to use online services such as subscription sites Ancestry.com **<ancestry.com>** and Archives.com **<archives.com>**, and the free FamilySearch.org **<familysearch.org>** (which has indexes and/or records for most US censuses, and links you to subscription sites to view some census records). Some census records are free at Internet Archive **<www.archive.org/details/us_census>**, though without a searchable index. Remember to check surname variations; census takers may have had a hard time spelling multisyllabic Greek names.

CITY DIRECTORIES: Once settled in America, your Greek ancestors might appear in local directories. Libraries often have print versions for the local area, as well as microfilm of directories for the local area and beyond. Online, use the links at the free Online Historical Directories **<sites.google.com/site/onlinedirectorysite>** and search the collections on Ancestry.com and subscription site Fold3.com **<fold3.com>**.

IMMIGRATION RECORDS: These encompass several types of records. Passenger lists could give you the passenger's name, origin and importantly, destination in America (later lists tend to provide more information). Resources for these include the Castle Garden **<castlegarden.org>** (pre-1892) and Ellis Island **<ellisisland.org>** (1892-1924) websites for New York arrivals, and Ancestry.com for all US ports. Remember that not all Greeks arrived in New York. Check lists for ports such as Boston, Philadelphia and New Orleans, as well as Canadian border crossings.

SURNAME CLUES

Certain Greek surname suffixes are associated with various parts of Greece, providing clues to where a family might have originated. Here are common place-based suffixes:

- **-akis:** Crete and the Aegean Islands
- **-akos:** Laconia
- **-as:** Macedonia and the Epirus
- **-atos or -etos:** Ionian islands
- **-eas:** Messenian part of the Mani peninsula
- **-allis or -ellis:** Dodecanese islands, mainly Rhodes
- **-iadia or -iades:** Asia Minor
- **-idis or -ides:** Asia Minor
- **-lis:** Turkey
- **-oglou:** Asia Minor
- **-ou:** Cyprus
- **-opoulos:** originally Peloponnesus, now widespread throughout Greece

Naturalization records include "first papers," or declarations of intention to naturalize, and "second papers," or petitions for naturalization. Not everyone filed for citizenship, but if your ancestors did, you may learn their birth date and place, date and port of arrival, and more (here, also, later records have more details). Naturalizations for 1906 and later are available for a fee through the Citizenship and Immigration Service Genealogy program **<www.uscis.gov/genealogy>**. Before then, records could be at any courthouse, so check court records where your ancestor lived. Run a place search of the Family History Library (FHL) catalog **<familysearch.org>** to see if it has microfilmed records for your ancestor's county. You can rent the film for viewing at a Family History Center **<familysearch.org/locations/centerlocator>**. Some state archives have naturalization records from their county courts; visit the website for your ancestor's state archives or call and ask. The aforementioned online services also have naturalization indexes and/or records for various regions of the country.

CHURCH RECORDS: The predominant religion among Greek-Americans is Eastern Orthodox Christianity. A number of others descend from Greece's small Sephardic and Romaniote Jewish communities (see Chapter 14 for more on Jewish research).

The Greek Orthodox Church not only served a spiritual role for the community, it was also the social center of Greek life. The Church provided Greek language schools, ladies' societies, Sunday schools and social functions, including modern-day festivals featuring food and dancing. The Church also helped Greek immigrants integrate into American society and develop their social and business networks.

Write or visit your ancestor's church to make your request for baptism and marriage records. The Greek Orthodox Archdiocese of America **<www.goarch.org>** can help you locate a parish where your ancestors lived. There are some obstacles, though: The church may not allow public access to its records, and the records are often handwritten in Greek and difficult to read. But don't let this deter you. It helps to call before you send a request, and you should consider making a small donation to cover staff time.

Going Greek

Once you've exhausted US sources and learned where your immigrant ancestors were from, you're ready to move on to records in Greece. Navigating these sources is a challenge, to say the least. I recommend Lica Catsakis's guides to family history research in Greece and her *Greek Gazetteer* (click Publications at **<www.greekgenealogy.org>**).

Fortunately, the Family History Library has microfilmed records including civil registrations and military records from a number of Greek counties. To see available film, check Catsakis's list of counties for which records have been filmed **<www.greekgenealogy.org/index_files/Page1631.htm>**, or type the town name (or simply Greece) into the FHL online catalog's place-names search **<www.familysearch.org/#form=catalog>**.

For civil vital registrations, which start in 1925, contact the municipality to which your ancestor's town belongs—or, in the case of a village, write to the community (*koinotis* or *koinotita*). Before 1925, write to your ancestor's church for records of births, marriages and deaths. Start with the church in his or her village, and if you don't get an answer, write the Greek Orthodox church headquarters in Athens for the name of the diocese (*mitropolis*) covering the village.

ORGANIZATIONS AND ARCHIVES

CHURCH OF GREECE
Aghias Filotheis 21, 10566 Athens, Greece
E-mail: contact@ecclesia.gr
<www.ecclesia.gr>

CYPRUS STATE ARCHIVES
CY-1461 Nicosia
Phone: +357 22 451045
Fax: +357 22 66 76 80
E-mail: mstatearchives@sa.mjpo.gov.cy
<www.mjpo.gov.cy>

EMBASSY OF GREECE
2221 Massachusetts Ave. NW, Washington, DC 20008
Phone: (202) 939-1300
Fax: (202) 939-1324
E-mail: gremb.was@mfa.gr
<www.mfa.gr/usa/en/the-embassy>

GENERAL STATE ARCHIVES OF GREECE
61 Daphne, PC 154 52 Psihiko, Greece
Phone: +30 210-6782200
Fax: +30 210-6782215
E-mail: archives@gak.gr
<www.gak.gr>

GREEK ORTHODOX ARCHDIOCESE OF AMERICA
8 E. 79th St., New York, NY 10075
Phone: (212) 570-3500
Fax: (212) 570-3569
<www.goarch.org>

HELLENIC HISTORICAL AND GENEALOGICAL ASSOCIATION
Box 710, Rye Beach, NH 03871
Phone: (603) 379-8140,
Fax: (603) 379-8141
E-mail: hellasgenealogy@papcoholdings.org
<www.helleniccomserve.com/genealogy.html>

HELLENIC LIBRARY AND HISTORICAL ARCHIVE
5 Aghiou Andreou St., 10556 Athens, Greece
Phone: +30 1 321 1149
Fax: +30 1 3667
E-mail: info@elia.org.gr
<www.elia.org.gr>

THE HELLENIC LITERARY AND HISTORICAL ARCHIVE
Aghiou Andreou 5, 10556 Athens, Greece
Phone: +30 210-3211149
Fax: +30 210-3213667
E-mail: info@elia.org.gr
<www.elia.org.gr>

HISTORICAL ARCHIVE OF CRETE
Jn. Sfakianaki 20, 73134 Chania, Greece
Phone: +30 28 210 52606
E-mail: mail@gak.chan.sch.gr
<gak.chan.sch.gr/history>

HISTORICAL SOCIETY OF PENNSYLVANIA: GREEK MANUSCRIPT COLLECTIONS
1300 Locust Street Philadelphia, PA 19107
Phone: (215) 732-6200
Fax: (215) 732-2680
E-mail: researchbymail@hsp.org
<www.hsp.org/collections>

NATIONAL ARCHIVES OF MALTA
Santo Spirito, Hospital Street, Rabat RBT 1043, Malta
Phone: +356 2145 9863
Fax: +356 2145 0078
E-mail: customercare.archives@gov.mt
<www.nationalarchives.gov.mt>

NATIONAL HELLENIC MUSEUM
333 South Halsted St., Chicago IL, 60661
Phone: (312) 655-1234
Fax: (312) 655-1221
<www.nationalhellenicmuseum.org>

NATIONAL HELLENIC RESEARCH FOUNDATION

48 Vassileos Constantinou Ave., 11635 Athens, Greece
Phone: +30 2107273700
Fax: +30 2107246618
E-mail: eie@eie.gr
<www.eie.gr/index-en.html>

NATIONAL STATISTICAL SERVICE
<www.statistics.gr>

SPEROS BASIL VRYONIS CENTER FOR THE STUDY OF HELLENISM

3140 Gold Camp Drive, Suite 50, Rancho Cordova, CA 95670
<www.loc.gov/rr/european/GrkColl/jcoles.html>

BOOKS

A Bibliographic Guide on Greeks in the United States, 1890–1968 By Michael N. Cutsumbis (Center for Migration Studies)

Carved in Stone: The Greek Heritage by Basil S. Douros (Five and Dot Corp)

Family History Research in Greece by Lica Catsakis (self-published)

The Genealogy of Greek Mythology by Vanessa James (Penguin)

The Greek Americans (Immigrant Experience) by Dimitris Monos (Chelsea House Publications)

Greek Gazetteer: A Dictionary of Towns, 2 volumes, by Lica Catsakis (LHC Bywater)

Greek Genealogical Research by Lica Catsakis (The Section)

Greek Immigrant Passengers, 1885–1910: A Guide and Index to Researching Early Greek Immigrants by Mary Voultsos (self-published)

Greek Immigrants, 1890–1920 by Rosemary Wallner (Blue Earth Books)

The Greeks in the United States by Theodore Saloutos (Harvard University Press)

A Guide to Greek Traditions and Customs in America by Marilyn Rouvelas (Nea Attiki Press)

A History of the Greeks in the Americas 1453–1938 by Paul Koken (First Page Publications)

A Lexicon of Greek Personal Names, multiple volumes, by P. M. Fraser and E. Matthews (Oxford University Press)

The Muslim and Christian Calendars by G.S.P. Freeman-Grenville (Bellew Publishing)

Studies in Greek Genealogy by Molly Broadbent (E.J. Brill)

Tracing Your Greek Ancestry by Antonia S. Mattheou (self-published)

WEBSITES

Cyndi's List: Greece
<www.cyndislist.com/greece>

Cyprus Genealogy Forum
<genforum.genealogy.com/cyprus>

D'Addezio Greek Genealogy Resources
<www.daddezio.com/grekgen.html>

Ellines.com: The Greek Connection
<www.ellines.com>

FamilySearch Research Wiki: Greece
<www.familysearch.org/learn/wiki/en/Greece>

Genforum Greece Genealogy Forum
<genforum.genealogy.com/greece>

GoGreece.com
<www.gogreece.com/society_culture/genealogy.html>

Greece Genealogy Forum
<genforum.genealogy.com/greece>

Greece GenWeb Project
<rootsweb.ancestry.com/~grcwgw>

Greece Research List
<www.feefhs.org/gr/grrl/grrl.html>

Greek Alphabet
<www.physlink.com/Reference/GreekAlphabet.cfm>

Greek Genealogy
<www.greekgenealogy.org>

Greek-English/English-Greek Dictionary
<www.kypros.org/cgi-bin/lexicon>

GreekFamilies.com
<www.greekfamilies.com>

A Guide to Greek Traditions and Customs in America
<www.greektraditions.org>

Hellenic Genealogy Geek
<hellenicgenealogygeek.blogspot.com>

Hellenic Genealogy Resources Facebook Group
<facebook.com/groups/101120679980726>

Hellenistic Resources Network
<www.hri.org>

Kefalonian Roots
<www.keffyroots.com/resaids.htm>

Lica Catsakis' Web Site
<www.licacatsakis.com>

Malta Certifikati: Public Registry
<www.certifikati.gov.mt>

Malta Genealogy Forum
<genforum.genealogy.com/malta>

MaltaGenealogy.com
<www.maltagenealogy.com>

Maltese Genealogy Services
<www.genealogyservicesmalta.com>

Mediterranean GenWeb Project
<sites.google.com/site/mediterraneangenweb>

Perry-Castañeda Library Map Collection: Greece Maps
<www.lib.utexas.edu/maps/greece.html>

The Republic of Cyprus on the Web
<www.pio.gov.cy>

Searchable maps of Greece
<www.nationsonline.org/oneworld/map/google_map_greece.htm>

Spartan Roots

CHAPTER THIRTEEN

Spain and Portugal

By Sunny Jane Morton

REGIONAL GUIDE

Since ancient times, the Iberian peninsula—encompassing Spain, Portugal and the long-contested Basque country—has been coveted and conquered by the Romans, Germanic tribes, Arabs, Holy Roman Empire and Napoleon. For genealogists today, tracing your ancestry in the Iberian region is a conquest with its own challenges: language barriers, decentralized records, lagging digitization and state takeovers of church registers, among others.

But those obstacles aren't insurmountable—technological weapons can help you break down language barriers, records access is gradually improving and the reward for tackling Spanish, Portuguese or Basque records likely will be well worth the struggle. The area's church and notarial records in particular are some of the world's richest genealogical treasures. Follow these four steps for your own successful assault on the formidable peninsula.

STEP 1 ✦ Using US Records

Identify your ancestor's city of birth or last foreign residence in US records. This city will become the target of your genealogical attack. Start by checking US marriage applications, delayed birth registrations, church records, obituaries, passenger lists or border crossings, naturalization paperwork, passport applications, SS-5s (Social Security applications), and after 1940, Alien Registrations.

No luck? Check the same sources for your ancestor's siblings. Then foray into lesser-known resources that might yield your ancestor's "real" surname or birth-

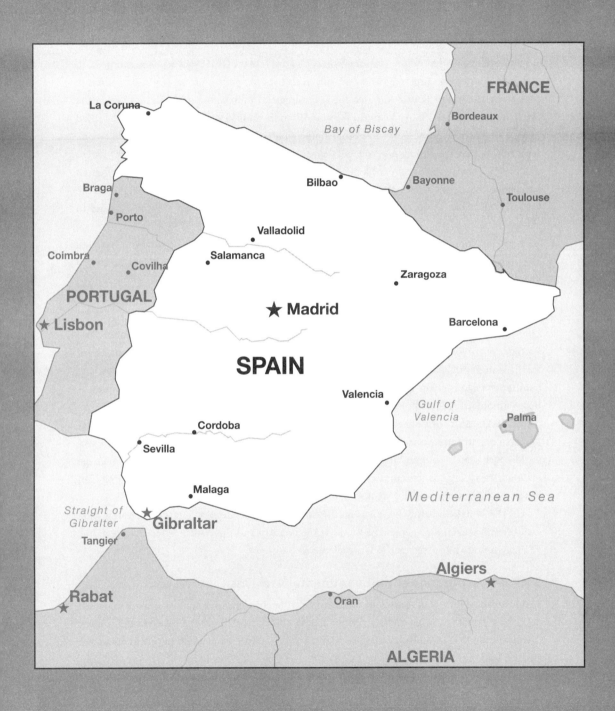

place. Fraternal organization records (particularly Portuguese), local histories, oral histories and Spanish colonial records have been collected by ethnic studies centers and genealogical societies, regional archives and museums, and the Family History Library (FHL) **<familysearch.org>**.

If you have an ancestral line that eventually leads back to Spain, it probably wanders through Mexico or Central or South America for several generations before arriving here. Even the Spanish who colonized St. Augustine, Fla., in 1565 (more than 40 years before the British settled Jamestown) arrived from Cuba and other points south. Before you're ready to tackle Spain's records, you may need to take a strategic detour through Latin American records. Portuguese and Basque immigrants are more likely to have stepped off the ship directly from their Iberian homeland. The largest waves of Portuguese settlers arrived in American fishing villages on the east and west coasts over the past two centuries. Basque arrivals quickly migrated inland to sheepherding regions of the American West.

Look for clues in larger migration patterns of incoming Spaniards, Portuguese and Basques. Did your immigrant ancestor live in one of these places? As a last resort, you might be able to guess at a region of origin based on where the neighbors came from.

STEP 2 ✦ Translation Tools

Like advanced weaponry, translation tools will do most of the fighting for you. Spanish and Portuguese are Romance languages with many similarities—you can see an animated map of the Iberian Peninsula's linguistic history here **<en.wikipedia.org/wiki/Iberian_Romance_languages>**. Don't go up against foreign-language reference materials or send off communications without using the following resources.

WORD LISTS: A cheat sheet of genealogical terms will help you read old records in a foreign tongue. Look to Family-Search's word lists **<wiki.familysearch.org/en/Translation_Services>** or do a web search on the terms genealogy word list and the language. Also turn to language dictionaries: George R. Ryskamp's *Finding Your Hispanic Roots* (Genealogical Publishing Co.) has an excellent section on old Spanish dialects.

LETTER-WRITING GUIDES: Again, FamilySearch is the place to look. On the Research Wiki **<wiki.familysearch.org>**, enter the name of the country and the phrase letter-writing guide. You may need to hire assistance to write a letter in Basque.

STEP 3 ✦ Geography and Governmental Archives

Spain is divided into 17 autonomous communities that encompass 50 smaller provinces, which in turn are home to towns or cities. Off the mainland, Spain includes the Balearic and Canary Islands. For mid-19th-century descriptions of most every little hamlet and parish in Spain, see Pascual Madoz's *Diccionario Geográfico-Estadístico-Histórico de España y Sus Posesiones de Ultramar* (view or download from our Google Library **<snipurl.com/ftm-google-library>**).

Availability and accessibility of Spanish government records varies by municipality and era. Some regions have their own historical languages or dialects (Basque, Catalan, Galician), and all have different archiving practices. Many records were lost during the civil war of 1936 to 1939. Some municipalities (such as Galicia) have put major effort into posting original images or indexes online. Others—namely Andalusia and Valencia—don't have extensive internet resources yet.

You can find municipal archives through Censo-Guía **<censoarchivos.mcu.es/ CensoGuia/directorioarchivosInicial.htm>** by following these steps (don't run this site through a web translator—it will limit the search function):

- From the *Tipo de Archivo* field, choose the type of archive (regional, parochial), then choose *España* for both *Área Geográfica* (geographic area) and *País* (country).
- In the box labeled *C.C.A.A./1a División*, look for the name of the autonomous community. *Provincia/2a División* asks for the province; *Municipios*, for the city; and *Núcleo de Población Menor*, for the name of a smaller population center.
- If you don't find an archive, delete the most specific levels of inquiry until you find one serving the larger area.

For the beginning Spanish researcher, the National Archives **<pares.mcu.es>** is most useful for web catalogs and directories that will help you locate records.

Portugal consists of the mainland and the Azores, Madeira and Cape Verde islands. Parishes are the basic unit of government; they

TIME LINE

1143	Portugal becomes independent; Alfonso I becomes first king.
1420	Portuguese ships sent by Prince Henry the Navigator begin voyages.
1478	Spanish Inquisition established.
1479	Ferdinand and Isabella unite Spain.
1492	Spain expels Moors; Columbus makes landfall in the New World.
1494	Treaty of Tordesillas divides New World between Spain and Portugal.
1497–1499	Vasco da Gama of Portugal becomes first European to sail to India.
1519–1522	Ferdinand Magellan of Portugal leads first circumnavigation of the globe.
1521	Cortés conquers Aztec Mexico.
1532	Portugal establishes first settlement in Brazil.
1533	Pizarro conquers the Incas.
1534	Ignatius Loyola founds The Society of Jesus in Spain.
1541	Fernando de Soto of Spain becomes first European to cross the Mississippi River.
1580	Portugal under Spanish rule (until 1640).
1588	English defeat Spanish Armada.
1605	Miguel de Cervantes publishes first part of Don Quixote.
1680	Portuguese establish colony at Sacramento, Calif.

1720	Spanish invade present-day Texas.
1755	Lisbon earthquake destroys many records.
1813	Mexico gains independence from Spain.
1818	Spain cedes Florida to the US
1822	Brazil becomes independent from Portugal.
1870	Spain begins civil registration.
1878	Portugal begins civil registration.
1898	Spanish-American War.
1904	Spanish surrealist artist Salvador Dalí born.
1907	Spaniard Pablo Picasso and Frenchman Georges Braque begin to establish Cubism.
1910	Portugal abolishes monarchy and establishes republic.
1928	António de Oliveira Salazar becomes dictator of Portugal.
1936	Spanish Civil War begins.
1939	Francisco Franco becomes dictator of Spain.
1951	Spain lifts ban on Basque language in schools.
1975	Juan Carlos restores Spanish monarchy.
1976	New Portuguese constitution created and multiparty elections held.

are grouped into councils, several of which make up one of 18 districts (plus two autonomous island regions, the Azores and Madeira). Search for existing towns, councils and districts at <www.freguesiasdeportugal.com>.

The Portuguese government seized ecclesiastical records in 1910, so today you'll find church records included with civil ones at district and national archives. Find a list of district archives at <dgarq.gov.pt/rede-portuguesa-de-arquivos/rede-dgarq/arquivos-regionais>. The National Archives <antt.dgarq.gov.pt> (Archivo Nacional, also known as the "*Torre do Tombo*") is a great resource for more-advanced genealogical research, as well as a catchall for records that didn't end up where they were supposed to. Learn more about its collections by typing the URL into an automatic translator, then clicking on Search the Torre do Tombo>Genealogy and Local History>Genealogy.

The Basque region straddles Spain and France and has complicated historical relationships with both countries. On the Spanish side are two municipalities, Navarre and the Basque Country (with three provinces, Álava, Biscay and Gipuzkoa). On the French side is Northern Basque Country (part of the Pyrénées-Atlantiques department), which is much less culturally Basque than the Spanish side.

For records on the Spanish side, check out the excellent National Archive System of Euskadi (Euskadi is what Basques call their own country), also known as IRARGI <www.snae.org>. If your ancestors came from Northern Basque Country, consult our guide to research in France in chapter 5.

STEP 4 ✦ Major Record Sets

Your go-to sources for tracing ancestors in this region are records documenting vital events. After conquering those, you can move on to several unique record sets.

CHURCH RECORDS: Catholicism was the religion in Spain and Portugal for hundreds of years, and the church kept thorough records dating to the 1500s or even earlier. Before modern civil registration, parish baptismal, marriage and burial records may be the only places to find your ancestors' names. Spanish church records are particularly famous for thoroughness: They may contain an individual's name, event date and location, parents' names, other relatives listed as godparents and a father's vocation.

Start your church record search online. FamilySearch has more than 10 million indexed baptisms, marriages and deaths in Spain (1500 to 1950) and more than a half-million in Portugal (about 1530 to 1910). You can search nearly 6 million Basque sacramental records (excluding Navarre) at **<dokuklik.snae.org/sacramentales.php>**, or search and order copies of these at church archives covering Viscaya **<www.aheb-beha.org>** and Guipuzcoa **<www. mendezmende.org/es>**. The FHL has filmed many Spanish and Portuguese church records. To find them, run a place search of its online catalog **<familysearch.org/catalog-search>** for the district/municipality or parish where your ancestor lived.

To track down original records in Spain, consult Guia de los Archivos de la Iglesia en Espana (download a PDF from **<www.mcu.es/archivos/docs/ArchivosIglesia.pdf>**). Also ask about parish records at diocesan archives. Diocesan boundaries are described in the Catholic Encyclopedia **<www.catholic.org/encyclopedia/view.php?id=10978>**; contact information for archives is at **<www.conferenciaepiscopal.es/index.php/iglesia-catolica-en-espana/ diocesis-espanolas.html>**. Search for parochial archives through Censo-Guía.

You can locate Portuguese parish records in district or national archives with the book *Inventário Colectivo dos Registos Paroquiais* by Maria José Moura (locate copies at libraries using WorldCat **<worldcat.org>**). View a directory of online Portuguese parish records at ETombo **<etombo.com>**.

CIVIL REGISTRATION: Spain (including the Basque region) and Portugal didn't require civil registration of vital events until 1870 and 1911, respectively. Some Spanish cities started earlier, and non-Catholics in Portugal registered with civil authorities as early as 1832. The records have great information, and sometimes life events are cross-referenced: A marginal note about an individual's marriage or death may appear in a birth record.

Most Spanish civil registrations are still in municipal archives, and haven't been filmed or indexed (though a small but growing collection is digitized on the FamilySearch website). Some were unfortunately destroyed in the 1930s civil war. Generally, you should write to the municipal archive for copies. Though it's now possible to order different types of civil registration data through the Ministerio de Justicia **<www.mjusticia.gob.es>**, the process is a bit complicated. If you don't read the language, consider hiring a Spanish genealogist to order these for you.

In Portugal, nearly all civil records from the past 100 years are still in the hands of district civil registries: Find a list on the Portugal page of FamilySearch's Research Wiki **<wiki.familysearch. org/en/Portugal>** (click Civil Registration). For records more than a century old, contact the district archive or library. The Basque government has a Spanish-language site **<www.justizia. net/registro-civil>** for ordering civil birth, marriage and death certificates. If you want original records, get contact information for district civil registries using the *Encuentra un Registro Civil* drop-down menu.

NOTARIAL RECORDS: Spanish *protocolos* are tough to find but literally packed with a lifetime's worth of legal events: wills, adoptions, lineage and nobility records, title transfers and sales of land or other personal property, marriage contracts, apprenticeship records and more. You have to identify which local notary your ancestor used and where his files may have ended up (if they were kept). District notarial archives and databases of wills exist in some places; in others, look for notarial records in provincial, ecclesiastical and private archives, and for filmed records at the FHL.

PASSAPORTES: These Portuguese emigration documents (of people leaving Portugal) contain information similar to what you'd find in a US passenger manifest: name, age, birthplace, date of application (usually filed shortly before leaving the country), parents' names, destination, occupation. Though these exist as early as 1757, the most accessible records seem to be for an era of heavy emigration traffic, the late 1800s to early 1900s.

Look for *passaportes* in both district and national archives. The FHL has filmed some of Madeira's *passaportes* (run a place-names search of the catalog and look under Emigration and

Immigration). The Azores government is in the process of digitizing its *passaportes*, beginning with municipality of Ponta Delgada (1875–1939); check its website **<www.azores.gov.pt>** for progress.

Once you've conquered these sources, you'll be in an excellent tactical position for forays into additional records: military files, censuses, passenger lists, Inquisition records and more. It might take a while to learn the ins and outs of research in Spain, Portugal and the Basque region, but be patient: As fellow Iberian conqueror Napoleon Bonaparte once said, "Victory belongs to the most persevering."

SPAIN RESOURCES

ORGANIZATIONS AND ARCHIVES

ARCHIVO DE LA CORONA DE ARAGON
C/Comtes 2 (Palacio de los Virreyes o del Lloctinent)
08002 Barcelona C/Almogàvers, 77
08018 Barcelona
Phone: +34 93 485 42 85
Fax: +34 93 300 12 52
E-mail: aca@cult.mec.es
<en.www.mcu.es/archivos/MC/ACA>

ARCHIVO GENERAL DE LA ADMINISTRACIÓN (GENERAL ADMINISTRATION ARCHIVE)
C/ Paseo de Aguadores, 2, 28871 Alcalá de Henares, Spain
Phone: +34 918 892 950
Fax: +34 918 822 435
E-mail: aga@cult.mec.es
<www.mcu.es/archivos/MC/AGA>

ARCHIVO GENERAL DE INDIAS (GENERAL ARCHIVE OF THE INDIES)
Avda. de la Constitución, 3, 41071 Sevilla, Spain
Phone: +34 954 500 528
Fax: +34 954 219 485
Email: agi1@cult.mec.es
<www.mcu.es/archivos/MC/AGI>

ARCHIVO GENERAL MILITAR DE SEGOVIA
Paseo de la Castellana, 109 28071-Madrid, Spain
Phone: + 34 91 213 2127
E-mail: portalcultura@oc.mde.es
<www.portalcultura.mde.es/cultural/ archivos/castillaLeon/archivo_150.html>

ARCHIVO GENERAL DEL PATRIMONIO
Palacio Real. C.P. 28071, Madrid, Spain
Phone: +34 91 454 87 00
E-mail: info@patrimonionacional.es
<www.patrimonionacional.es/Home/ Colecciones-Reales/Archivo-General-de-Palacio.aspx>

ARCHIVO GENERAL DE SIMANCAS
C Miravete, 8, 47130 Simancas, (Valladolid), Spain
Phone: +34 983 590 003
Fax: +34 983 590 311
E-mail: ags@cult.mec.es
<www.mcu.es/archivos/MC/AGS>

ARCHIVO HISTÓRICO NACIONAL (NATIONAL HISTORICAL ARCHIVE)
Serrano 115, 28006 Madrid, Spain
Phone: +34 917 688 500
Fax: +34 915 631 199
E-mail: ahn@cult.mec.es
<www.mcu.es/archivos/MC/AHN>

ARCHIVO DE LA REAL CHANCILLERÍA DE GRANADA

Plaza del Padre Suárez, 1, 18009 Granada
Phone: +34 958 00 26 00
E-mail: informacion.arch.gr.ccd@
juntadeandalucia.es
<www.juntadeandalucia.es/culturaydeporte/
archivos>

ARCHIVO DE LA REAL CHANCILLERÍA DE VALLADOLID

C/Chancillería, 4, 47071 Valladolid, Spain
Phone: +34 983 250 232
Fax: +34 983 267 802
E-mail: arch@cult.mec.es
<www.mcu.es/archivos/MC/ACV>

ASOCIACION DE DIPLOMADOS EN GENEALOGIA, HERALDICA Y NOBILIARIA (ASSOCIATION OF GRADUATES IN GENEALOGY, HERALDRY AND NOBILITY)

C/Alcalá, 20, 2nd desp. 7-B, 28014 Madrid, Spain
Phone: +34 915223822
E-mail: info@adghn.org
<www.adghn.org>

ASOCIACION DE HIDALGOS A FUERO DE ESPAÑA (ROYAL ASSOCIATION OF GENTLEMEN OF SPAIN)

C/Jenner, 6, Bajo Dcha., 28010 Madrid, Spain
Phone: +34 91 542 81 46
Fax: +34 91 542 85 23
<www.hidalgosdeespana.com>

BIBLIOTECA NACIONAL DE ESPAÑA

Paseo de Recoletos 20-22, 28071 Madrid, Spain
Phone: +34 91 580 78 00
Fax: +34 91 516 89 28
<www.bne.es>

GENEALOGICAL SOCIETY OF HISPANIC AMERICA

Box 3040, Pueblo, CO 81005
E-mail: info@gsha.net
<www.gsha.net>

THE HISPANIC GENEALOGICAL SOCIETY

Box 231271, Houston, TX 77223
Fax: (281) 449-4020
E-mail: joguerra@hispanicgs.com
<www.hispanicgs.com>

SOCIETY OF HISPANIC HISTORICAL AND ANCESTRAL RESEARCH

Box 490, Midway City, CA 92655
<shhar.net>

SPANISH AMERICAN GENEALOGICAL ASSOCIATION

Box 794, Corpus Christi, TX 78403
Phone: (361) 855-1183
E-mail: sagacorpus2005@yahoo.com
<sagacorpus2005.tripod.com>

BOOKS AND AUDIO

"The Best in the World: Catholic Church Records of Spain, Portugal, and France" lecture by Peggy Ryskamp (Audiotapes.com)

"Catholic Marriage Dispensations in the Diocesan Archives of Spain & Mexico" lecture by George R. Ryskamp (Audiotapes.com)

Finding Your Hispanic Roots by George R. Ryskamp (Genealogical Publishing Co.)

"Genealogical Research in the Archives of Spain" lecture by George R. Ryskamp (Audiotapes.com)

Hispanic Surnames and Family History by Lyman D. Platt (Genealogical Publishing Co.)

Historical Dictionary of Spain by Angel Smith (Scarecrow Press)

"Inquisitions and Archival Resources of Late Medieval/Early Modern Spain" lecture by Lawrence H. Feldman (Audiotapes.com)

"Las Islans Canarias, Spain's Stepping Stone to the New World: Its Geography, History, and Genealogical Significance For America" lecture by Paul Newfield III (Audiotapes.com)

Mexican and Spanish Family Research by J. Konrad (Ohio Summit Publications)

"Natural de España: Connecting Your Ancestors with Spain" lecture by George R. Ryskamp (Audiotapes.com)

"Notaries and Notarial Records in Northern New Spain" lecture by George R. Ryskamp (Audiotapes.com)

"The Province of Texas and Available Records in the Archivo General de Indias in Sevilla, Spain" lecture by Peter E. Carr (Audiotapes.com)

"Researching Spanish Archives Without Going to Spain" lecture by Alfred E. Lemmon (Audiotapes. com)

"Spanish Colonial Records of Northern New Spain (Northern Mexico, Southwestern United States, Florida, and Louisiana)" lecture by George R. Ryskamp (Audiotapes.com)

The Spanish Frontier in North America by David J. Weber (Yale University Press)

Tracing Your Hispanic Heritage by George R. Ryskamp (Hispanic Family History Research)

WEBSITES
Azores GenWeb
<rootsweb.ancestry.com/~azrwgw>

Censo-Guía
<censoarchivos.mcu.es/CensoGuia/portada. htm>

CIDA Database
<www.mcu.es/archivos/MC/CIDA>

Doug da Rocha Holmes' Portuguese Genealogy
<www.dholmes.com/rocha1.html>

Freguesias de Portugal
<www.freguesiasdeportugal.com>

Geneall
<www.geneall.net/P>

Genealogía Española-España GenWeb
<www.genealogia-es.com>

Genealogy of New Spain
<newspaingenealogy.com>

Hispanic Genealogy Blog
<hispanicgenealogy.blogspot.com>

LusaWeb
<www.lusaweb.com>

PARES, Portal de Archivos Españoles
<pares.mcu.es>

Perry Castañeda Library Map Collection: Spain
<www.lib.utexas.edu/maps/spain.html>

Sí, Spain
<www.sispain.org>

Spain Mailing Lists
<rootsweb.ancestry.com/~jfuller/gen_mail_ country-spa.html>

Spanish Archives
<www.cultura.mecd.es/archivos>

Spanish-English Dictionary
<www.freedict.com/onldict/spa.html>

Spanish GenWeb
<www.genealogia-es.com>

Spanish Postal Codes
<www.correos.es/comun/ CodigosPostales/1010_s-CodPostal.asp>

BASQUE RESOURCES

ORGANIZATIONS AND ARCHIVES

BASQUE MUSEUM AND CULTURAL CENTER
611 Grove St., Boise, ID 83702
Phone: (208) 343-2671
<www.basquemuseum.com>

CENTER FOR BASQUE STUDIES
University of Nevada-Reno/322, Reno, NV 89557
Phone: (775) 784-4854
Fax: (775) 784-1355
E-mail: basque@unr.edu
<basque.unr.edu>

SISTEMA NACIONAL DE ARCHIVOS DE EUSKADI (BASQUE NATIONAL ARCHIVES)
Rekalde Jauregia, PK 220 E-20570, Bergara, Spain
<www.snae.org>

BOOKS
Basque History of the World by Mark Kurlansky (Penguin)

WEBSITES
Basque Genealogy Homepage
<home.earthlink.net/~fybarra>

Buber's Basque Page
<buber.net/Basque>

Dokuklik
<dokuklik.snae.org>

The Etxeto Basque Family Genealogy Home Page
<www.etxeto.com>

Euskal Herria: The Basque Country
<www.ehu.es/~wmppitoj/bc2.html>

PORTUGAL RESOURCES

ORGANIZATIONS AND ARCHIVES

AMERICAN-PORTUGUESE GENEALOGICAL SOCIETY
Box 644, Taunton, MA 02780
<apghs.org>

ARQUIVO NACIONAL DA TORRE DO TOMBO (NATIONAL ARCHIVES OF TORRE DO TOMBO)
University Mall, 1649-010 Lisbon, Portugal
Phone: +351 210 03 7100
Fax: +35 1217937230
E-mail: mail@dglab.gov.pt
<antt.dgarq.gov.pt>

ARQUIVO REGIONAL DA AZORES
alácio Bettencourt, Rua da Rosa, 49, 9700-171 Angra do Heroísmo, Portugal
Phone: +351 295 401 000
Fax: +351 295 401 009
<www.bparah.azores.gov.pt>

ARQUIVO REGIONAL DA MADEIRA
Caminho dos Álamos 35, Santo António, 9000, 064 Funchal, Portugal
Phone: +351 291 708 400
Fax: +351 291 708 402
E-mail: arm@arquivo-madeira.org
<www.arquivo-madeira.org>

J.A. FREITAS LIBRARY
Portuguese Union of the State of California, 1120 E. 14th St., San Leandro, CA 94577
Phone: (510) 483-7676
E-mail: webmaster@mypfsa.org
<www.mypfsa.org/library>

PORTUGUESE AMERICAN HISTORICAL AND RESEARCH FOUNDATION
277 Industrial Park Road, Franklin, NC 28734
Fax: (828) 369-3751
E-mail: portugal@portuguesefoundation.org
<portuguesefoundation.org>

PORTUGUESE GENEALOGICAL SOCIETY OF HAWAII

810 N. Vineyard Blvd., Room 11, Honolulu, HI 96817
Phone: (808) 841-5044
<www.portugueseancestry.com/genealogy/html/phgs.cfm>

PORTUGUESE HISTORICAL AND CULTURAL SOCIETY

Box 161990, Sacramento, CA 95816
E-mail: mariwgt@att.net
<www.sacramentophcs.com>

PORTUGUESE HISTORICAL MUSEUM

1650 Senter Road, San Jose, CA 95112
Phone: (408) 287-2290
<www.portuguesemuseum.org>

BOOKS

Historical Dictionary of Portugal, 3rd edition, by Douglas L. Wheeler (Scarecrow Press)

Our Portuguese Heritage: An Informal Genealogy of 3,000 Families on Martha's Vineyard by Marianne Thomas (Community History Project)

The Portuguese Making of America: Melungeons and Early Settlers of America by Manuel Mira (Portuguese-American Historical Research Foundation)

WEBSITES

Azores GenWeb
<rootsweb.ancestry.com/~azrwgw>

Azores: Source of Immigration to the Americas
<www.lusaweb.com/azores>
ETombo
<etombo.com>

Finding Your Portuguese Roots
<www.lusaweb.com/Genealogy/tabid/172/Default.aspx>

Perry Castañeda Library Map Collection: Portugal
<www.lib.utexas.edu/maps/portugal.html>

Portugal Mailing Lists
<rootsweb.ancestry.com/~jfuller/gen_mail_country-por.html>

Portuguese Ancestry
<www.portugueseancestry.com>

Portuguese-English Dictionary
<www.freedict.com/onldict/por.html>

Portuguese Genealogy Project of Martha's Vineyard
<history.vineyard.net/mvpgp>

Portuguese Passenger Ship Master List
<www.dholmes.com/ships.html>

Ship List Database
<www.portugueseancestry.com/lwi/genealogy/shiplists/shiplist.cfm>

CHAPTER FOURTEEN

YOUR EUROPEAN JEWISH ANCESTORS

By Schelly Talalay Dardashtl

I f you've started researching your Jewish ancestors, you might've heard that all the records were destroyed, or that Ellis Island clerks changed your family's surnames, essentially cutting you off at the genealogical pass.

Don't believe the rumors. In reality, there's not a single documented case of an Ellis Island official changing an immigrant's surname. Archives hold impressive collections of records. And a wealth of online resources can help you fulfill the goals you probably share with every Jewish family historian: to learn the fate of lost branches, create memorials for relatives without resting places and connect with distant kin around the world.

That's not to say Jewish genealogy is easy. Cultural differences, language barriers, religious persecution, forced conversion and genocide have created black holes in every Jewish family's history. But those roadblocks needn't stop you from discovering and honoring your past. With these seven research strategies to guide your genealogical journey, you'll find that your family's ties are stronger than any outside forces.

LEARN YOUR HISTORY

Jewish history, unfortunately, is riddled with tragic events that complicate the work of genealogists. Marauding Crusaders destroyed many European Jewish communities. Massacres, mass conversions, the Inquisition and 1492 Expulsion shattered lives in Iberia. The Russian pogroms and the tragedy of the

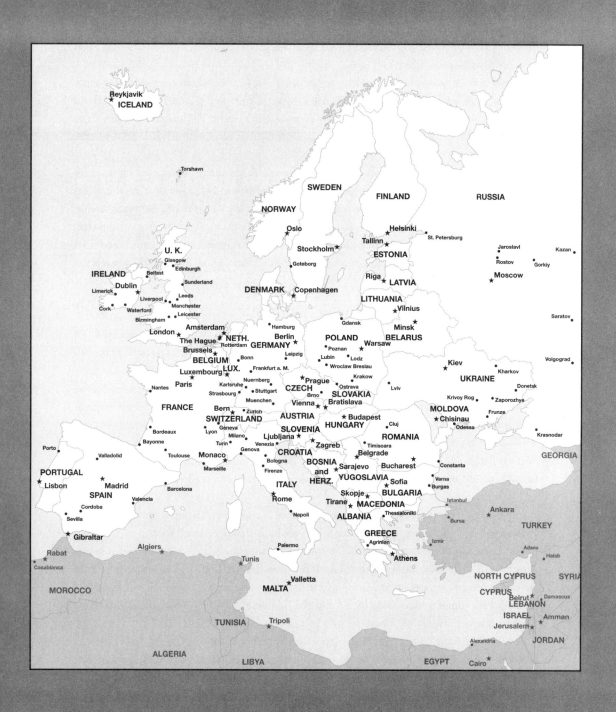

Holocaust affected our history forever. This Day in Jewish History **<thisdayinjewishhistory. blogspot.com>** documents historical events in detail; see the time line on the following pages for a rundown of some major events.

Many actions spurred survivors to move elsewhere—sometimes to the next village, or more often, far from home. That means you'll need to cast a wide net to find information about your family. From the Middle Ages, Sephardic communities existed in major European cities (such as Hamburg, Vienna and Warsaw), and some Ashkenazi families made their homes in the Mediterranean.

To understand and decipher Jewish records—from Hebrew tombstones to Jewish marriage contracts (*ketubot*)—it's useful to learn basic tenets and traditions of Judaism, such as life events and the Jewish calendar. Knowing the Jewish day ends at sunset, for example, helps you understand death records. An online calendar conversion tool such as Steve Morse's **<stevemorse. org/jcal/jcal.html>** lets you translate Jewish dates to the civil calendar. Remember, too, that Jews use BCE (before common era) and CE (common era) instead of BC and AD when referring to civil years.

FOLLOW THE GROUP

Jews fall into two major groups—Ashkenazim and Sephardim—with further subdivisions. Because of each group's unique origins and migrations, your genealogical research will take different paths depending on the group your ancestors belonged to.

The first Jewish immigrants to the New World were Sephardim, who originated in the Iberian Peninsula. Ashkenazi Jews from Western Europe began arriving in the United States as early as the 1840s. About 95 percent of Jewish immigrants to America—predominantly Ashkenazi—came in a wave starting in 1881, following Russian pogroms, and then after each World War. Although Ashkenazim in much of Europe generally were assimilated and spoke secular languages, Yiddish was the lingua franca for those in Eastern Europe: Russia, Lithuania, Poland and Germany.

Sephardim spoke Ladino, a mix of Hebrew, Spanish and other languages sometimes called Judeo-Spanish or Judezmo. The term Sephardic generally describes any Jews not of Ashkenazi origin, including those who lived in the former Ottoman Empire, the Mediterranean, North Africa, the Middle East, the Balkans and Asia. But Jews from Iran, Iraq, Afghanistan and India are more correctly referred to as Mizrahi, Oriental or Eastern Jews. Roman Jews make up the oldest Jewish community outside Israel, and the Romaniote Jews have resided in Greece for more than two millennia.

Ladino-speaking Sephardim began to arrive in the New World in the late 1500s as *conversos*—the Spanish word for those forced to convert to Catholicism during the Inquisition. Columbus' ships included *converso* crew. Sephardim settled in Brazil, the Caribbean and New Amsterdam.

BREAK DOWN LANGUAGE BARRIERS

Jewish records can appear in Hebrew, Yiddish, Ladino, German, Polish, Russian, French, Italian, Spanish, Catalan, Hungarian, Romanian and more—whatever language was spoken wherever a Jewish community existed. Vital records kept by Jewish communities are likely to be in Hebrew, Yiddish or Ladino as well as the secular language, which may have changed as borders changed. You'll want to examine dual-language records carefully, because certain details might appear in only one language.

Sephardic records are especially challenging. Turkey is an excellent example of how convoluted the quest can be. Ashkenazi and Sephardi communities have existed side by side in what's now Istanbul since the 1400s. Turkish was originally written with Arabic letters; since 1928, it's employed the Latin alphabet. Sephardic records were written in Turkish, Hebrew, Ladino and solitreo, an obsolete script, while Ashkenazi and civil records are found in Turkish, Hebrew, Yiddish and Eastern European languages. (The Ashkenazi community kept its communal records in the language it knew best.)

To learn more about Jewish languages worldwide, visit Jewish Language Research **<www.jewish-languages.org>** for maps, text, audio samples and additional links. As you trace your family into areas whose languages you don't speak, FamilySearch's Letter Writing Guides **<familysearch.org/learn/wiki/en/Category:Letter_Writing_Guides>** can help you contact foreign repositories.

TIME LINE

1492	Jews are expelled from Spain. Columbus, with conversos Jews aboard, reaches the New World.
1628	First Jews settle in Barbados. By 1710 there are two synagogues in the English colony.
1648–1649	Chmielnicki cossack massacres in Poland.
1650	Twelve Jewish families granted permission to settle in Curacao. Jews settle in Jamaica, permitted to own land and practice their religion.
1654	Jews expelled from Brazil; 23 land in New Amsterdam.
1655	Jews allowed to resettle in England, from which they had been barred since 1290.
1700s	Rise of Hasidism in Russia and Poland.
1732	Congregation Mickve Israel, oldest synagogue in Western Hemisphere, built in Curacao.
1760	Jewish merchants and their families settle in New Orleans.
1791	Jews granted citizenship in France. Beginning of Jewish Emancipation in Europe.
1820s	Rise of Reform Judaism in Germany.
1858	Edgardo Mortara, a little boy, is abducted in Italy after forced conversion, creating worldwide protests.
1868	Benjamin Disraeli becomes English prime minister. Queen Victoria makes him Earl of Beaconsfield.
1881	Czar Alexander II assassinated in St. Petersburg, Russia. Pogroms and persecution of Jews follows; 2 million Eastern European Jews will emigrate to America through 1914.

1917	Balfour Declaration pledges British support for a Jewish national homeland. United States enters World War I against Germany. Russian Revolution.
1919	Jewish delegations to the Paris Peace Conference after World War I seek rights for European Jews.
1922	British Mandate on Palestine approved by League of Nations.
1931	Three million Jews live in Poland, making it the largest Jewish population outside the US
1933	Rise of Adolf Hitler. German Nazis boycott Jewish businesses.
1935	Germans pass Nuremberg Laws restricting rights of Jews.
1939	Germany invades Poland, starting World War II. *Steamship St. Louis*, carrying 907 Jewish German refugees, is turned back by US and Cuba. US Jewish population estimated at 4,770,000.
1940	Nazis establish ghettos in Poland.
1941	*Einsatzgruppen* (special units) follow German troops into Soviet Union, perpetuating systematic murder.
1942	Nazi leaders refine the "Final Solution"—the genocide of the Jewish people—at Wannsee Conference.
1945	Nuremberg War Crimes Tribunal estimates that 6 million Jews have been murdered by the Nazis.
1947	Ancient scrolls are discovered at Qumram near the Dead Sea. UN approves partition of British Mandate Palestine into Jewish and Arab states.

TRACE THE NAMES

In Jewish families, given names offer clues to past generations—sometimes more so than the surnames. Ashkenazim generally name children after recently deceased relatives, so you can try to estimate Ashkenazi relatives' years of death by matching infants to ancestors. Sephardim name offspring after the living as well as the dead.

Ashkenazi given names often changed as families migrated—Hebrew or Yiddish names gave way to colloquial diminutives or secular versions. The JewishGen Given Names Database <**www.jewishgen.org/databases/givennames**> helps you find alternate forms of monikers based on local and Jewish vernaculars. For example, searching for the name David turns up possible Yiddish nicknames of Debele, Dovitke, Tevele and Dovet.

The roots of European Jewish surnames are relatively recent, following civil laws passed in the late 18th century that required Jews to take fixed surnames. Many unrelated families adopted common names, so knowing the name of the ancestral village is often more helpful than searching for a surname.

Sephardic surnames, on the other hand, can be ancient—some appear in Spanish archival records as early as the 10th century. Many modern Sephardic names bear close resemblance to their original forms, indicating descent from a particular family. In Sephardic research, the surname is key to finding family in Spain or Portugal as well as Italy, Greece and Turkey. See the sidebar on page 249 for clues to deciphering Jewish surnames.

Sephardic given names often follow established patterns. The eldest son is traditionally named for the paternal grandfather; eldest daughter for the paternal grandmother; second male child for the maternal grandfather; second female child for the maternal grandmother; next child for a paternal uncle or aunt; and the next child for a maternal uncle or aunt. But a recently deceased grandparent or sibling often takes precedence over a living relative. Some Sephardim commonly name children after their own living parents—a great honor.

Try the Sephardic name search engine at Sephardim.com **<www.sephardim.com>**. The Jewish History Channel Blog **<ha-historion.blogspot.com>** has good information on Sephardic names.

REVIEW AVAILABLE RECORDS

Both Ashkenazi and Sephardic Jews have lengthy paper trails to follow—once you've identified your family's ancestral town. You might find this in immigration records, draft registration cards, Social Security applications or other documents. When you know the town, you can determine where its documents are located today. Jewish-Gen's ShtetlSeeker **<www.jewishgen.org/communities>** can help you find a town with phonetic searches and maps. Records may be in surprising locations. In Morocco, for example, civil registration wasn't required until the 20th century and, with major immigration to France and Israel, many communal records were sent to those countries.

Some resources and documents are specific to Ashkenazim or Sephardim, but marriage, divorce, birth and circumcision records exist for both groups. They may provide three

1948	Israel is founded as a nation and is recognized by the United States.
1950s	Hundreds of thousands of Jews from Europe and Asia come to Israel.
1956	Sinai campaign by Israel, France and England.
1960	Adolph Eichmann stands trial in Israel for crimes against the Jews and humanity during World War II.
1967	Israel is victorious over Egypt, Jordan, Syria and Iraq in Six Day War.
1969	Golda Meir elected prime minister of Israel.
1973	Egypt and Syria attack Israel on the Day of Atonement, starting the Yom Kippur War, which Israel wins.
1978	Israel-Egypt Peace Treaty.
1985	Operation Moses, airlift of Ethiopian Jews to Israel.
1987	Uprising of Palestinian Arabs, known as the Intifada, begins on Judea, Samaria (West Bank) and Gaza.
1989	Soviet Union permits Jews to emigrate on their first application for visa.
1991	Breakup of Soviet Union leads to rise of nationalism and outbreaks of anti-Semitism.
1992	Operation Solomon brings almost all Ethiopian Jews to Israel.
1993	Israel signs Agreement with the PLO.
1994	Israel-Jordanian Peace Treaty.

generations of names in one record through the use of patronymics (the child's name derives from the father's name, such as Moshe Leib ben David Leibovich, indicating the father's and grandfather's names). Many of these European records have been microfilmed and are available at the Family History Library **<familysearch.org>**. Other records, such as circumcision, may have been kept privately by the mohel, the person who performs the circumcision. But some communities kept mohel registers, which indicate the date of circumcision, the parents and the mohel.

Jewish birth records include the baby's name, sex, date (civil and Hebrew), names and residence of parents and grandparents, and sometimes the mother's maiden name, relatives' occupations and name of the mohel.

A Jewish marriage record will generally show the date, place, the names of the bride and groom, the dowry, parents (with patronymics giving you another generation), and sometimes occupations and previous residences. In England, many synagogues kept separate marriage registers, now transcribed and published, for both Sephardic and Ashkenazi congregations. Iberian marriage contracts will normally list several generations for both bride and groom. And don't overlook Christian records—because of forced conversion, they might document your ancestor's union.

Gravestones show the death date, the deceased's given name, and his or her father's name. Some Sephardic stones contain much more information. Cemetery registers, if they still exist, may also be useful.

Holocaust records are valuable for both Ashkenazi and Sephardic research. Some Sephardic communities were nearly destroyed in addition to the decimated Eastern European Ashkenazi communities. See the next section for more information on the repositories that hold records of the Shoah.

Records specific to Eastern Europe include cadastral records and maps—real estate maps showing where families lived in a town or village, sometimes for generations. Depending on the time period, Jewish records might've been kept by the parish church. So if you're searching prior to civil registration, your Jewish ancestor's vital records might be within the church records.

For Sephardic researchers, records may go back to the 10th century. Note that many smaller Spanish archives are only now beginning to go digital. In Lerida a few years ago, for example, the archive had just one computer and was attempting to catalog more than 10,000 documents. Inquisition records are maintained in dedicated archives, but notarial records identify accused or sentenced individuals as Jew or *converso* and can provide other details.

Every Spanish town's archives holds notarial records. These extremely detailed files might include records of debts, real estate transfers, marriage settlements and divorces. Jews and *conversos* are noted, and variations of names can appear, as well as other towns of residence. Because of conversions, Catholic Church records are a next stop for baptism, marriage and death records.

RESEARCH IN REPOSITORIES

You'll find Jewish records in a number of different places, from websites to centuries-old archives. The worldwide Jewish genealogy community is made up of many dedicated volunteers who are transliterating and translating records. Projects might be as narrow as births from one small town or as gigantic as the 3 million Pages of Testimony at the Yad Vashem Holocaust Memorial.

JewishGen <www.jewishgen.org> hosts many databases, some of which are searchable for free on Ancestry.com <ancestry.com>. You may also have luck with Jewish Records Indexing Poland <www.jri-poland.org>, which has some 3 million vital records. The Family History Library holds microfilm of original records used by Jewish volunteers to create accessible, searchable databases, while other groups work directly with Eastern European archives to create indexes. You can search many of these on JewishGen.

SURNAME SUFFIXES	
Jews often adapted the naming conventions of the local population, so surnames may give you a clue to an ancestor's origins. Use our chart to decode common suffixes and prefixes.	

-son, -sohn	son of (Ashkenazi)
ben-	son of (Hebrew)
ibn-	son of (Arabic)
-abi, -abu	father of (Hebrew, Arabic)
-zadeh	father of (Iranian)
-ian, -nia	son of (Iranian)
-chi	occupational suffix (Iranian)
-i	geographical locator (Iranian)
-vitch	son of (Slavic, Russian)

Yad Vashem: The Holocaust Martyrs' and Heroes' Remembrance Authority <www.yadvashem.org> holds International Tracing Service (ITS) documents, concentration camp records, a comprehensive library and a database of *Shoah* victims' names. The US Holocaust Memorial Museum <www.ushmm.org> also has ITS records.

The Center for Jewish History <www.cjh.org> in New York City holds records and library resources of the American Jewish Historical Society <www.ajhs.org>, YIVO Institute <www.yivoinstitute.org>, Leo Baeck Institute <www.lbi.org>, American Sephardi Federation <www.americansephardifederation.org> and the Jewish Genealogical Society of New York <www.jgsny.org>. Also in New York, the Museum of Jewish Heritage <www.mjhnyc.org> preserves and celebrates 20th-century Jewish life and culture. You can view 650 digitized Holocaust memorial books—or *yizkor*—online at the New York Public Library website <legacy.www.nypl.org/research/chss/jws/yizkorbooks_intro.cfm>.

The Central Archives for the History of the Jewish People Jerusalem <cahjp.huji.ac.il> holds the collections of hundreds of Jewish communities as well as local, national and international Jewish organizations. The Central Archives has a large collection of vital record registers from Germany from the end of the 18th century onward, as well as registers from France, Italy and Poland.

Sephardim.com has an extensive name index and an active discussion group. Sephardicgen <**sephardicgen.com**> has links to sources, names, news lists and country resources, plus information on Spanish notarial records, Inquisition archives and *ketubot*. JewishGen also has Sephardic information at <**www.jewishgen.org/infofiles/sefard5.htm**> and <**jewishgen.org/sephardic/names.htm**>.

GO GENETIC

In 2007 Simon and I co-founded the Iberian Ashkenaz Y-DNA project <**www.familytreedna.com/public/IberianSurnamesofAshkenaz**> to find more people like us. The project has more than 250 members, and Sephardic or *converso* Y-DNA matches were located for more than 75 percent of participants.

Simon and I discovered Ashkenazi families from Eastern, Western and Central Europe with indicators of Sephardic heritage, such as Spanish or Portuguese surnames, an oral history of Sephardic ancestors, children named after living grandparents or Mediterranean genetic disorders. The families couldn't verify possible Sephardic roots through archival records, so we used DNA.

Simon's male cousin was tested, and his matches were Ashkenazi Jews from villages near his own, where Latvia, Belarus and Lithuania meet. Two Hispanic men in Mexico and Texas matched him, too. Of the Ashkenazim who found matches, none had any idea they had paternal Sephardic roots.

The most important element of DNA testing for investigating Jewish ancestry is the size of the comparative database (that is, how many other samples your profile will be compared to). FamilyTreeDNA **<www.familytreedna.com>** has the largest Jewish comparative databases and the largest general DNA database, according to founder Bennett Greenspan, with records for Ashkenazim, Sephardim, Levites and Kohanim. JewishGen links to FamilyTreeDNA studies at **<www.jewishgen.org/DNA/genbygen.html>**. Another study, the DNAShoah Project **<www. dnashoah.org>**, aims to reunite families separated by the Holocaust. It's free to join, and more than 1,000 samples are already in the collection—all potential ties to your past.

RESOURCES

ORGANIZATIONS AND ARCHIVES

AMERICAN JEWISH HISTORICAL SOCIETY, NEW ENGLAND ARCHIVES
101 Newbury St., Boston, MA 02116
Phone: (617) 226-1245
Fax: (617) 226-1248
E-mail reference@ajhsboston.org
<ajhsboston.org>

THE AMERICAN SEPHARDI FEDERATION
15 W. 16th St., New York, NY 10011
Phone: (212) 294-8350
Fax: (212) 294-8348
E-mail: info@americansephardifederation.org
<www.americansephardifederation.org>

BEIT HATFUTSOT: THE MUSEUM OF THE JEWISH PEOPLE
Box 39359, Tel Aviv 61392, Israel
Phone: +972 3-7457800
<www.bh.org.il>

CENTER FOR JEWISH HISTORY
15 W. 16th St., New York, NY 10011
Phone: (212) 294-6160
Fax: (212) 294-6161
E-mail: gi@cjh.org
<www.cjh.org>

CENTRAL ARCHIVES FOR THE HISTORY OF THE JEWISH PEOPLE
Sprinzak Building, Givat Ram, Hebrew University, Box 39077, 91010 Jerusalem, Israel
Phone: +972 2-6586249
Fax: +972 2-6535426
E-mail: archives@vms.huji.ac.il
<sites.huji.ac.il/archives>

THE JACOB RADER MARCUS CENTER OF THE AMERICAN JEWISH ARCHIVES
3101 Clifton Ave., Cincinnati, OH 45220
Phone: (513) 221-1875
Fax: (513) 221-7812
<www.huc.edu/aja>

JEWISH GENEALOGY SOCIETY OF NEW YORK

Box 631, New York, NY 10113
Phone: (212) 294-8318
E-mail: info@jgsny.org
<www.jgsny.org>

LEO BAECK INSTITUTE

15 W. 16th St., New York, NY 10011
Phone: (212) 744-6400 or (212) 294-8340
E-mail: lbaeck@lbi.cjh.org
<www.lbi.org>

MUSEUM OF JEWISH HERITAGE

Edmond J. Safra Plaza, 36 Battery Place,
New York, NY 10280
Phone: (646) 437-4202
E-mail: info@mjhnyc.org
<www.mjhnyc.org>

ROUTES TO ROOTS

136 Sandpiper Key, Seacaucus, NJ 07094
E-mail: mweiner@routestoroots.com
<www.routestoroots.com>

SOUTHERN JEWISH HISTORICAL SOCIETY

Box 71601, Marietta, GA 30007
E-mail: info@jewishsouth.org
<www.jewishsouth.org>

US HOLOCAUST MEMORIAL MUSEUM

100 Raoul Wallenberg Place SW, Washington,
DC 20024
Phone: (202) 488-6130
Fax: (202) 314-7820
E-mail: resource-center@ushmm.org
<www.ushmm.org>

YAD VASHEM

Box 3477, 91034 Jerusalem, Israel
Phone: +972 2-6443720
Fax: +972 2-6443719
<www.yadvashem.org.il>

YIVO INSTITUTE FOR JEWISH RESEARCH

15 W. 16th St., New York, NY 10011.
Phone: (917) 606-8217
<www.yivoinstitute.org>

BOOKS

Abraham's Children: Race, Identity and the DNA of the Chosen People by Jon Entine (Grand Central Publishing)

Avotaynu Guide to Jewish Genealogy edited by Gary Mokotoff and Sallyann Amdur Sack (Avotaynu)

A Dictionary of Jewish Names and Their History by Benzion C. Kaganoff (Jason Aronson Publishers)

Dictionary of Jewish Surnames from Galicia by Alexander Beider (Avotaynu)

Dictionary of Sephardic Surnames, 2nd edition, by Guilherme Faiguenboim, Paulo Valadares and Anna Rosa Campagnano (Fraiha)

Discovering Your Jewish Ancestors by Barbara Krasner-Khait (Heritage Quest)

The Encyclopedia of Jewish Genealogy, Volume I: Sources in the United States and Canada (Jason Aronson Publishers)

A Field Guide to Visiting a Jewish Cemetery by Rabbi Joshua L. Segal (Jewish Cemetery Publishing)

Finding Our Fathers: A Guidebook to Jewish Genealogy by Dan Rottenberg (Genealogical Publishing Co.)

Finding Your Jewish Roots in Galicia: A Resource Guide by Suzan F. Wynne (Avotaynu)

From Generation to Generation: How to Trace Your Jewish Genealogy and Family History by Arthur Kurzweil (Jossey-Bass)

The Galitzianers: The Jews of Galicia, 1772–1918 by Suzan Wynne (Wheatmark)

German Name-Change Gazetteer by Otto Kredel and Franz Thierfelder (Avotaynu)

Getting Started in Jewish Genealogy, 2010 Version by Gary Mokotoff (Avotaynu)

How to Document Victims and Locate Survivors of the Holocaust by Gary Mokotoff and Benjamin Meed (Avotaynu)

Jewish Roots in Poland: Pages from the Past and Archival Inventories by Miriam Weiner (Routes to Roots Foundation)

A Practical Guide to Jewish Cemeteries by Nolan Menachemson (Avotaynu)

Scattered Seeds: A Guide to Jewish Genealogy by Mona Freedman-Morris (RJ Press)

Sephardic Genealogy: Discovering Your Sephardic Ancestors and Their World by Jeffrey S. Malka (Avotaynu)

Sourcebook for Jewish Genealogies and Family Histories by David S. Zubatsky and Irwin M. Berent (Avotaynu)

Where Once We Walked, revised edition, by Gary Mokotoff and Sallyann Amdur Sack (Avotaynu)

WEBSITES

American Jewish Historical Society
<www.ajhs.org>

Avotaynu: The International Review of Jewish Genealogy
<www.avotaynu.com>

Beth Hatefutsoth: Museum of the Jewish Diaspora
<www.bh.org.il>

Consolidated Jewish Surname Index
<www.avotaynu.com/csi/csi-home.htm>

Cyndi's List: Jewish
<cyndislist.com/jewish>

Czestochowa-Radomsko Area Research Group
<www.crarg.org/search-holocaust-records.php>

DoroTree
<www.dorotree.com>

Genealogy Resources on the Internet: Jewish Mailing Lists
<rootsweb.ancestry.com/~jfuller/gen_mail_jewish.html>

Hebrew Immigrant Aid Society
<www.hias.org>

JewishGen
<www.jewishgen.org>

Jewish Historical Archives and Jewish Genealogical Societies
<www.iajgs.org>

Jewish History Channel Blog
<ha-historion.blogspot.com>

Jewish Names
<www.jewfaq.org/jnames.htm>

Jewish Web Index
<www.jewishwebindex.com>

JewishGen
<www.jewishgen.org>

Judaism and Jewish Resources
<shamash.org/trb/judaism.html>

ShtetlSeeker
<www.jewishgen.org/communities>

Southern Jewish Historical Society
<www.jewishsouth.org>

Tracing the Tribe: The Jewish Genealogy Blog
<tracingthetribe.blogspot.com>

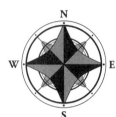

CHAPTER FIFTEEN

Appendices

ONLINE TRANSLATORS

Once you've successfully traced your immigrant ancestors back to their distant homelands, you may hit a new roadblock: foreign-language records and web resources. Thankfully, you don't have to become fluent in your ancestor's tongue. Instead, take advantage of affordable—if not free—online tools for getting quick and accurate translations. Many online translators are continually being upgraded and enhanced to encompass more languages and user-friendly features. Keep in mind that translation tools are most effective at conveying the essence of a text and are often stumped by slang and jargon. If you encounter a nonsensical translation, try feeding the text or URL into another service and compare the results. These five popular online translators boast a variety of language and translation options.

BABYLON <translation.babylon.com>
- **Cost:** $10 a month for a subscription; $118 to buy the software
- **Languages:** 75, including 1,400 online dictionaries; claims to translate slang and jargon
- **Features:** Translates web pages and documents. Program enables you to control+right-click on a word in any application and view an immediate translation. Mac and PC compatible. Audio pronunciations also are available.
- **Tips:** Babylon offers free dictionaries for download and a free trial of its software online.

BING TRANSLATOR <microsofttranslator.com>

- **Cost:** Free
- **Languages:** More than 30; uses automatic language detection, making it possible to browse the web in a language you don't recognize
- **Features:** Translates basic text and full web pages. Download a special translator to translate your documents within Microsoft Office (compatible with Windows only).
- **Tips:** Bing rivals Google with its translation bot ("Tbot") for Windows Life Messenger, which enables you to chat with someone in differing languages, while it automatically translates the conversation. It also offers four different layout options for side-by-side web translation.

FREETRANSLATION.COM <freetranslation.com>

- **Cost:** Free for basic use; upgrade for $9.95 a year
- **Languages:** About 10; doesn't use automatic language detection
- **Features:** Translates basic text. Professional translation is available for a fee.
- **Tips:** FreeTranslation.com also makes a free iPhone app.

GOOGLE TRANSLATE <translate.google.com>

- **Cost:** Free
- **Languages:** About 70; uses automatic language detection
- **Features:** Translates basic text and full web pages, and allows you to upload documents (in a wide range of formats) for translation.
- **Tips:** As an alternative to going back and forth between a site and a translator, Google has devised a button you can add to your browser bookmarks that will translate sites (or selected portions of sites) with just a click.

WORLDLINGO <worldlingo.com>

- **Cost:** Free for basic use; myWorldLingo subscription $4.95 to $6.95 a month
- **Languages:** 32
- **Features:** Translates basic text, documents and websites up to 500 words. Professional translation in 141 languages is available for a fee.
- **Tips:** WorldLingo is worth using only if you pay for the subscription, which allows for unlimited translations of text, documents, e-mails and websites in 15 or 32 languages, depending on your subscription.

PASSENGER ARRIVAL RECORDS

By Lisa A. Alzo

Sailing vessels and steamships carried our ancestors to America by the millions during the 19th and early 20th centuries. They arrived at more than 100 ports all along the coasts—among the busiest were Boston, Baltimore, New York, Philadelphia, Charleston, New Orleans, Galveston and San Francisco—and overland from Canada and Mexico. To retrace the journey of ancestors who braved the arduous ocean crossing is to claim your family's place in an American historical saga. But you'll need to know which records to search for and how to avoid pitfalls along the way. Here, we'll explain how to trace your immigrant ancestor.

STEP 1 ✦ Search at Home

Through family stories or initial research, you might already know (or think you know) a few things about the immigrants in your family tree. But you'll want to find out as much as possible about those folks so you can locate them in immigration records. Some key facts to look for:

- immigrant's name
- date and place of birth
- year or date of immigration
- port of entry
- town or village the immigrant came from
- place the immigrant settled in the United States
- names of family members
- religion (this may give clues to the home parish)
- native language

You won't necessarily need all these details to track your ancestor. But the more identifying information you have, the easier it'll be to tell if a record names your ancestor or someone else.

Start your research at home with family papers you have. Also ask relatives what they remember about your ancestors, especially those who immigrated. Examine records you find for immigration clues.

STEP 2 ✦ Examine US Records

Don't worry if you didn't learn much from home sources and relatives. Next, you'll look for clues in records your ancestor left once he settled in America. In particular, search these records:

CENSUSES: Censuses were taken every ten years, beginning in 1790. Depending on the census, you might discover the year of immigration, whether your ancestor applied for naturalization, his country of birth (rarely, a town of origin) and more. Census takers asked for each person's country of birth starting in 1850 and parents' birthplaces starting in 1880. Citizenship status and year of immigration were reported beginning in 1900.

Don't be alarmed if a census lists a different homeland than your family stories claimed. It's possible the census or the story is wrong, or that the nationality your ancestors identified with differed from the ruling country at the time. For example, during much of the 1800s, Czech ancestors would've been citizens of Austria.

VITAL RECORDS: Birth, marriage and death records may provide you with a date and place of birth (though possibly only the country), the parents' and other relatives' names, and maybe the parents' places of birth. The availability of vital records varies by state: Some states, particularly New England, mandated birth, marriage and death registration in the 1800s; others waited until the early 1900s. Towns and counties may have recorded vital events earlier on their own. In addition, states typically restrict access to records for 50 to 100 years after they're created, though you may be able to get an "uncertified" copy (fine for genealogy, but not useful for official purposes).

The Family History Library (FHL) **<familysearch.org>** might have microfilmed vital records for your ancestor's area; run a place search of the state or county and look under the vital records heading. To rent FHL microfilm, visit a branch Family History Center.

Few states have put vital records online, though some have indexes that can help you identify the right record to order. See a sampling of these sites at **<familytreemagazine.com/article/10-vital-records-web-sites>**. Visit Where to Write for Vital Records **<www.cdc.gov/nchs/w2w.htm>** to find out how to order vital records from each state. Usually, you request old records from the state archives and more-recent ones from the vital records office. Check with county clerks or town halls for locally kept records. Fees typically range from $15 to $35.

SOCIAL SECURITY APPLICATIONS: If your ancestor applied for a Social Security number (SSN), his application (called an SS-5), will provide his place of birth (if known) along with other information. Because Social Security began in 1937, it's a good resource for recent kin.

Start by searching for your ancestor's SSN in the Social Security Death Index on subscription site Ancestry.com **<ancestry.com>** or at the free FamilySearch.org **<familysearch.org>**. Not everyone who had an SSN is named in this index. It includes people with Social Security numbers whose deaths were reported to the Social Security Administration (SSA). Most died in 1962 and later, when the SAA began computerizing its records. Note that some sites are removing recent deaths from their SSDI databases due to privacy concerns.

Next, get the SS-5 by filling out the SSA's form at **<www.socialsecurity.gov/online/ssa-711.pdf>**. You'll need to provide at least the applicant's full name, birth date and SSN. If you don't know the SSN, include as much other information as possible. You'll need to pay a nonrefundable fee of $27 if you supply the correct SSN, or $29 if you don't.

NATURALIZATION RECORDS: Not all immigrants became citizens, but if your ancestors did, those papers can break your immigration research wide open. Later records, especially after 1906, offer the most detail, including the applicant's birth date and place, current address, vessel and port of embarkation, and US port and date of arrival. Earlier records should at least provide a country of origin and the date and port of arrival.

An immigrant's first step to becoming a citizen involved going to any courthouse to file a Declaration of Intention ("first papers"), in which he renounced his allegiance to his homeland and declared his intention to become a US citizen. After meeting residency requirements, an immigrant could formally petition for citizenship by filing a Petition for Naturalization ("second papers"). This could be filed at the same court where he filed his first papers or at another court entirely.

Naturalization records after 1906 are easier to locate because courts had to forward copies to the federal government. If the person's birth date was more than 100 years ago, you can get copies of post-1906 naturalizations from the US Citizenship and Immigration Services **<www.uscis. gov/genealogy>**. You can search digitized records for some US regions at Ancestry.com (these include pre-1906 naturalizations filed in federal district courts). The records are on microfilm at the National Archives and Records Administration **<archives.gov>** and through the FHL.

The Alien Registration Act of 1940 required resident aliens to register their addresses and places of employment with the government. Use the UCSIS genealogy service to request the resulting Alien Registrations (A-Files) of people born more than 100 years ago.

STEP 3 ✦ Locate Passenger Lists

Passenger lists are the Holy Grail of immigrant research. They can tell you when your ancestor arrived on US shores, what ship he sailed on, when and from where he departed, and more. Starting in 1820, all US-bound ships had to keep lists of passengers, known as customs lists. They were printed in the United States and shipping company personnel filled in passenger information—usually a name, sex, age, occupation and nationality—at the port of departure. That's why you want to search for the name the immigrant used back in the old country.

Later laws required more-detailed records called immigration passenger lists, starting in 1891. In addition to basic information, they give last residence, final US destination, name and address of a relative in the United States and more.

US immigrants arrived at more than 300 ports, with New York being the busiest. In 1855, the first immigrant inspection station opened at Castle Garden in New York City. Its famous successor, Ellis Island, opened in 1892; some 40 percent of Americans have an ancestor who passed through Ellis Island's doors. (Contrary to popular belief, officials there didn't change immigrants' names.) Search Ellis Island passenger arrivals from 1892 to 1924 free at **<ellisisland.org>**. Ancestry.com's immigration records collection includes surviving customs and passenger lists from all US ports of arrival, including border-crossing records from Canada and Mexico. See the next article for help searching Ancestry.com's immigration records.

If you have trouble finding your kin in an online database, try dropping search parameters; for instance, drop the first name. Try various spellings (it's not uncommon for names to be transcribed incorrectly) and search for women's maiden names. Also look for family members your ancestor might have traveled with.

For greater search flexibility, use Stephen P. Morse's free One-Step search tools **<stevemorse. org>** for passenger lists on Ellis Island and Ancestry.com. For example, Morse's forms enable you to perform "sounds like" searches on first and last names, as well as towns of origin Morse doesn't store data on his site—he simply offers a way to search what's hosted elsewhere. So you must log in with your username and password to view results in the Ellis Island database, and you must be an Ancestry.com subscriber (or use the site at a subscribing library) to see matches from its databases.

To use microfilmed passenger records, you'll need to know the port and date of arrival, and (ideally) the ship name. National Archives facilities have passenger list microfilm, as does the FHL. Large public genealogy libraries often have passenger lists from nearby ports. Once you've found this key to researching your immigrant ancestor, you're ready to tell your family's chapter in America's history.

ANCESTRY.COM'S IMMIGRATION COLLECTION

By David A. Fryxell

In addition to its rich collections of censuses, vital records, newspapers and other resources, subscription genealogy site Ancestry.com **<ancestry.com>** has built up an impressive collection of immigration records to help you solve the often-intractable problem of "crossing the pond." The site divides its Immigration and Travel collection into six categories of databases: Passenger Lists, Citizenship and Naturalization Records, Border Crossings and Passports, Crew Lists, Immigration and Emigration Books, and Ship Pictures and Descriptions.

Within these categories, some databases are indexes; many link to images of original records. You can search all these databases at once, by category or one at a time. And because you can pop back and forth with other Ancestry.com records, you can easily cross-reference data about an ancestor: Find your ancestor's year of naturalization or how many years the 1900 census says he'd been in America, for example, and you can use that information to locate his naturalization and passenger list records. Best of all, you can use most of the Immigration and Travel Collection free at libraries offering Ancestry Library Edition.

Setting Sail

To get started searching Ancestry.com's immigration records, from the home page, hover over Search on the navigation bar. Select Immigration and Travel from the menu that drops down. If the Advanced search form isn't already displayed, click Show Advanced in the green bar above the search blanks to give yourself the most options. To search only a single category of records, use the links under Narrow by Category on the right.

If you want to search just a single database—say you know your ancestor sailed from Germany and you want to find him in Hamburg Passenger Lists, 1850–1934—scroll down a little and click the View All in Card Catalog button on the right. It's a big list, 339 databases at last count, ranging from "19th-Century Emigration of 'Old Lutherans' from Eastern Germany to Australia, Canada, and the United States" to "Wuerttemberg, Germany Emigration Index."

Among the most popular—and, not coincidentally, the largest—immigration and travel databases you'll find on Ancestry.com are:

- New York Passenger Lists, 1820–1957
- Passenger and Immigration Lists Index, 1500s–1900s
- UK Incoming Passenger Lists, 1878–1960
- Selected US Naturalization Record Indexes, 1791–1966, 1790–1974 and 1794–1995

Other popular databases cover Canadian passenger lists (1865–1935) and border crossings from Canada to the United States (1895–1956) and Mexico to the United States (1895–1957). Most US ports are represented among passenger lists, including the major ones such as Boston, Baltimore, Philadelphia and New Orleans. You can even trace your ancestor's travels back to his hometown in the old country, if he's in the database of US passport applications (1795–1925).

Anchoring Your Searches

Ancestry.com's frequently updated search interface lets you enter a variety of facts about your ancestor—the more the better—and produces a list of results in order of relevance, ranked by stars.

Because of the inaccuracies inherent in old records, the search uses a sort of "fuzzy" logic, assuming that the criteria you enter aren't exact. Search filters built into the search form give you more control: Click Exact to make Ancestry.com search for, say, "Harold Higgins" and not "Harold Higgens" or "Hal Higgs." You also can choose Exact plus any combination of Soundex matches (last names only), phonetic matches, names with similar meanings or spellings, and records where only initials are recorded (first and middle names only). Soundex is a system for grouping similar-sounding names together, helping you catch those variant spellings that can make records difficult to find.

Filters in the search form also let you refine place searches—including birthplace, residence, place of arrival and departure, and place of origin—to encompass adjacent counties or states.

Our ancestors birth dates tend to "wander" quite a bit in historical records. That's why, when you include a birth date in your search, the Ancestry.com search engine assumes an automatic "fudge factor" of five years before and after the date you type in. Or you can still check Exact for either birth or migration date, and select your own fudge factor of one, two, five or ten years.

The advanced search form also has a check box where you can universally "Match all terms exactly." But don't go wild with that Exact option until you've at least seen what results you get from casting a broad net. When you specify "Exact," records that don't contain that piece of information simply get skipped: A passenger list that doesn't enumerate ages (or that doesn't give your ancestor's age) won't be included if you enter an "Exact" birth year, even if you choose a plus/minus range.

Even with the "exact plus" options, you may want to use "wild card" characters to account for oddball spellings not ordinarily caught by Soundex. This can be especially important with immigration records, which often involve unfamiliar foreign names and places, as well as accent marks. Use wild cards to substitute for letters in the name you're searching for. A question mark (?) serves as a single-character wild card, while an asterisk (*) replaces zero or more characters.

Keep a few rules in mind when searching with wild cards: You can use a wild card at the beginning or end of a name, but not both. You must use at least three actual characters in an asterisk search; searching for Jo* produces only an error message. But it's fine to use more than one wild card in a search: Typing *Leibo?i?z* retrieves Leibowitz, Leibovitz and Leibowicz. Searching for *Leibo** not only brings up those names, but also Leibold, Leibovsky and more.

You can even search without a name at all. For example, you could search for all Lithuanian passengers born in 1881 who arrived at New York in 1897. You might use this technique to circumvent the genealogical brick wall of surnames changed in America. My ancestor whom I knew as Oscar Lundeen, for example, was born Oscar Ingelsson—who would have guessed?

Refining Your Search

After you click Search, you'll get a ranked list of possible matches to your search terms. You also might see a note prodding you to enter more data to improve your search. Once you've run that initial search, you can speed up your record viewing and search refining by using "hot keys" **<blogs.ancestry.com/ancestry/2008/10/10/hot-keys-in-the-new-search-user-interface>**.

Save any promising-looking records to your Ancestry.com Shoebox, using the button at the top of the record viewer, for later scrutiny. If nothing looks like your ancestor or you have too many results to wade through, refine your search by adding more information: an ancestor's country of origin, for example, or a date range. The Keyword field accepts single words, multiple words or phrases enclosed in quotation marks. If you know the name of the ship your ancestor sailed on, try entering it in the Keyword box. If you think you know your ancestor's town or province in the old country, type it into the Origin box and see if Ancestry.com "suggests" a complete place name (such as Thanet, England, United Kingdom). If not, try entering the place as a Keyword (don't make it Exact, since spelling variants are common).

As you accumulate clues, you may want to focus on a single category or database. To view search results from a particular category, such as Crew Lists, click the box to the left of your search results. When viewing by category, the box lists search results by specific database. If you click on the name of a database (Minnesota Naturalization Records Index, 1854–1957, for example), you'll see only results from that resource; selecting Learn More About This Database jumps to a page where you can start a fresh search in just that database.

GENEALOGY GLOSSARY

To better research your European ancestors, here's a handy cheat sheet of common family history-related terms in English, Dutch, French, German and Spanish.

Numbers

English	Dutch	French	German	Spanish
one	een	un	eins	uno
two	twee	deux	zwei	dos
three	drie	trois	drei	tres
four	vier	quatre	vier	quatro
five	vijf	cinq	fünf	cinco
six	zes	six	sechs	seis
seven	zeven	sept	sieben	siete
eight	acht	huit	acht	ocho
nine	negen	neuf	neun	nueve
ten	tien	dix	zehn	diez
eleven	elf	onze	elf	once
twelve	twaalf	douze	zwölf	doce
thirteen	dertien	treize	dreizehn	trece
fourteen	veertien	quatorze	vierzehn	catorce
fifteen	vijftien	quinze	fünfzehn	quince
sixteen	zestien	seize	sechszehn	dieciséis
seventeen	zeventien	dix-sept	siebzehn	diecisiete
eighteen	achttien	dix-huit	achtzehn	dieciocho
nineteen	negentien	dix-neuf	neunzehn	diecinueve
twenty	twintig	vingt	zwanzig	veinte
thirty	dertig	trente	dreißig	treinta
forty	veertig	quarante	vierzig	quarenta
fifty	vijftig	quinze	fünfzig	cincuenta
sixty	zestig	soixante	sechzig	sesenta
seventy	zeventig	soixante-dix	siebzig	setenta
eighty	tachtig	quatre-vingts	achtzig	ochenta
ninety	negentig	quatre-vingt-dix	neunzig	noventa
hundred	honderd	cent	hundert	cien
thousand	duizend	mille	tausend	mil
million	miljoen	million	million	millón

Dates

English	Dutch	French	German	Spanish
year	jaar	année	Jahr	año
month	maand	mois	Monat	mesa
day	dag	jour	Tag	día
date	datum	date	Datum	fecha
January	Januari (archaic: louwmaand)	janvier	Januar	enero
February	Februari (archaic: sprokkelmaand)	fevrier	Februar	febrero
March	Maart (archaic: lentemaand)	mars	Marz	marzo
April	April (archaic: grasmaand)	avril	April	abril
May	Mei (archaic: bloeimaand)	mai	Mai	mayo

June	Juni (archaic: zomermaand)	juin	Juni	junio
July	Juli (archaic: hooimaand)	juillet	Juli	julio
August	Augustus (archaic: oogstmaand)	août	August	agosto
September	September (archaic: herfstmaand)	septembre	September	septiembre
October	October (archaic: wijnmaand)	octobre	Oktober	octubre
November	November (archaic: slachtmaand)	novembre	November	noviembre
December	December (archaic: wintermaand)	décembre	Dezember	diciembre
Monday	Maandag	lundi	Montag	lunes
Tuesday	Dinsdag	mardi	Dienstag	martes
Wednesday	Woensdag	mercredi	Mittwoch	miércoles
Thursday	Donderdag	jeudi	Donnerstag	jueves
Friday	Vrijdag	vendredi	Freitag	viernes
Saturday	Zaterdag	samedi	Samstag, Sonnabend	sábado
Sunday	Zondag	dimanche	Sonntag	domingo

Relationships

English	Dutch	French	German	Spanish
aunt	tante	tante	Tante	tía
brother	broer, broeder	frère	Bruder	hermano
brother-in-law	zwager	beau-frère	Schwäger	cuñado
child	kind	enfant	Kind	niño
cousin	nicht (f), neef (m)	cousine	Kusine, Base (f), Cousin, Vetter (m)	prima (f), primo (m)
daughter	dochter, dr.	fille	Tochter	hija
family	familie	famille	Familie	familia
father	vader	père	Vater	padre
father-in-law	schoonvader	beau-père	Schwiegervater	suegro
grandchild	kleinkind	petit-enfant	Enkelin, Enkel	nieta, nieto
grandfather	grootvader, opa	grandpère	Grossvater	abuelo
grandmother	grootmoeder, oma	grandmère	Grossmutter	abuela
grandparents	grootouders	grands-parents	Grosseltern	abuelos
great-aunt	oudtante	grand-tante	Grosstante	tía abuela
great-grandfather	overgrootvader	arrière grandpère	Urgrossvater	bisabuelo
great-grandmother	overgrootmoeder	arrière grandmère	Urgrossmutter	bisabuela
great-uncle	oudoom	grand-oncle	Grossonkel	tío abuelo
husband	echtgenoot, man	époux	Mann, Gatte	esposo, marido
mother	moeder	mère	Mutter	madre
mother-in-law	schoonmoeder	belle-mère	Schwiegermutter	suegra
niece	nicht	nièce	Nichte	sobrina
nephew	neef	neveu	Neffe	sobrino
parents	ouders	parents	Eltern	padres
orphan	wees	orphelin	Waise	huérfana, huérfano
sister	zus, zuster	soeur	Schwester	hermana
sister-in-law	schoonzus	belle-soeur	Schwägerin	cuñada
son	zoon, zn.	fils	Sohn	hijo
stepfather	stiefvader	beau-père	Stiefvater	padrastro
stepmother	stiefmoeder	belle-mère	Stiefmutter	madrastra
uncle	oom	oncle	Onkel	tío
widow	weduwe	veuve	Witwe	viuda
widower	weduwnaar	veuf	Witwer	viudo
wife	echtgenote, vrouw	épouse	Frau, Gattin	esposa, marida

INDEX

265

ABOUT THE CONTRIBUTORS

LISA A. ALZO

Eastern European genealogy specialist Lisa A. Alzo received the Association for Women in Slavic Studies 2002 Mary Zirin Prize for excellence in scholarship and serves on the Board of Directors for the Czechoslovak Genealogical Society International. Her books include *Three Slovak Women*, *Slovak Pittsburgh* and *Cleveland Slovaks* (with John T. Sabol). She's written numerous articles for genealogy publications, including regular contributions to *Family Tree Magazine*, and blogs regularly at The Accidental Genealogist.

JAMES M. BEIDLER

German research expert and Pennsylvania resident James M. Beidler frequently contributes to *German Life* magazine and is active in the Federation of Genealogical Societies.

SHARON DEBARTOLO CARMACK

Sharon DeBartolo Carmack is a Certified Genealogist and partner in the research firm of Warren, Carmack & Associates. She specializes in Irish and Italian genealogical research. Sharon is the author of 16 books, including *You Can Write Your Family History*. She is also a contributing editor for *Family Tree Magazine*. She is a member of the Association of Professional Genealogists and the Association of Writers and Writing Programs.

SCHELLY TALALAY DARDASHTI

Journalist and genealogist Schelly Talalay Dardashti writes Tracing the Tribe: The Jewish Genealogy Blog **<tracingthetribe.blogspot.com>**. She has tracked her family history through Belarus, Russia, Lithuania, Spain, Iran and elsewhere.

DAVID A. FRYXELL

David A. Fryxell founded *Family Tree Magazine* and continues to write for the magazine as a contributing editor.

NANCY HENDRICKSON

Nancy Hendrickson is the author of *Discover Your Family History Online*, *Remembering Old California*, *Events This Day in History* and S*an Diego Then and Now*. Learn more about her genealogy coaching at **<AncestorNews.com>**.

LISE HULL

Lise Hull is an American freelance writer and researcher specializing in British heritage. Her work has been published by *Everton's Family History* and *Genealogical Helper* magazines, *Celtic Heritage,* Military *History Quarterly*, *History Today*, *Pembrokeshire Life*, *Activity Wales*, *Faces, Scottish Journal*, *US Scots*, *AntiqueWeek*, and other print and online publications

CECILE WENDT JENSEN

Certified Genealogist Cecile Wendt Jensen, **<www.mipolonia.net>**, is the lead developer of the Polonica Americana Research Institute and author of books including *Sto Lat: A Modern Guide to Polish Genealogy*.

THOMAS MACENTEE

Thomas MacEntee is a genealogist specializing in the use of technology and social media to improve genealogical research. He provides consulting services through his business High-Definition Genealogy and is the creator of **<GeneaBloggers.com>**.

RHONDA R. MCCLURE

Rhonda R. McClure is a nationally recognized professional genealogist and lecturer specializing in New England and celebrity research as well as computerized genealogy. She has been a contributing editor to numerous magazines and is the author of ten books.

SUNNY JANE MORTON

Sunny Jane Morton is a writer and family historian who loves helping people tell their family stories. She is a contributing editor to *Family Tree Magazine* and the author of *My Life & Times*.

DIANA CRISMAN SMITH

Diana Crisman Smith has written for numerous genealogical publications, including current regular columns in the *National Genealogist*. She serves as Treasurer of the International Society of Family History Writers and Editors (ISFHWE) and Genealogical Speakers Guild (GSG), as well as webmaster (and founding member) of the Great Lakes Chapter of the Association of Professional Genealogists. She's a Past District Director of APG.

MAUREEN A. TAYLOR

Maureen A. Taylor is an internationally known photo identification expert and genealogist. She is a contributing editor to *Family Tree Magazine* and has written the Photo Detective blog, **<blog.familytreemagazine.com/photodetectiveblog>** since 2001. She is the author of several books including *Family Photo Detective*. Her website is **<www.maureentaylor.com>**.

Second edition ISBN: 978-1-4403–3347-7

Other Family Tree Books are available from your local bookstore and online suppliers.
For more genealogy resources, visit **<shopfamilytree.com>**.

17 16 15 14 13   5 4 3 2 1

DISTRIBUTED IN CANADA BY FRASER DIRECT
100 Armstrong Avenue
Georgetown, Ontario, Canada L7G 5S4
Tel: (905) 877-4411

DISTRIBUTED IN THE U.K. AND EUROPE BY
F&W Media International, LTD
Brunel House, Forde Close,
Newton Abbot, TQ12 4PU, UK
Tel: (+44) 1626 323200,
Fax (+44) 1626 323319
E-mail: enquiries@fwmedia.com

DISTRIBUTED IN AUSTRALIA BY CAPRICORN LINK
P.O. Box 704, S. Windsor, NSW 2756 Australia
Tel: (02) 4560-1600
Fax: (02) 4577-5288
E-mail: books@capricornlink.com.au

PUBLISHER/EDITORIAL DIRECTOR: Allison Dolan
EDITOR: Grace Dobush
COVER DESIGNER: Julie Barnett
INTERIOR DESIGNER: Laura Spencer
PRODUCTION COORDINATOR: Debbie Thomas